Antoni Abad

megafone.net/2004-2014

Antoni Abad

megafone.net/2004-2014

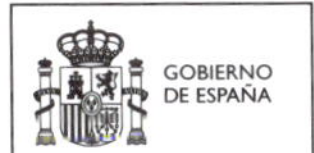

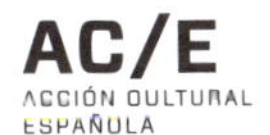

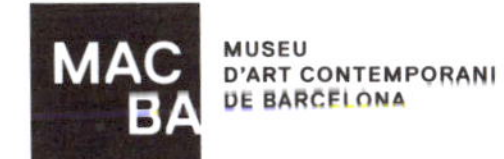

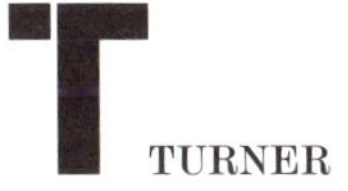

Acción Cultural Española (AC/E) here offers a critical review of *megafone.net*, the initiative launched by Antoni Abad in March 2004. This art and social communication project has been live online for a decade, making use of social relationships and smartphones to offer exposure and a means of expression to communities who dwell on the margins of modern social networks.

megafone.net encourages this demographic to record its experiences and opinions in sound and images (videos and photographs), either in person or by smartphone. Those recordings are immediately fed to the web and are thereby transformed into a digital megaphone of experiences, opinions and voices that would otherwise be lost.

Years before the public used information and communication technology *en masse* to make itself heard, and well before public institutions actively adopted policies to reduce the digital divide in society, *megafone.net* emerged as a pioneering project offering a practical and creative means of providing a digital platform for the voice and image of those who have been socially isolated, whether because they belong to a marginal group, because they suffer from functional or sensory limitations, or simply lack access to such technology.

AC/E congratulates Antoni Abad for conceiving such a necessary project for a society like ours, where the influence of the social majority and its capacity to exercise real pressure on collective decision-making clears the way for creative initiatives such as *megafone.net* and for public bodies to articulate proposals that offer media presence to minorities.

We wish to thank the authors of these essays, as well as the creators of the show—Cristina Bonet, Roc Parés, and Soledad Gutiérrez—for their ability to bring a narrative structure to the materials assembled by this project, thereby allowing both the reader and the viewer to grasp its significance. Finally, we extend our thanks to the Museu d'Art Contemporani de Barcelona (MACBA) for counting on AC/E to promote beyond its frontiers a genuinely modern and engaged vision of our country.

Teresa Lizaranzu
President
Acción Cultural Española (AC/E)

The Museum, the Internet, and the Megaphone

Since its foundation in 1995, the Museu d'Art Contemporani de Barcelona (MACBA) has been attentive to the relationship between art and information networks. From the very start, the role of the Internet as a public digital space and that of the museum as a public cultural service defined the guidelines for an enterprising project which was to involve all departments in the development of the museum's functions. In fact, Antoni Abad was the first artist to participate in MACBA's pioneering foray into the Internet as a platform for experimentation and creation; this was carried out in collaboration with the Universitat Pompeu Fabra.

Beyond Richard Meier's emblematic white building, MACBA has found in the Internet a platform in which to develop a method complementing on-site work whereby artists can reach a new audience. This started in 1996 with *Sisyphus*,[1] where Abad linked the antipodes of Barcelona and Wellington (New Zealand); it continued with the online exhibition *Remote Connection* (2001)[2] and the appearance of *Z* (2002)[3] before reaching Radio Web MACBA (2006)[4]. These are just a few examples of what has already been achieved through the basic principles of the museum-Internet dimension. Now, after twenty years in which the Internet has assumed a markedly commercial character, MACBA is dedicating an exhibition and the present publication to *megafone.net*, a participative, non-profit project that deliberately sets itself apart from the corporate world.

megafone.net addresses the complexities of cultural production and artistic practice in the twenty-first century: issues such as regionalism versus internationalization or cultural identity versus the culture industry are present in the critical nature of its works. Yet these are not discussed in any systematic way, nor are they the subject of any dissident manifestos: *megafone.net* is created from collective performances in which these complex themes emerge from the associations and the questioning of boundaries between the artist, cultural institutions, technical devices, and local communities.

This book offers a wide variety of viewpoints regarding *megafone.net*'s first decade. This diversity is a small-scale reflection of the contributions of over 260 participants who have collaborated with Abad to create this confluence of art and social communication involving thirteen communities (which are, themselves, quite heterogeneous) between 2004 and 2014. MACBA's role in this publication is specifically to procure a protected space where this plurality of voices appears not only as an object of study, but also as a veritable interaction between active participants, devices, and temporalities that have made *megafone.net* what it is today. *megafone.net* is a collectively produced project made up of ephemeral

1. http://iua.upf.edu/?q=ca/node/157.

2. A selection of net.art curated by Roberta Bosco and Stefano Caldana in the context of the exhibition *Antagonisms*: http://www.macba.cat/ca/expo-conexion-remota.

3. The digital fly, a veritable social network *avant la lettre* with which Abad himself parasitized the MACBA in 2002 and 2003: http://www.macba.cat/ca/expo-zexe.

4. A pioneering online radio project that explores the potential of the Internet and the medium of radio as platforms for exhibition and creation: http://rwm.macba.cat.

links that Latour[5] would have categorized as uncertain, fragile, and controversial. And those are the very attributes that justify MACBA's continued solidarity and its commitment to the future of this project.

This critical review would not have been possible without the support of Acción Cultural Española (AC/E) and the collaboration of the Mobile World Capital Barcelona. The Laboratorio Arte Alameda and the Centro Cultural de España in Mexico, Matadero Madrid, and the Pinacoteca do Estado de São Paulo are bringing this work to life again in some of the contexts that generated it over the course of its history with the participation of AC/E. I wish very particularly to thank the artist for his generosity, as well as Roc Parés' contribution to the scientific publishing of this volume, and the involvement of Cristina Bonet, who insured the curatorial work and coordination with MACBA, along with Soledad Gutiérrez and the audiovisual teams that were fundamental to this project.

Bartomeu Marí
Director
Museu d'Art Contemporani de Barcelona (MACBA)

5. Bruno Latour, *Reassembling the Social: An Introduction to Actor-Network-Theory*, Oxford: Oxford University Press, 2005.

**megafone.net/2004–2014**
Roc Parés

Introduction

This book seeks to familiarize the general public and scholars of contemporary culture with _megafone.net_, a collectively created series of geographically disperse, interdisciplinary and innovative works that have been internationally recognized as pioneering in twenty-first-century art and social communication networks.[1]

Begun in 2004, these art projects involving online communities, conceived and directed by Catalan artist Antoni Abad,[2] continue into their tenth year still in a process of constant evolution. This is therefore a perfect time for an overall evaluation of that period; for this purpose we have brought together some of the most significant of many texts published until now, as well as others especially commissioned for this book from scholars, participants, and collaborators in these projects. The viewpoints and methodologies expressed here range from art history and criticism to ethnography by way of communication theory and social and political thought. We are confident that this group of texts will allow readers to take in the complexity of _megafone.net_ and to appreciate its techno-cultural relevance.

Throughout the last ten years the work of _megafone.net_ has been continually developing novel communication strategies devised specifically for each community at risk of social exclusion. With this book we propose to highlight the special quality of these projects that stubbornly refuse to promote consumerism, a characteristic trait that distances _megafone.net_ from the vast majority of generic communication platforms and conventional social networks. We can begin by observing that _megafone.net_ is characterized by its innovative use of interactive media (smartphones, computers, networks) and by its conception of art as a free, non-profit public service that offers up the experience of vulnerable groups to society as a whole.

Despite this book's diversity of materials and viewpoints, readers are very likely to discover a certain complicity in the defense of the Internet as a digital public space and a resistance to the reduction of identity to mere spectacle—this, most of all, has been achieved through the work of _megafone.net_.

Away from the art market, a new international generation of media artists, often working in collaboration, exhibits the same utopian fury and radical innovation that once characterized the modern 'avant-garde' groups. Regardless of whether we will call the innovative art of the present 'avant-garde' or not, we must still acknowledge the critical

1. In 2006, Antoni Abad received a Golden Nica in the Digital Communities category for the _megafone.net_ (then called _zexe.net_) project, _canal*ACCESSIBLE_. This is the highest prize in the most prestigious contest for electronic art in the world: the Ars Electronica Prize. The jury consisted of Steven Clift (United States), Andreas Hirsch (Austria), Peter Kuthan (Austria) and Lara Srivastava (Canada). Archives of the Prix Ars Electronica: http://90.146.8.18/en/archives/prix_archive/prixJuryStatement.asp?iProjectID=13731.
2. Antoni Abad i Roses was born in Lleida in 1956 and lives in Barcelona, the city where he has developed much of his professional art career in quite diverse areas, including sculpture, photography, video, and art specifically created for the Internet.

and experimental scope of their enterprise within and beyond the Internet, despite
(or because) of the fact that they don't fit into any of the '-isms' that serve as chapter
heads to art history survey books.

_Eduardo Kac[3]

…We may fear a world in which, rather than generalized democracy, there develops
an aristocracy around the poles where knowledge, money, and power concentrate, and a
mass of consumers, and an even larger mass of non-consumers, those who are excluded
from both consumption and knowledge…

In a capitalist world, where the aim of everything is to accumulate capital, the role of
images in the media, like television or Internet, is to make people consume.

_Marc Augé[4]

When bodies gather as they do to express their indignation and to enact their plural
existence in public space, they are also making broader demands. They are demanding
to be recognized and to be valued; they are exercising a right to appear and to exercise
freedom; they are calling for a livable life. These values are presupposed by particular
demands, but they also demand a more fundamental restructuring of our socio-economic
and political order.

_Judith Butler[5]

Forerunners of *megafone.net*

First steps on the Internet

megafone.net emerged when Antoni Abad decided to make a risky investment of
the creative capital he had accumulated in the form of international prestige over his
25-year career as an artist. That recognition reached its apex in 1999 when Harald
Szeemann selected him for the Venice Biennial, and the opportunity to invest that
capital came in 2004 when the Spanish Cultural Center in Mexico invited him to
put on a solo exhibition of his work. At that time, the most visible part of Abad's
oeuvre consisted of experimentation with audiovisual language in the form of video
installations shown in galleries[6]. Rather than accept the invitation as such, he made
a bold counteroffer: to convert the exhibition area into a space for social research
and experimentation. The decision to invest his prestige as a visual artist in a cultural
medium for which there were no recognized referents at that time was not made
lightly. Abad has been working since 2001 on a project that is a clear example of
social art and networks. We are referring to Z^7, an authentic Web 2.0 experiment

3. 'Interactive Art on the Internet', in Karl Gerbel and Peter Weibel (ed.), *Mythos Information. Welcome to
the Wired World*, Vienna/New York: Springer-Verlag, 1995, pp. 170–79.
4. Ignasi Aragay, 'Entrevista amb Marc Augé', *Barcelona Metròpolis*, October-December 2009:
http://w2.bcn.cat/bcnmetropolis/arxiu/ca/page9763.html?id=21&ui=278 [accessed March 2013].
5. Judith Butler, 'For and Against Precarity', *Tidal*, no. 1, December 2011: www.e-flux.com/wp-content/
uploads/2013/05/7.-Butler_Precarity.pdf [accessed March 2013].
6. Especially with Antoni Estrany in Barcelona, Oliva Arauna in Madrid, and Brito Cimino in São Paulo.
7. Originally hosted on its own specific domain, *zexe.net*, the fly can still be found and downloaded
(although it is not entirely compatible with current operating systems) at: http://megafone.net/Z.

avant la lettre[8], and a direct forerunner of the digital art and community projects that make up *megafone.net*.

Z was a project based on the conceptualization, design and development of a computer program called *z.exe* that would run on the personal computer of any user who decided to install it. *Z* is a piece of software art that is still conceptually valid today: it works with a custom-made program (of course the code itself is now obsolete) that manifests itself visually and sonically as a fly. That fly operated as an agent infiltrated into the computer user's interface in such a way that it only appeared when he or she connected to the Internet. When it did, it made it more difficult for programs to run and questioned the users' connection to their computers and to networks. But Abad's fly was more than just an audiovisual gimmick created to subvert computer interactivity; anyone installing the fly obtained access to a communication channel connecting them with all other *z.exe* users and involving them in a community. Each fly entering the community had a 'genetic code' that determined its appearance (phenotype) and behavior (genotype). That genetic code linked each fly to the rest of the community as if it were part of a family tree rooted in the 'mother' fly launched on the Internet on May 13, 2001. The activity of all the flies (exhaustively measured in terms of pixel displacement, new installations or 'births,' removals or 'deaths,' connection durations or 'flight hours') was constantly sent to a central server (*http://zexe.net*) where anyone could follow the swarm's movement in real time. This server also offered graphic illustrations of the total population, family relations, and geographic distribution of the digital flies. But beyond the statistical information stored on the server, the flies allowed their users to exchange text messages using a P2P (peer to peer) protocol that kept the messages between flies from passing through a central server. This peculiarity in the network's architecture was a deliberate decision by the artist. Unlike most commercial interpersonal communication services from that period, *z.exe* cost its users nothing, was completely publicity free, and configured horizontally, in other words, decentralized. Abad's decision to use the P2P protocol should be understood as a purely esthetic one. In appearance, there is no difference between sending and receiving messages directly from fly to fly or indirectly, as is customarily done through centralized instant messaging. But the choice of this protocol allows the creation of a horizontal, non-hierarchical communication platform that expresses the deliberate intention of the artist not to be placed in a central position. In other words, the choice of P2P has no implications for how the system appears to work, but enormous implications from a political standpoint. As we will see, this esthetic decision set the guidelines for Antoni Abad's subsequent projects, especially those he has carried out with *megafone.net* communities.

With the digital fly, Abad began his successful career in the creation of online communities. Over fifteen thousand people throughout the world had their own flies, and only 10% were installed in the GMT + 1 time zone that includes Abad's Barcelona base. The *Z* project went through different phases of development involving highly prestigious institutions such as Le Fresnoy-Studio national des arts contemporains in Tourcoing, France, and Museu d'Art Contemporani in Barcelona. It also received support from Spain's Ministry of Foreign Affairs. Among

---

8. While *Z* began in 2001, the concept of web 2.0 was not presented until the O'Reilly Web 2.0 Conference (San Francisco, California, October 5-7, 2004): http://web2con.com/pub/w/32/presentations.html [accessed August 2013].

Z's multiple public presentations, three were especially worthy of mention: first, the 1999 international exhibition *Net Condition*[9], possibly the twentieth century's most important net.art exhibition, organized by ZKM of Karlsruhe, the ICC in Tokyo, the 1999 Steirischer Herbst Festival in Graz, and MECAD in Sabadell. Second, the exhibition prepared for the international cyber-culture congress *Ligações/Links/ Liaisons*, organized by José Bragança de Miranda and Maria Teresa Cruz at the Museu de Arte Contemporânea de Serralves in Oporto (2001)[10]. And finally, *The Real Royal Trip/El real viaje real*, an exhibition curated by Harald Szeemann at MoMA's PS1 in Queens, New York (2003)[11], where Abad distributed ten million adhesive labels with the image and URL from which to download the fly installation file and follow that community's statistics.

As a result of its successful reception by the public, *Z* received outstanding international awards. In 2003, a specialized jury awarded it an honorable mention in the Net Vision/Net Excellence category of the prestigious Prix Ars Electronica in Linz, Austria[12]. The previous year, after *Z* was shown at MACBA, Abad had received the Premi Ciudad de Barcelona in the multimedia category[13].

Another important aspect of the *Z* project is that it already benefited from the collaboration of Daniel Julià and Eugenio Tisselli as programmers and Mery Cuesta as disseminator. These three collaborators have been very present in Abad's career. Daniel Julià has worked with Abad as a computer programmer on several projects. Two of the most outstanding were a piece of net.art called *1.000.000* (1999)[14] and a delightful small-format video installation entitled *Pluto* (2002). Abad won the Arco Electrónico prize in 1999 for *1.000.000*, making it the first piece of net.art acquired for a collection in Spain (Fundación Sanitas)[15]. Both Eugenio Tisselli and Mery Cuesta have been key figures in the development of *megafone.net* (we will discuss their involvement further on).

9. One of the curators from the team that organized this outstanding exhibition was Claudia Giannetti, who invited Abad to present *Z*: http://on1.zkm.de/netcondition/navigation/barcelona [accessed August 2013].
10. José A. Bragança de Miranda & Maria Teresa Cruz (eds.), *Crítica das ligações na era da técnica: ligações, links, liaisons*, Lisbon: Tropismos, 2002.
11. Kevin Power & Octavio Zaya (eds.), *The Real Royal Trip/El real viaje real*, New York, MoMA PS1, 2004.
12. Ed Burton (United Kingdom), Joshua Davis (United States), Casey Reas (United States), Steve Rogers (United Kingdom), Yukiko Shikata (Japan), jury members for the Net Vision/Net Excellence category of the Prix Ars Electronica 2003, stated: 'Antoni Abad builds on human nature to care for a "pet" to create an extremely unusual and organic network. That the instantiation of the network is a fly makes it intriguing. It shows a very original train of thought that is supported by excellent execution. Of particular note is the possibility to see the global level of activity of the network, clearly although not exclusively following daytime around the world.' Archive of the Prix Ars: http://90.146.8.18/en/archives/prix_archive/ prixJuryStatement.asp?iProjectID=12341 [accessed August 2013].
13. That year, the jury for the multimedia category consisted of Vicent Partal (president), Claudia Giannetti and Lluís Reales. Its award statement reads: 'For the creativity and innovation of a project that marks an evolution in net.art, creating a brilliant metaphor for the network using virtual flies. The jury has also valued the use of open-source technologies for its creation.' www.bcn.cat/cultura/ premisciutatbcn/2002/#multimedia [accessed March 2014].
14. *1.000.000* was originally created for issue no. 4 of the objectual magazine *La Ruta del Sentido*, a monographic issue dedicated to sex. According to Abad, this project 'offers unlimited virtual and free love.' *Mostra d'Arts Electròniques 2000 = Artes electrónicas = Electronic arts*, exhibition catalogue, Centre d'Art Santa Mònica, Barcelona: Departamento de Cultura de la Generalitat de Catalunya, 2000, pp. 60 and 61. This project is still available at http://aleph-arts.org/1.000.000 [accessed August 2013].
15. Regarding this piece, Roberta Bosco observed: 'His works for the Internet were very widely accepted, and *1.000.000*, windows with lips sending kisses, became the first piece of net.art sold in Spain.' Roberta Bosco, 'La revolución digital. Artistas del ciberespacio y alrededores', *El País*, October 21, 2006: http://elpais.com/diario/2006/10/21/babelia/1161387550_850215.html [accessed August 2013].

To conclude this brief review of *Z* as a direct forerunner of the *megafone.net* projects, I refer to the final paragraph of the text I wrote for its presentation in Porto in 2001: 'In sum, Abad invites us to participate in an art proposal that we can take on as an experience in the field of social communication. It is the artist who furnishes a specific and unique way of taking part in the network. For our part, we can understand it as an extension of his sculptural thinking, an expansion of his audiovisual work, or as research into the relational esthetics and involvement with information and communication technology.'[16]

We have already seen that *megafone.net* (2004-ongoing) is not Antoni Abad's first piece of net.art, nor was his *Z* fly from 2001 or even *1.000.000* from 1999. For Abad, the Internet became a space for artistic creation several years earlier, during the so-called 'heroic period'[17] of net.art. As he himself recounted[18]: 'There is another crucial moment, in 1996 [...] when Roc Parés invites me to do a project specifically for the Internet within the now disappeared MACBA on line, a project driven by the Universitat Pompeu Fabra and MACBA. The result was a renewed interpretation of *Sisyphus*, a video-projection from 1995. The new version adapts to the Web and is located between two Internet servers, one in Barcelona and the other in the Antipodes, in New Zealand. The virtual space overpowers *Sisyphus* and nothing takes place any more in the physical space. To enjoy this experience it is essential to connect to the Internet.' As Abad explained, his first piece of net.art was launched in 1996 simultaneously on the servers at the MACBA in Barcelona and the Museum of New Zealand Te Papa Tongarewa, in Wellington. To properly appreciate this work, Internet users had to connect simultaneously to those two extremely distant parts of the planet[19]. The now nonexistent platform Abad mentioned above was, indeed, *MACBA en línia*, a techno-cultural project carried out in 1996 as a collaboration between MACBA (founded in 1995) and the Audiovisual Institute at the Universitat Pompeu Fabra (founded in 1994). Regarding this first online project by Abad, artist and theorist Octavi Comeron wrote: 'In the different versions of *Sisyphus* (1995), artist Antoni Abad portrays him as a perpetual tight-rope act, or as a denizen of cyberspace pulling a rope with all his strength from Barcelona while, at the antipodes, in Wellington (New Zealand), his exact double is pulling the other end of the rope in the opposite direction. In any case, this is always about a "chronic" activity, one that is permanently incomplete—a cyclical movement or eternity at play. And despite it all, Camus said that we must imagine this hero of meaningless work, this figure bordering on the absurd, as "happy" in this infinite process.'[20]

We must keep very much in mind that in 1996, only 0.9% of the world's population was connected to the Internet, and the number of servers was around

16. José A. Bragança de Miranda & Maria Teresa Cruz (eds.), *op. cit.*, 2002.

17. The expression 'heroic period' of net.art is attributed to Olia Lialina (http://art.teleportacia.org/exhibition/miniatures) and refers to the first period of artistic experiments with the Internet, spanning the period between 1994 and 1999, approximately.

18. Montse Badia, "SOFTWARE SOCIAL. An Interview with ANTONI ABAD". *A*DESK Magazine*, no. 104. October 2012: http://www.a-desk.org/spip/spip.php?article1604.

19. As is evident in the minutes of the following congresses: The Annual Conference of the Museum Computer Network (Ottawa, Canada, 1998) and ISEA 96 Rotterdam. 7th International Symposium on Electronic Art: http://archives.isea-web.org/?page_id=1651.

20. Octavi Comeron, 'Arte y postfordismo: notas desde la Fábrica Transparente', Madrid: Trama, 2007.

nine and a half million[21]. That was the moment when the unstoppable avalanche of electronic commerce began and Google was still two years away[22].

The transition to Internet works using smartphones

We have already seen that Abad was building a solid oeuvre of net.art that earned him international recognition as he gradually distanced himself from the art-gallery circuit where his professional art career had begun and on which he had based his economic subsistence. The transition from the twentieth to the twenty-first century called for a redefinition of his working context based on a careful tracking of technological developments and financing that gradually looked to public funding and private sponsors.

In 2000, Abad began exploring the possibilities of the Internet on mobile devices and had already commissioned Daniel Julià to adapt his *Z* fly to work with WAP[23]. Abad and Julià experimented with Nokia 7110 cell phones, an innovative and advanced device that the Finnish manufacturer had put on the market in 1999 and promoted with the appearance of a very similar device in the film *Matrix*. WAP provided cell phones with data access that allowed nearly 750 million cell-phone users around the world to connect to the Internet. The WAP fly was no more than an animated image on those cell phones' low-resolution (96 x 65 pixels) monochrome screen, but it paved the way for online work with smartphones that Abad has continued to develop ever since. For the next four years, Abad focused on the development of his other fly, that is, the *Z* fly that users could see and use when connecting their personal computers to the telephone network through a modem (usually at 56,000 bits/second). In 2002, the constant attention required to track the activity of the swarm of flies led Abad to commission a WAP for tracking the statistics of that community on his cell phone. All of this laid the technical, ethical and esthetic foundation[24] for the work with communities now known as *megafone.net*, which was still called *zexe.net* in the early years because it was hosted on the domain originally created by the *Z* fly where the public downloaded the *z.exe* software.

The origins of *megafone.net*

In June 2003, Abad launched a first test of his definitive platform with programming by Eugenio Tisselli. This platform had to serve as a basis for trying out what was supposed to be his first project involving communities, namely the motorbike

21. Matthew Gray, *Internet Growth Summary*: http://stuff.mit.edu/people/mkgray/net/internet-growth-summary.html [accessed August 2013].

22. www.google.com/intl/en/about/company [accessed August 2013].

23. Wireless Application Protocol or WAP. The WAP was the first attempt to bring basic web functions to mobile devices of that period. The first WAPs date from 2000: http://technical.openmobilealliance.org/Technical/wapindex.aspx [accessed August 2013].

24. 'Antoni Abad is the creator of *Z*, an audiovisual piece which shows that the Internet is a digital public space where the technological determinism and increasing penetration of electronic commerce do not prevent the launch of an esthetic proposal of an experimental character, which eschews profit motives and promotes communications in the interpersonal sphere.' Roc Parés, 'Un parásito digital llamado *Z* se propaga por la red e invade ordenadores en todo el mundo con el consentimiento de los usuarios' ['A digital parasite named *Z* is propagated through the Internet and invades computers throughout the world with users' consent'], *Cultura* supplement, *La Vanguardia* (February 19, 2003).

couriers of São Paulo (promised for 2004 and later postponed until 2007); this is why he called it *Ensayo general* (Dress Rehearsal). This first workshop in 2003 was held at La Casa Encendida in Madrid with the participation of ten collaborators who generated channels such as HORATIU, which followed the daily life of a boy from Madrid's Lavapiés neighborhood; YNTQ, which explored the right to appropriate the images of other people in public spaces, and LABO, which reflected the eviction of squatters from Laboratorio 3 and the subsequent occupation by squatters of Laboratorio 4, also in Lavapiés[25].

There is some risk that our society's constant technological transformation might make the merits of these pioneering experiences difficult to properly appreciate. And here I refer to the words of Eugenio Tisselli, the programmer and writer who dedicated ten years (from 2000 to 2010) to the technical development of Abad's projects. Tisselli details the steps taken in 2003 to facilitate the direct uploading to the Internet of images taken with the first camera-equipped cell phones (Nokia 7650): 'first of all, we examined exactly how the photos taken by participants in *zexe.net* could be sent directly from cell phones to a webpage, that is, without need of any intermediate step. Current cell-phone networks allow the transmission not only of voice but also of data codified as digital signals. Moreover, cell-phone service providers offer the possibility of sending text messages (SMS) or multimedia (MMS) from a phone with data net access to an email address. It is precisely this capacity that we exploit in *zexe.net*. When we examine the format of an e-mail, we discover that it includes various important elements: the addresses of the sender and recipient, the date, text, and occasionally, attached files. It was clear that this format was ideal for our purposes so we created an application on the *zexe.net* server to receive all emails sent by participants from their phones, separate all their elements and, depending on the sender and recipient, place them in the proper place in a database. In this way participants only had to worry about sending their texts, images, sounds, or videos to the required address using the tools available on their own phones. We made the first transmission tests in 2003 for the first *zexe.net* project in Madrid, which Abad quite appropriately called *Ensayo general* (Dress Rehearsal)[26].'

In this detailed description of how the first test was operated, we already find some of the technical characteristics of *megafone.net*. At the same time, if we look back at the repercussions it had in the media, we will also find a very structured discourse that foreshadows the proposal's key concepts. Take, for example, the article about *Ensayo general* that Stefano Caldana and Roberta Bosco, journalists specializing in contemporary art and new media, published in *El País* in 2003: 'Abad's latest work in this field was presented a few days ago at the Casa Encendida art center in Madrid. It was the final act of a workshop the artist taught under the name *Ensayo general*. "The aim is to socially liberate cell phones by creating a straightforward, efficient, economical, instant and wireless audiovisual communication device. To do so, we use the latest wireless communication protocols that allow immediate publication on the Internet of multimedia messaging through cell phones with built-in cameras," stated Abad. Thanks to those cell

25. That is how it was described in a review signed by Europa Press and published in *La Vanguardia* (June 20, 2003), with the title 'El arte según el móvil.'
26. Eugenio Tisselli, *zexe.net: une cartographie numérique du monde*, Geneva: Centre d'Art Contemporain de Genève and Seacex, 2008.

phones, participants in the Madrid workshop became chroniclers of their own reality and initiated a participatory community forum in constant flux. Internet users are welcome to take part, although only with texts for the time being. "The goal is to offer the system, once it has been developed, to communities that do not have a voice in mainstream media and could even use it to improve their own internal relations."'[27]

The communities of *megafone.net* (formerly *zexe.net*)

Returning to 2004, when the Spanish Cultural Center in Mexico invited Abad to present a solo exhibition of his work, we will recall that Abad had transformed that invitation to exhibit his video installations by inviting taxi drivers from Mexico City to gather at the cultural center (located in the very heart of the city's historic center) and carry out his first art and mobile communication project (*sitio*TAXI*) with a community stigmatized by the media. That change not only involved persuading the center's director, Ángeles Albert, to reassign a space and budget originally intended for a contemporary art exhibition in order to carry out an unprecedented experimental proposal; it also marked a definitive step for Abad in the direction of a workshop dynamic as a form of public art. Regarding those first projects, the lecturer, curator, and art critic Martí Peran pointed out: 'More than an art project, these are workshops. The concept is important enough, given that it leads us directly to a second weighty consideration: the project's conception as the production of services. […] The workshop thus has a purely technical first dimension, which is already very efficient because of the novelty of providing access to these devices to users who, in most cases, have never had contact with them. […] It is here that we proposed the idea of art becoming a mechanism for the production of services: building devices, platforms, or tools that would allow users to develop an appropriate and efficient use value for their needs, desires, and imagination. In the context of these observations, it is even feasible to interpret projects as a possible type of public art: one that does not project anything into the general public's domain, yet also refrains from imposing a critical viewpoint from the unassailable podium of art. On the contrary, it inhabits the cracks and embodies the demands that already exist in the social body, thereby acting as a catalyst for action and to strengthen expectations of reaching a successful conclusion.'[28]

As Peran accurately observes in these fragments, Antoni Abad's strategic shift towards the 'production of services' becomes the principle characteristic of a working methodology that began with seventeen Mexican taxi drivers in 2004 and that has continued to be refined and adapted to the needs of different communities with which Abad and his collaborators continue to develop *megafone.net* today. Let us now focus on the assessment of this strategic shift that the lecturer and critic Alberto López Cuenca offered in his first article on Abad's endeavour in Mexico: 'but instead of simply reproducing iniquities in gallery spaces, these strategies must address social agents as subjects (not as objects of artistic representation), awakening in them mechanisms of reflection and representation that allow them to speak in the first person and consciously position themselves within the network of

27. Stefano Caldana and Roberta Bosco, '*Ensayo general* une el móvil y la comunicación distribuida', *El País* (July 3, 2003).
28. Martí Peran, *canal*GITANO*, Lleida, Centre d'Art la Panera (May 2005).

social relations. In this case, the artistic interventions are no longer a matter
of esthetics or compassion but rather of real, concrete activation that directly
addresses social conflict. In this sense, a project such as *sitio*TAXI* emerges
precisely as a reaction to realities that are distorted or even hidden by prejudice and
the media. What matters is not so much the project's institutional visibility as the
effect this initiative has had on the views of the taxi drivers who took part, and on
their perception of themselves and their environment.'[29] In this paragraph, López
Cuenca reveals what most legitimizes *megafone.net*'s *modus operandi* when he
points out that the participants are not called on as objects of artistic representation
but rather as subjects.

Clearly, beyond the reception of *megafone.net* by critics of contemporary
art and culture, it is the participants in these projects who bring meaning to the
platform. It is they who, by appropriating the resources supplied by the artist,
become present in a network from which they were previously absent, undertaking
individual actions that are interwoven, and collective actions that have been planned
through debate among the individuals to whom the project has conferred the status
of equals. Presence and agency had been denied them for various educational,
economic, and political reasons that involve fractures of all kinds, especially the so-
called digital divide. An example is offered by Antoni Jové (coordinator of the Centre
d'Art la Panera) and Maria López Fontanals (specialist in cultural communication for
the Lleida City Hall) in their observations of the *canal*GITANO* meetings in Lleida:
'Actually, one could say that for some participants, as they themselves explained,
the project was little more than mere entertainment—albeit with some implicit
dangers such as displaying themselves publically on the Internet—with a cell phone
as final compensation.' However, the majority of them, for example, the Associació
Trampolí, concluded that the experience of having accepted Antoni Abad's proposal
had been a fruitful process of exploration and introspection. This is how the Trampolí
girls put it: '*canal*GITANO* helped us to express things we would never have said.'[30]

*canal*GITANO* was the second project, following *sitio*TAXI*. Abad began with
the Gypsy community in his hometown[31] and then continued with the Gypsies in
León over the course of 2005. The paradigmatic mobility of the Gypsy community
as well as Abad's tendency to consider his own art career as a process of
nomadism[32] and progressive dematerialization[33] imbue these works with a poetics of
displacement redolent of Borges and the Situationists. Such displacement involves
immersion in other worlds and is never free of conflict. According to Abad, 'in the
Gypsy world, those who have the right to express themselves in the name of
the community are the patriarchs. Instead, I set out to give the youth a voice. At first this
proposal was not well received, but eventually the patriarchs accepted that, in this
project, the youths should represent the community. In the case of Lleida, it was very

29. Alberto López Cuenca, 'El taxista como etnógrafo', *ABC Cultural*, no. 642 (May 15, 2004).
30. *canal*GITANO*, Lleida: Centre d'Art la Panera, 2005.
31. See note 2.
32. A significant example is Abad's 1990 participation as artist-in-residence in The Nomad Residency at
the Banff Centre for the Arts, in the Rocky Mountains of Canada.
33. Dematerialization in the sense assigned to that term by Lucy R. Lippard (1973), combined with the
hyperbolic discourse on the passage from atoms to bits by authors such as Nicolas Negroponte (founder
of the MIT Media Lab in 1985), which was so in vogue when Abad was studying the European Media
Master in Audiovisual Creation and Technology at the Audiovisual University Institute of the Universitat
Pompeu Fabra, in Barcelona (1995–97).

difficult to find young Gypsy women who wanted to participate. The community tried to censure a few of the women whose images had been published. But the conflicts were eventually resolved in every case.'[34]

That same year (2005), Abad began working with a new community: sex workers from the city of Madrid. The project was entitled *canal*INVISIBLE* and involved ten people who worked as prostitutes on the streets of the Spanish capital. The obvious friction between the visibility of an art project and the invisibility of the human aspects of a paradigmatically vulnerable group generated a highly interesting mosaic of images loaded with an intimate emotional intensity. Once again, Abad applied the workshop methodology, allowing questions of gender to be expressed directly by the group, avoiding the interference of social agents who view that reality from ideological perspectives based on prejudice and alleged moral superiority. As is customary by now in *megafone.net* projects, the online platform also has a forum open to participation by Internet users. Compared to other groups, participation in this case was one of the highest and it is possible to discern a great contrast between the search for complicity among prostitutes and the tendency towards transgression detectable in the anonymous commentaries of certain Internet users. In working with this group, *megafone.net* found an ally in Hetaira,[35] an association that allowed it access to a community marked by fear and on the edge of legality.

Perhaps the largest community to work with *megafone.net* was that formed by some forty physically handicapped individuals in the city of Barcelona. Coordinated by Mery Cuesta, this project managed to involve participants and organize collective actions ('commando' teams) to explore the city's most peripheral neighborhoods. It was in 2006 that Abad proposed this project to the art center Arts Santa Mònica in Barcelona's central Rambla neighborhood. Regarding this project the jury statement of the Ars Electronica Prize[36] observed: 'It is in an elegant way that this project unites several of the key factors that define outstanding "digital communities". A group of Barcelona people in wheelchairs documents road blocks and other obstacles on their way as well as the—rare—positive examples of easy access for people in wheelchairs. Doing this they make the best use of existing technology to work for change. This project tells us a lot about access in its most basic forms as well as in relation to technology and networks: it supports the fight for physical access to buildings and infrastructure for a marginalized and handicapped group of people, it promotes the awareness of their problems and takes the collaborative use of technology right in the hands of the concerned people themselves. The technology they use represents the most common form of ubiquitous computing: mobile phones with digital cameras. The web platform of *canal*ACCESSIBLE* serves as the binding element of this community, and maps their findings and observations to the physical geography of Barcelona. All of this is done with a simple interface, providing easy-to-use access to that constantly growing and up-to-date base of information. They will use the prize money of the Golden Nica not only for further improvements of the usability of their interface but also give it to the implementation of similar projects in countries of the global South—an investment in replicability and in bridging the global digital divide.'

34. See note 15.
35. Colectivo Hetaira: www.colectivohetaira.org [accessed August 20113].
36. See note 1.

In 2006, Abad also responded to an invitation from TEOR/éTica to participate in *Estrecho dudoso*—a cultural event in Costa Rica—with the project *canal*CENTRAL*. On that occasion, the community consisted of 22 Nicaraguan immigrants who transmitted information from cell phones to San José, Costa Rica. According to the Costa Rican press[37], 'The contents of Canal Central are very varied, ranging from a chronicle of the eviction of Nicaraguan families from a squat or a poem about migrant women to a recipe for making tasty *vigorón*. Among the 22 migrants participating in the project are housewives, a security guard, a boxer, a secretary and an accountant. They each have their own section or channel with their name or pseudonym. For example, Azucena's channel is called Mariposa and includes an interview with a security guard or two children: "A little brother and sister, one *tico* and the other, *nica*." There are also thematic sections with titles such as *Bacanal, Vivienda* or *Papeles. Bacanal* is about how the so-called "pinoleros" have fun, while *Papeles* contains advice, reflections and ironic observations by immigrants about how to obtain one's documents in Costa Rica. The telephones employed by participants in this initiative run on an experimental GPRS network belonging to the Costa Rican Electricity Institute—a sponsor—which makes it possible to send multimedia contents (voice recordings and videos) as well as photographs and texts.'

In May 2007, Abad managed to launch what was supposed to have been his first project with communities: *canal*MOTOBOY*, in the city of São Paulo. This project marked a change of methodology, shifting from the individual use of mobile devices (each participant with one phone) to a collective use metaphorically represented by the megaphone employed in protests and demonstrations. The cell phone passed from one participant to another at weekly meetings. In the future, this variation will make it possible to carry out projects with very limited resources, even without institutional support or sponsors. Two aspects of this project should be emphasized. First, the Brazilian community of motorbike couriers is the one that has managed to maintain the most continuous flow of uploads. In fact, at the time of writing (late August 2013) they are still going on[38]. On my web browser in Catalonia (on August 28, 2013, at 18:11:03) I see that Crispim, in Brazil, has stopped his bike and posted to *canal*MOTOBOY* from his cell phone: a white SUV has turned over on the asphalt of Avenida Sumaré, taking down a streetlight in the process. Crispim comments that this is the first avenue in São Paulo to have a lane for motorbikes and he labels his concise but eloquent report #*accidentes*. The sustainability of *megafone.net*'s projects depends on a variety of factors, but here the commitment of some of the project's original participants has been key to maintaining the platform. The second aspect to be emphasized is structural: the use of labels or tags.[39] Thanks to the labeling of messages with tags proposed by the participants themselves, *canal*MOTOBOY* is the first *megafone.net* project to use metadata (information about information). This constitutes a qualitative leap in the organization of contents because metadata allows the community to create its own taxonomy: a true *folksonomy*. The shift from a top-down organization of information (taxonomy) to a bottom-up organization (*folksonomy*) implies a major

37. Doriam Díaz, 'Migrantes nicas muestran su realidad a través de internet', *La Nación* (November 22, 2006): www.nacion.com/ln_ee/2006/noviembre/22/aldea903683.html [accessed August 2013].
38. *www.megafone.net* [accessed August 2013].
39. Mery Cuesta and Eugenio Tisselli, *zexe.net: 44 tags per a descriure el món*, Sala d'Exposicions de la Rambla de Girona, 2007.

advance with regard to the community's autonomy, above and beyond the creation of contents.

In 2008, the city of Geneva invited Antoni Abad to work on a new project of collective cartography, generating a collective map of accessible Geneva with a group of people with physical disabilities. The success of *canal*ACCESSIBLE* in Barcelona (2006) made it possible to replicate the experience with major support from institutions and associations, including the Centre d'Art Contemporain Genève. One immediately visible characteristic of this new project was the degree of organizational maturity in the planning, methodology, and coordination of workshops. The smartphones had also improved, with more versatile cameras and GPS systems. Moreover, *GENÈVE*accessible* had different nuances from the previous projects, largely due to its evident connection to public institutions, including the fact that Geneva's mayor, Patrice Mugny, made the opening speech at the project's presentation[40].

*canal*TEMPORAL*: in 2009, Abad traveled to Colombia at the invitation of Felipe Londoño, director of the International Festival of the Image in Manizales. This trip had a very ambitious objective: to bring together two historically opposed communities, the *displaced* and the *dissociated*. The two groups defined themselves as follows:

Displaced: men, women, boys, girls, youths, adults, and the elderly, mostly peasants forced by armed conflict in Colombia to abandon their lands, communities and birthplaces to save their lives.

Dissociated: men, women, boys, girls, youths, adults, and the elderly, mostly peasants who formerly belonged to different illegal armed groups in Colombia and have decided to abandon armed struggle and return to civilian life through processes of social integration and employment.

Abad was warned that bringing these two communities together could have dire consequences and even threaten the participants' physical wellbeing. For this reason the first meetings of the two groups were held on different days, even though they were both using *megafone.net*. After a few meetings, Abad pointed out the striking similarities between the descriptive labels (tags) being generated by each group and suggested they hold joint meetings. One of the participants confirmed that this was the right moment, despite the fact that such meetings would have been impossible just a year earlier. Nevertheless, in order to protect the participants' freedom of movement and expression, their cell phones' GPS systems were deactivated. Later on, the work with these two communities was maintained by the Universidad de Caldas (a collaborator in the original project) although outside the context of *megafone.net*.

*canal*SAHARAUI* (2009): a group of young Sahrawis from the Tinduf refugee camp in Algeria transmit their experiences on the Internet using cell phones. Given the logistical difficulties of their geopolitical context in the Sahara Desert, with

---

40. Program of the *Cycle de conférences, projections et performances autour du projet et de l'exposition 'GENÈVE*accessible - Antoni Abad'*, which includes the speech by the mayor of Geneva, Patrice Mugny: www.centre.ch/images/images_cac/content/expositions/2010/createurs_singuliers.pdf [accessed March 2014].

water rationing, an intermittent electrical supply, and no cell-phone coverage, this project used the megaphone variant, that is, collective use of available cell phones. They also had to resort to delayed publication, using the wifi coverage offered by an Italian NGO. *canal*SAHARAUI* was part of the ARTifariti International Art and Human Rights Meeting in Western Sahara organized by the Ministry of Culture of the Sahrawi Arab Democratic Republic (SADR) and the Asociación de Amistad con el Pueblo Saharaui in Seville. This experience has given *megafone.net* some of its most extraordinary images, and here I am referring to what we see when we open *http://www.megafone.net/SAHARA*, expand the image of a territory we imagine to be uninhabited, and discover photographs, texts, and audiovisual recordings by people who live there in the desert refugee camps.

And from the striking images of *canal*SAHARAUI* we move to the absence of any image in the access interface for *The Blind Point of View*. The Internet is an interactive audiovisual medium that has progressively assigned more weight to images than text. With this development, it has become increasingly less accessible to people with impaired vision. As is explained at *http://www.megafone. net/BLINDVIEW*, 'The Blind Point of View* is an interactive, community-based GPS cellphone project that invites the blind and visually impaired to share their own news and opinions of the difficulties and facilities they find in their day-to-day lives. The *Blind Point of View* project will hold not only information on barriers and accommodations, but will also be a repository for storytelling posts, designed to build a more nuanced location-specific overview of the cityscape, as experienced by blind and visually impaired people who interact with it on a regular basis. Using software especially designed for cell phones with built-in GPS, participants can register and publish, on a webpage, geo-located images and sounds of architectural obstacles and barriers they encounter on the streets, as well as examples of good adaptation.'

The project was carried out in Barcelona, and once again, it relied on the web programming of Eugenio Tisselli, with a cell phone application programmed by Lluís Gómez (computer engineer and specialist in free and open-source software). Abad worked with Tisselli and Gómez to develop this project in cooperation with a community calling for an active presence in both the urban and the digital public spheres. At the same point in history (2010) that the Arab Spring was becoming known to the world through images recorded and published from smartphones, the group that took part in *The Blind Point of View* reminded us that many obstacles and conflicts exist beyond appearances.

In 2011, Abad returned to New York where, with the support of the Queens Museum of Art, he organized *you*PLURAL*. There, a group of immigrants used cell phones to make public their experiences, opinions and expectations through audiovisual chronicles. This new project characterized by its diversity of origins and languages was launched with the support of Immigrant Movement International and the Fundación Botín. Among *you*PLURAL*'s publications we find curiosities such as photos of people fishing on the Hudson River, pink magnolias blooming on the corner of 45th Avenue and 70th Street, complaints about the price of gasoline on a service station sign in Long Island, and protests against evictions on Livingston Street. All of this is part of a polyglot mosaic in which citizens express themselves with great spontaneity--a wake-up call about the economic recession and social inequalities in what was formerly called the First World.

At the time of writing (August 2013), another project, *MONTRÉAL*in/accessible*, is still underway. This new work involving telecommunications engineer Matteo Sisti Sette as a *megafone.net* programmer began in 2011 and maintains the dynamic that began in Barcelona (*canal*ACCESSIBLE*, 2006) and Geneva (*GENÈVE*accessible*, 2008). It is no surprise that at a moment when commercial social networks such as Facebook, Instagram, and Twitter are blossoming the projects organized by *megafone.net* are still being called for and recognized throughout the world. The unstoppable dynamic of corporate social networks will continue, leaving space for social groups united by shared interests to form their own digital communities.

Conclusions

Mobility, which is *megafone.net*'s main characteristic, manifests itself through the new and paradoxically primitive though ubiquitous computing devices, as used by its different participants with innumerable nuances: from the mobility of taxi drivers or motorbike couriers that cross borders between neighborhoods to the mistrusted mobility of the Gypsies' itinerant commerce; from the imposed mobility of the displaced, dissociated and emigrants to the promiscuous mobility of prostitutes and transsexuals; and, from the limited mobility of those with physical disabilities to Antoni Abad's own free thinking, which is in constant motion at the crossroads of art, technology and society.

The second general characteristic of *megafone.net* is that it offers a voice, and a listening ear. In other words, it practices a human form of interactivity. What characterizes the interactivity of these projects surpasses the interaction between a person and a computer, and even surpasses human interaction with computers, cell phones or networks. *megafone.net* promotes collective communication; moreover, it seeks to make this sustainable. Its workshops do not teach participants digital literacy the way job training does. They are, instead, personal encounters where communities define their problems and needs and adopt the mobile devices and web platform offered to them as an adaptable framework for action.

The third most outstanding characteristic of *megafone.net* is resistance: resistance to discrimination in any form. By developing proactive but resistant processes, *megafone.net* renews, with each new collective, the will and desire to intervene in society. It thus seeks to affect the manner and procedures through which streets and squares, computers and networks, languages and protocols, political parties and borders, urban codes and plans determine, configure and delimit people's lives. Each community exercises its own resistance, but it may be possible to define two major lines of action: resistance to the corporate behavior of mainstream media—that turns people into consumers and products—and resistance to bureaucratic behavior in networks, which turns citizens into a homogenous mass of users or simple human resources.

The beauty of *megafone.net* lies not only in some of the many moments captured in images, texts, and videos. Its interest lies not only in its well-adapted and publicity-free interfaces, nor in its non-hierarchical communication protocols, nor even in the prodigious technology hidden beneath the shiny covers of its mobile devices. The beauty and interest of *megafone.net* is really the rebellious solidarity of its efforts, collective efforts to foster expression and open dialog that, as the maximum exercise of freedom, has a capacity for transformation that extends beyond its author's intentions[41].

Up to now, in these first ten years of existence, **254** people have participated in *megafone.net*, generating **61,072** files or uploads[42]. But beyond those figures, and beyond questions of accessibility or capacity to participate in critical thought, *megafone.net*'s projects are a collective, diverse, and living reality and an outstanding example of an artistic endeavour concerned with digital communities.

41. I refer to Antoni Abad as author because he is ultimately responsible for the *megafone.net* project.
42. *www.megafone.net* [accessed August 2013].

Roc Parés i Burguès lives and works in Catalonia since 1983. Artist and researcher in the field of interactive communication. Doctor of Audiovisual Communication from the Universitat Pompeu Fabra (2001) and Bachelor of Fine Art from the Universitat de Barcelona (1992). His artworks have been presented at the Centro de Cultura Contemporánea de Barcelona, the Museo Nacional Centro de Arte Reina Sofía in Madrid, the Centro Cultural de Belém, the Tate Gallery in London, the Art Gallery of Ontario, the National Museum of Photography, Film and Television in Bradford, Brandts Danmark of Odense, and the Centro Cultural de España in Mexico, among others. He is a lecturer at the Department of Communications and researcher at the DigiDoc Interactive Communications Group in the Universitat Pompeu Fabra. He has been lecturer in Interactive Communications and Electronic Art for several undergraduate and postgraduate, master and doctoral programs. He currently co-directs the Master of Digital Arts course (MUAD) and lectures for the Interdisciplinary Master in Cognitive Systems and Interactive Media (CSIM), both at the UPF in Barcelona.

Participants and collaborators *megafone.net/2004–2014*

261 participants **54.254** publications of audio, photos, video, and text **project** Antoni Abad **programming** *megafone.net* Matteo Sisti Sette **computer programming** 2003–10 Eugenio Tisselli **smartphone programming 2008–10** Lluís Gómez **documentary** Glòria Martí

2004–05/14 México DF: *sitio*TAXI*

taxistas participantes Alejandro García Pineda, Alejandro Fabila Sagaseta, Antonio Sabbagh Macedo, Arturo Olguín Luna, José David Morín Luna, Miguel Ángel Ortiz López, Eugenio Alderete Boy, Juan Gerardo Herrera Zamora, Javier Vargas González, Jorge Alberto Barrera Urrutia, José Guel Serrano, Juan Montzi Hernández, Marcos Arturo González Espinosa, Miguel Ángel Perea Alarcó, Pedro González Mercado, Pedro González Mariscal, Rosa María López Sánchez **talleristas** Andrea Martínez, Morelos León, Mariel Quevedo, Quetzal Castillo, Aldo Francisco Córdoba, Lucía Italia Rodríguez, José Vladimir Cortés **agradecimientos** Ángeles Albert, César Martínez, Germán Rostan, Saúl Ruiz, Josefo, Humberto Jardón, Fabián Garré, Juan Antonio Montiel, Miriam Quintanilla, Roc Parés **coordinación** Jorge Morales **patrocinio** Fundación Telefónica **organización** Centro Cultural de España en México, Centro Multimedia del Centro Nacional de las Artes, Conaculta México

2005 Lleida: *canal*GITANO*

joves gitanos participants Antonio de la Rosa Jiménez, Adán Giménez Giménez, Jesús Giménez Cortés, Juan Antonio Giménez Castro, Efraín Salazar Cortés, Samuel López Jiménez, Ángel Giménez Castro, Miguel, Jere, Moises, Richard, Jimmy, Jonathan Reyes, Rubén, Lorena, Naima, Francisco, Paio, Paco Salazar, Pepote, Richard, Jesús Pubill, Soraya, Sulamita, Toño Salazar Ardura, Trampolí **sociologia** Jordi Garreta, Alba Cazorla, Glòria Noe, Mireia Garra **comunicació** María López **agraïments** Associació Futur, Associació Trampolí, Associació Prosec, Universitat de Lleida, Marta Rincón, Hermes Carretero, Alex Pilis, Helena Ayuso, Anna Roigé, Roser Sanjuán **coordinació** Antoni Jové **patrocini** Nokia España **organització** Centre d'Art la Panera

2005 León: *canal*GITANO*

jóvenes gitanos participantes Diana García Borja, Elena, Toño y Carmela, Guadalupe, Isaac, Isabel Jiménez Hernández, Jonatan Jiménez Pérez, José Jiménez Jiménez, Alfredo Jiménez García, Enrique Díez Barrul, Teresa García León, Tamara Coray Romero, Juan Roque Jiménez Vargas, Rosario, Susi **geografía humana** José Somoza, Jessica de la Fuente, Alejandro Santos, Victoria Labarga, Susana Abad, Ignacio Arias, Jaime Iglesias **agradecimientos** Fundación Secretariado General Gitano, Hogar de la Esperanza, Universidad de León **coordinación** Raúl Ordás **organización** Museo de Arte Contemporáneo de Castilla y León

2005 Madrid: *canal*INVISIBLE*

trabajadoras sexuales participantes Sirena, Margarita, Caminante, Gata, Libertina, Brandy, Camelia, Traviesa, Dátil, Orquídea, Chiquitina, Salomé **agradecimientos** Blanca Rosillo, Amaya de Miguel, Elvira Villa, Juan López-Aranguren, Rubén Lorenzo, Colectivo Hetaira **coordinación** Herminia Gonzálvez, Rocío Gracia, María Nieto, Vanesa Casas **organización** La Casa Encendida

2006–13 Barcelona: *BARCELONA*accessible*

participants amb diversitat funcional Antonio Ortega Caraballo, Carlos Vidal Wagner, Antonio Centeno, José Conrado, Craig Grimes, David Rodríguez Vilalta, Íñigo Álvarez, Eugeni Boix Prats, Francisco Nieto, Josep Gallart, Javier Touzon, Jesús González, Joan Prat Julián, Joaquín Esteban, Jordi Pie Bolívar, Josep Xarau, Maria Rosa Pane, Juan Cantón, Khalid Zerguini Jassid, Lucia Tevar Jimenez, Marga Alonso, Marta Boltó Grau, Martín Leates, Mercè Campeny, Miguel Ángel Sánchez, Nicolás Basadonna, Oriol Bono i Costa, Óscar Rodríguez, Pilar Cruz, Holger Strauss, Rosa Bonastre, Salvador Pi Puig, Sonia Guerrero, To Monreal, Mireia García Godia, Antonio Vargas Punti, Joan Basums **col.laboren** Servei de Cartografia de l'Ajuntament de Barcelona, Departament de Benestar Social de la Generalitat de Catalunya **espai** Gnopolis Disseny **fotomatón** Pere Pratdesaba **curador** Miguel von Hafe Pérez **agraïments** Gema Hasen-Bey, Javi Creus, Ángel Aguilar, Jono Bennett, Leticia Pérez, Albert Cano, Michel Tofahrn **assistents de coordinació** Iban Calzada, Mar González, Pilar Cruz **coordinació** Mery Cuesta **patrocini** Nokia España, Amena **organització** Centre d'Art Santa Mònica

2006–07 San José de Costa Rica: *canal*CENTRAL*

inmigrantes nicaragüenses participantes Alejandra Selva Bolaños, Azucena Mercedes Blessing Fuentes, Carlos Ernesto Cálix Calderón, Esmeralda Jaime Peralta, Milena Lazo Coronado, Hazel Sáenz Arriaza, Ramón Bravo Gil, Eugenio Jarquín Salazar, Alonso Mejía Sánchez, Eva Martha Gozález Carvajar, Lester Ramírez Martínez, Yesenia Rodríguez, Daniela López Membreño, Miriam Morales García, Lesbia Sánchez Bolaños, Guadalupe Álvarez Molina, Luis Enrique Balladares Orozco, Olinda Bravo Ramírez, Claudia **colabora** Municipalidad de San José **equipo** Pedro Leiva, Fiorella Resenterra, Zulay Orozco, Cayetana Cores, Ruth Sibaja, Jaime Alvarado, Jafhis Quintero, Jean Pierre Ratton, Federico Herrero, Alexis Seas, Geiner Núñez, Guillermo Acuña **curadoras** Virginia Pérez-Ratton, Tamara Díaz Bringas **coordinador** Elvis Martínez **patrocinio** Sociedad Estatal Acción Cultural Exterior de España, Instituto Costarricense de Electricidad **organización** Fundación TEOR/éTica

2007–14 São Paulo, Brasil: *canal*MOTOBOY*

motoboys participantes Adriana Maria de Oliveira, Alexandro de Moraes Lima, Andrea Sadocco Giannini, Fernando, Tadeu Luiz dos Santos Scabio, Cleyton Pedro Perroni, Bruno Crispim, Anderson do Prado Gil, Franscisco Djalma Souza, Edison Cordeiro da Silva, Luiz Fernando Bicchioni, Mirtão, Neka, Renato Roque de Loreto Junior, Ronaldo Simão da Costa, Tadeu Ferreira dos Anjos, Viralata **equipe CCSP** Henrique Siqueira, Mónica Calderón, Douglas Freitas, João Mussolin **sem a participação de** Regina Silveira, Augusto Stiel Neto, Inês Raphaelian, Ana Tomé, Marta Rincón, Alex Pilis, Lucas Bambozzi, Karla Brunet, Glòria Martí, Gerald Kogler, Philippe Bertrand e Teresa Lenzi **o** *canal*MOTOBOY* **não teria o gás merecido / curador adjunto** Eliezer Muniz dos Santos **coordenação** Ronaldo Simão da Costa **patrocínio** Sociedad Estatal Acción Cultural Exterior de España **organisação** Centro Cultural de Espanha em São Paulo, Centro Cultural São Paulo

2008 Genève, Suisse: *GENÈVE*accessible*

personnes à mobilité réduite Alireza Kabirlaleh, Alexandre Baumgartner, Franco Gamba, Corinne Billaud-Antoniadès, Daniel Rabina, Nadia Habibi, Florence Odier, Numa Poujouly, Hermane Ntsoli, Laurent Kneubühl, Christian Gobe, Christian Mordasini, Calogero Curreri, Paul Pham, Paolo Daga, Ursula Farah-Muller, Jean-Vincent Tache, Tao Pham, Zigzag **équipe CAC** Katya García-Antón, Marie-Avril Berthet, Maxime Lassagne **forum Créateurs Singuliers** Laura Györik Costas **coordination projet** Joëlle Oudard **coordination émetteurs** Numa Poujouly, Laurent Kneubühl **sponsorisation** Pro Infirmis, Association Handicap Architecture Urbanisme, Swisscom, Fondation Hans Wilsdorf, BFEH, Seacex, Migros, Prohelvetia, Fondation Transport Handicap *GENÈVE*accessible* **a été soutenu par** Centre d'Art Contemporain, Ville de Genève

2009–10 Manizales, Colombia: *canal*TEMPORAL*

participantes desplazados y desmovilizados Ángel, Dana, Deambulante, Gujago, Jack, Juantiburón, Lagordis, Llanerita, Malkamikuna, Minutos, Poli, Xixgu, Yanacona **logo** Ravi Poovaiah adaptado por Sergi Botella **agradecimientos** Asociación Abriendo Horizontes, Felipe Londoño, Ricardo Andrés Delgado, Juliana Morales, Consuelo Rozo **coordinación** David Zapata **colaboración** Centro de Estudios y Desarrollo Alternativo en Territorios, Conflicto y Violencia Social **apoyo** Institut Ramón Llull **organización** Universidad de Caldas, Vicerrectoría de Proyección Universitaria, Facultad de Artes y Humanidades, Departamento de diseño Visual

2009–11 Tinduf, Argelia: *canal*SAHARAUI*

refugiados saharauis participantes مشاركون صحراويون لاجئون Ahyeb, Ahziba, Anhabuha, Brahimsalem, Chbla, Fatimetu, Fatma, Fatu, Galia, Glana, Hamada, Jaddu, Jatuha, Kabara, Kabara S, Koria, Lamira, Magla, Mamia, Mula, Salca, Tekbr, Zagma, Zeina **agradecimientos** شكر وامتنان Ahmed Fadel, Saleh Brahim, Salka Ala-ti, Azman Mohamed, familia Krikiba, Chaska Mori, Eugenio Tisselli, Glòria Martí, Jorge Fernández, Edi Escobar, Roc Parés, Afapredesa, Pililli Narbona **coordinación** تنسيق Kabara Abderraman, Fatma Kori **apoyo** دعم Aso-ciación de Amistad con el Pueblo Saharaui de Sevilla, Hangar Barcelona, Ministerio de Cultura de la República Árabe Saharaui Democrática, Unión Nacional de Mujeres Saharauis **organización** تنظيم Artifariti

2010–11 Barcelona: *The Blind Point of View*

participants amb diversitat visual Boualem Hamamda, Elisa Botet, Felipe Yagüe, Iván Molinos, Joan Miquel Roig, Jordi Noguera, José Ángel Carrey, Meritxell Aymerich, Neus Salvat, Paquita García, Pepa Casas, Xavier Blanch **agraïments** Johana Vásquez, Lorea Iglesias **col.laboren** Associació Discapacitat Visual Catalunya, l'Associació Catalana per a la Integració del Cec, Centre Cívic Golferichs **suport** Ajuda Activitats Culturals d'Impacte Social, Obra Social de la Fundació "la Caixa"

2011–13 New York: *you*PLURAL*

participant migrant workers 参加民工 Anna Lu, Manuel Martagón, María Canela, Francis Low, Jun Ying Zhai, Eva Liu, Plinio Garrido, Fiona Yuen, Irene Liu, Vicencio Márquez, Shurong Qian, Louise Lear, Chuankui Jiang, Tony Talachas, Yitao Yang, Gary Yuen **thanks to** 感谢 Fiona Yuen, José E. Rodríguez, Nung-Hsin Hu, Tania Bruguera, Jing Sun **coordination** 协调 Manuel Molina *you*PLURAL* **has been supported by** 由 Immigrant Movement International, Queens, New York; Fundación Botín, Spain; New New Yorkers Program of the Queens Museum of Art, New York 支持

2012–13 Montreal, Canada: *MONTRÉAL*in/accessible*

personnes à mobilité réduite Ali Akbor Chowdhury, Anna Tkaczewska, Arseli Dokumaci, Henry Desbiolles, Joeroul, Laurence Parent, Linda Gauthier, Marie-Eve Veilleux, Mélanie Benard, Julien Gascon-Samson **collaboration** Joëlle Rouleau, Antonia Hérnandez, Ben Spencer **remerciements** RAPLIQ **coordination projet** Kimberly Sawchuk, Laurence Parent *MONTRÉAL*in/accessible* **a été soutenu par** Office of the Vice-President of Research and Graduate Studies, Concordia University, Montréal; Concordia University Chair, Tier One, in Mobile Media Studies; Mobile Media Lab, Concordia University, Montréal; FQRSC, Mediatopias Research Group, Montréal; GRAND-National Centres of Excellence, Canada

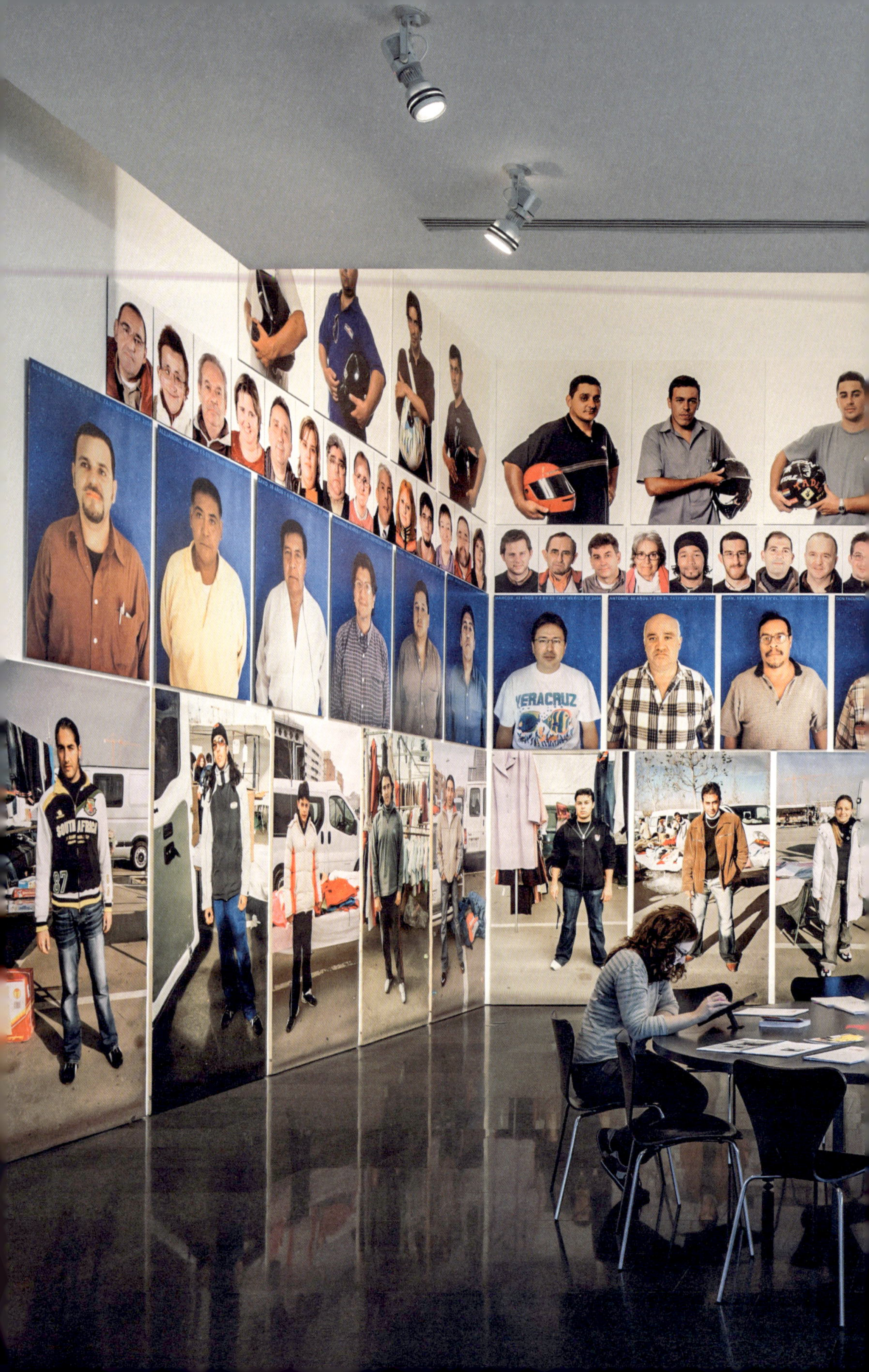

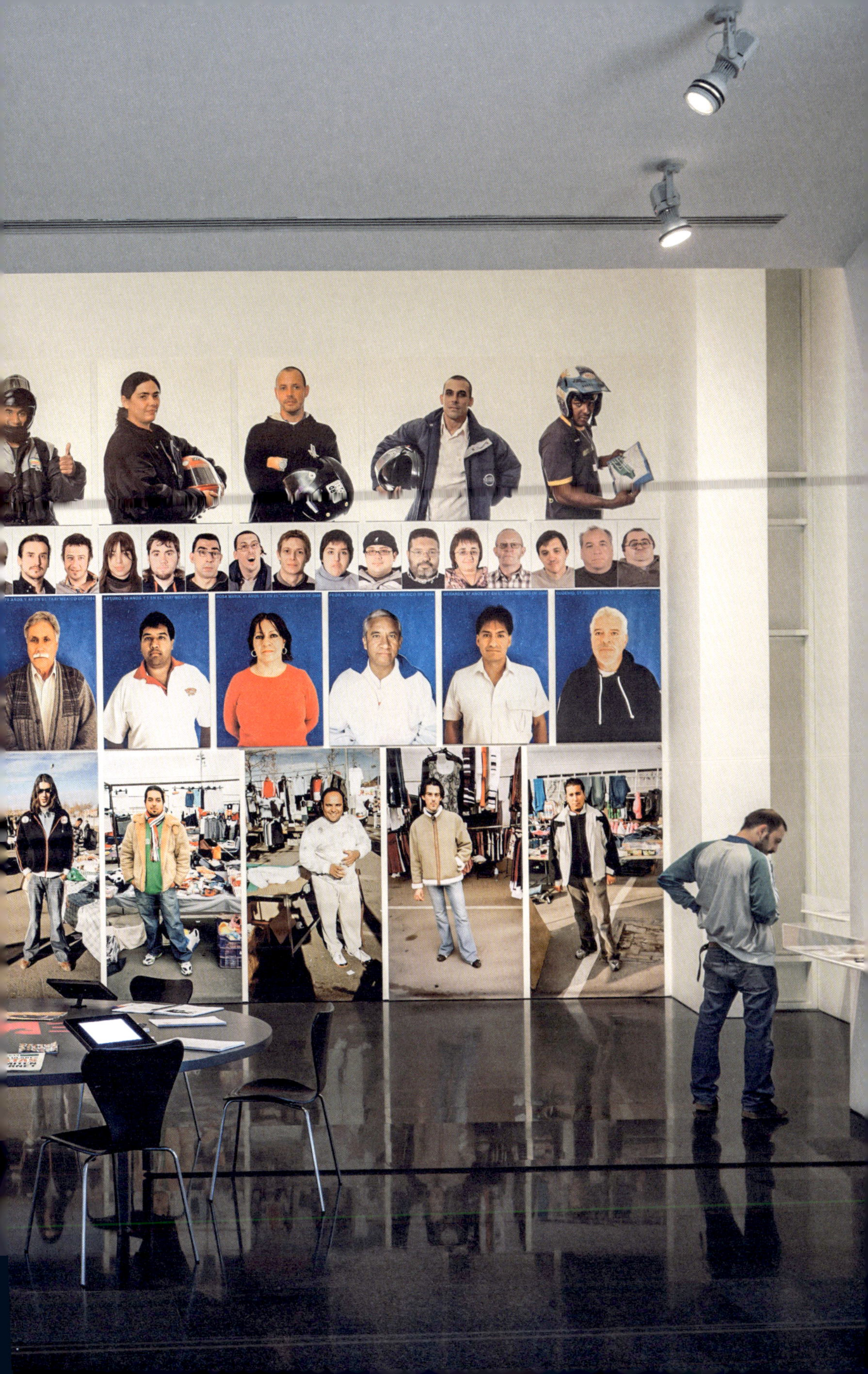

*sitio*TAXI*

Jorge Morales Moreno

[Originally published in *sitio*TAXI*, Spanish Cultural Center in Mexico City, April 2004]

To understand *sitio*TAXI*, you need to imagine yourself mixing high-tech communication media with considerable amounts of art, and industrial doses of sociology. Imagine yourself immersed in a gigantic asphalt jungle, one with no beginning and no end, completely filled with every sort of building and fragmented into thousands of streets and avenues leading everywhere and nowhere. To this interminable jungle add millions of 'urbanauts' of all ages, stressed by infernal working hours and rhythms, marching this way and that like armies of ants. Finally, imagine yourself at the wheel of a taxi, routinely driving incredibly long fares for ten to twelve hours a day.

Once you are inside this scenario, you will be asked to record everything you consider relevant with a sophisticated cell phone—voices or sounds, fixed or moving images—and transmit them via the Internet to a web page: *www.zexe.net/TAXI* where they will be published with no intermediaries! There you have the basic ingredients of the social and artistic experiment that Catalan artist Antoni Abad (*b.* 1956) has been carrying out in our city since March 13.

Getting back to the cocktail you mixed in the first paragraph, we find three possible ways of understanding this event: one from a technological viewpoint, another as art and yet a third, from a social perspective; these are its three basic components.

I.

From a technological perspective, *sitio*TAXI* is an extremely innovative and libertarian event (not to use the word 'democratic,' which has fallen practically into disrepute in our country lately). It is innovative not so much in its choice of technological tools as in how it employs them. Let us put it this way: the combination of cell phones capable of sending multimedia messages directly to the Internet and the Net itself as a worldwide forum for publications and information turns this project's participants, flesh-and-blood taxi drivers (some with over twenty years' experience) into its central protagonists, as well as intermediaries between the limitless jungle (the city) and its world of life (everyday existence). The message lies not in the medium (cell phones, Internet, web pages) but rather in its users, who involve themselves in the project and thus become its message through what they see and consider pertinent, relevant or meaningful in a day's work.

In that sense, *sitio*TAXI* makes it possible for the person on the street—the authorless and thus anonymous gaze—to publish on the World Wide Web (www) with neither barriers nor censors. This, then, is direct and free web access, so this project's innovative character lies in its reassignment of the use of cutting-edge technology, something still elitist and with restricted use in our country, to empower other perspectives, voices, and views, allowing them to present and express themselves on the Internet's public forum.

And *sitio*TAXI* is libertarian in its validation of guru McLuhan's prophecy. Never before in Mexico has the use of communication technology 'broadened,' 'expanded' or 'extended' the natural potential of human communication. Out of nowhere, *sitio*TAXI* has made it possible for the taxi driver's voice, gaze, ear, and awareness of everything to surpass and transcend the limitations of the human body and occupy the screens of any terminal, any working computer anywhere in the world. Technology is here working as a humanizing element.

II.

From the standpoint of art, *sitio*TAXI* behaves like both an object and an action, each within a framework of metaphorical terrains.

It is an object in the sense that all of the information transmitted by its participants ends up on a web page that can be seen by anyone who so wishes. That makes it a public and collective visual object with no Author. A postmodern work of electronic art, multimedia that can stand up to any sort of reading as long as it does not try to be linear or textual. Its central element is neither an artist/creator nor its medium, as we have seen, let alone the institutions that have made it possible. In any event, this artwork's center is on the edge, in the fortuitous broadcasters that become a part of the project strictly as a result of destiny.

Anyone who enters the web page will find more than simply a catalog of images associated with the inexhaustible world of the taxi. They will also discover a work in motion, something that changes every time a message (graphic, text, or audio) is posted. It is thus a work that is only complete when it has viewers who, as generally occurs with contemporary art works, 'read' it in their own way. They will draw on what interests them and carry away what impresses them.

In action, *sitio*TAXI* steals the necessary means to access major-league mass communication from a limited circle of high-tech users and offers them to a group of strategic social agents—who are, by the way, sufficiently stigmatized by mainstream media—without subjecting them to harsh processes of elimination, and without demanding specialized or technical training, just as Prometheus stole fire from the gods and offered it to the simple, common people of his time.

Here we have the repurposing of a technological implement, something I consider to be very common in the history of art, and something that directly affects the user's experience: freed of the fetters associated with its original function, it becomes a means for experimenting, exploring, playing, and creating, revealing the close relationship between art and technology and bringing out the artist's defiant and visionary role in that relationship. Far from accepting its rules or instructions, the artist approaches the technology of his time as a set of tools for creative action.

Antoni Abad confirms all of this with this real-time art in motion. He steals means of communication (cellular or Internet) from their technological Olympus and distributes them among the taxi drivers of Mexico City, possibly the most populous urban center in the world. And once again, the instrument becomes a tool for exploring, an interface and pretext for experimenting and creating. In this experiment, the artistic gaze (through the medium) has taken root amongst the taxi drivers: day by day, they create mosaics of city images, with the greatest diversity and wealth of colors, subjects, and scenes, accompanied by audio, video, and text. Their gazes converge on an electronic site where they generate arbitrary and complex collages that present the city as it is: arbitrary, immense, diverse, full of contrasts, scenes and subjects.

Thus, we take stock of how the artistic gaze invades the workaday world (one rooted in routine, monotony and predictability), making each moment, scene, day, night, and instant unique and different, memorable and unrepeatable—worthy of publication on the Internet. Life then takes on a greater meaning, or a new one as the case may be, and that is one of *sitio*TAXI*'s most interesting and incisive proposals: its impact on the social world, its mark on those who took part, and the possibility it offers for social communication without intermediaries. It illustrates how media can be used to foster and facilitate collective creation to broaden people's free and direct expression as in the art world: without control, unfettered, with neither instructions nor rules.

III.

Finally, from a social perspective, that is, from a sociological standpoint, *sitio*TAXI* can be seen as a two-way window, with two channels—interactive, more or less like Alice's looking glass.

On one side, it is a window opened by art that also serves as a show window and a projection of life stories that speak of coming and going, and of the existence of concrete social agents who experience the city like all of us, except that they reconnoiter it every single day, kilometer by kilometer. These life stories are not only the expressions of taxi drivers; they are also fragments of a (social) way of being, of a guild-based way of looking, of a lifestyle, a way of structuring, representing, staging and experiencing the city. We see in them a social and possibly local imagery that speaks to us of identity, a community with shared features. We then discover representations of that way of being: symbols, expressions, subjects, objects, icons, manifestations. Let the readers see this for themselves on pages from this project, including, for example: *sitio*CHAMBA*, *sitio*AMPARO*, *sitio*TALACHAS*, *sitio*TARJETÓN*, *sitio*RETROVISOR*. They will find images *in flagrante* of bribes, car accidents, couples kissing during their trip, taxis being repaired in the street, videos of cars running a red light, large gatherings of taxi drivers without license plates, jammed avenues at any time of the day, and so on.

Antoni's wager was that this window could serve to offer an alternative image of the guild. That is, that they could make it their own and, from there, counteract the adverse information they so frequently receive through the official media apparatus. What we see, then, is not necessarily political. Instead, we are offered fragments of a social personality from which we can derive many elements that speak, in turn, of the context in which that social personality resides.

And that, precisely, is the other side of the window: in these arbitrary scenes of life, we find insolent reflections—incongruities, inconsistencies—of the social structure or operating system of all society. The attentive viewer will detect what is on 'the other side of the window': that which explains that in this world of everyday life there is shelter, pressure to pay bribes, a hack license, an official organization and another in the wings, control, numbers, license plates, initials, quotas, and power. That viewer will notice that the taxi world is part of a social order that imposes features, behavior, patterns, and sequences on it. Many of these characteristics speak irremediably of a social system that is arbitrary, baroque, complex, bureaucratic, arduous, expensive, inefficient, slow, and unfair—one to which we have all contributed, and toward which we have become immune, indifferent, and permissive.

*sitio*TAXI* thus opens a window onto interactive sociological exploration: a two-way gaze that runs from the particular—the cell phone of a Mexico City taxi driver on any given day—to the general, to the way we Mexicans have organized our city, what we have turned it into, and all the contradictions and anomalies employed in that process. It offers the possibility of reawakening our sensitivity to all this, eschewing habit and indifference and recovering, anew, our capacity for amazement and surprise.

Jorge Morales Moreno, sociologist and Master of Architecture with doctoral studies in historiography, is undergraduate and postgraduate lecturer in Design at the Universidad Autónoma Metropolitana-Azcapotzalco. He is also professor of Art History at the Escuela Nacional de Pintura, Escultura y Grabado 'La Esmeralda.' In 2001 he was a visiting professor at the Faculty of Environmental Studies at York University (Ontario, Canada) and in 2011, at the Department of History of Art and Architecture at the University of Pittsburgh (Pennsylvania, United States).

Orchestrating the Collective Buzz: Chronicle of a Turning Point in the Inner Workings of *megafone.net*

Mery Cuesta

My first job in the art world as a newcomer to Barcelona was as an assistant to Antoni Abad. I spent hours in his studio laboring under the picturesque title of 'Digital Disseminator,' that is, publicizing and vitalizing one of his pioneering projects in the digital setting: the virtual *Z* fly, which earned him the Ciutat de Barcelona Prize in 2003. We continued to maintain a sunny friendship until, in 2006, Antoni invited me to coordinate *canal*ACCESSIBLE*, one of *megafone.net*'s characteristic collaborative projects. This time, it focused on Barcelona's physically handicapped.

One glance at *megafone.net* is enough to reveal that Antoni combines aspects of an orchestral director and an alchemist of technology. The trajectory of *megafone.net*, interlinking one channel to the next since 2004, is the story of a continuous process of technological refinement, similar to working with a chorus: tuning it, one rehearsal at a time, so that it sounds with a clear, unanimous voice that is ever more musical.

Around 2007, halfway between *canal*ACCESSIBLE* and *canal*MOTOBOY*, Antoni made a change that served to strengthen the musicality of the collective voices that make up *megafone.net*. Here I am referring to a transition from the system of tag-based descriptions of files sent to the *canales* by participants, to one in which individual participants could freely designate files in their own way. Let us see how this turning point occurred.

Soon after I finished coordinating *canal*ACCESSIBLE* (which had required me to stop and chat with total strangers in wheelchairs on the Rambla, teach people with reduced motor skills to operate cell phones, call meetings, generate positive feelings there and elsewhere, write accounts of all that was taking place under the pseudonym *Leoparda* and much, much more), Antoni assigned me a titanic task: to apply descriptive tags, one by one, to the over 27,000 uploads that six communities from different parts of the world had been publishing on *megafone.net* since 2004. These were not only sound, text and video files from *canal*ACCESSIBLE*, but also from Mexico City taxi drivers, Gypsies in Lleida and León, Nicaraguan emigrants in Costa Rica, and prostitutes in Madrid.

megafone.net's enormous bank of uploads required the development of an interface that would allow users to consult them, because one photo swimming among 27,000 others with no way to fish it out might just as well not exist. So in collusion with a sociologist and two geographers, Antoni supplied me with a list of 44 words arranged in four areas: Activities, Spaces, Beings, and Objects. With those 44 tags I was supposed to categorize all of the uploads. 'Description' was the name given to this task of manually associating one or more tags to each file uploaded by the different *canales*' participants. At first, it seemed that a mechanical method would soon develop to facilitate this process of description but that was not at all the case; it required a careful exercise of judgment and determination, as Pilar Cruz (my colleague in this arduous undertaking) and I soon discovered. The doubts that arose and the interesting observations emerging around the semiotics of the image and the nature of photographic representation became the subject of my graphic novel *44 tags para describir el mundo* ('44 Tags to Describe the World'), published in 2008 by the City Government of Girona on the occasion of Antoni's retrospective show there.

In the end, *megafone.net*'s *canales* make up a choral narrative that is constructed and developed in a fragmentary way. The thrilling experience of description clarified certain kinds of collective behavior in which individual participants were unwittingly involved. For example, it confirmed that when a community is offered the opportunity to express itself publically, it does not know what to say at first, but then, it gradually arrives at a unanimous narrative. From Mexican taxi drivers to 'nicas' in San José de Costa Rica, all coincided in first addressing their human environment and their family moments of relaxation and entertainment. Later, they began to take on their specific problems, especially with regard to their work.

The collective buzz designated the tag OCIO (leisure) number 1 in the ranking for all of *megafone.net*; it was the one most frequently used. MÚSICA and CALLE (music and street) were also among the most frequently employed (around 30% of the files were created on the street). OCIO was probably number 1 in the ranking because we applied it to all activities carried out in free time: from playing soccer to watching it at home. But beginning with *canal*MOTOBOY*, Antoni took a pioneering step—remember, this was 2007— by adding a function that allowed each participant to describe his or her own images with tags or *palavras chave* ('key words' as they were called on that occasion) that each of them could choose with total freedom. From then on, description became an individual act. The astounding result was an increased clarity in the community's image on *megafone.net*. Once they could describe their own uploads, the *motoboys*[1] categorized their OCIO activities with various terms, including FESTA, AMIGOS, CULINÁRIA, LAZER, FINAL DE SEMANA and SAMBA (party, friends, cooking, leisure, weekend, and samba). Their descriptive system had the great advantage of being much more eloquent with regard to that community's environment and idiosyncrasies.

It was fascinating to see how the language shifted from systemic to organic as the *motoboys* made their changes. Another example was the curious lexical adaptation the *motoboys* found to designate children: MINHA VIDA (my life). One of them began describing photos of his young daughter as MINHA VIDA and it caught on with the rest, who adopted the same tag for photos of their own children. This was a beautiful case that allows us to observe the lexical interchange between two descriptions of reality: the anthropological one dictated by a list of 44 designations, and the intimate one implemented by the *motoboys*. Where anthropology was insufficient, MINHA VIDA arose.

---

1. *Motoboy* is the popular name given to motorcycle couriers in Brazil.

Here, then, is one of the steps orchestrated by Antoni in his quest to improve the tuning and musicality of the choral mass. Since that turning point, diverse technological variations and transformations have taken place to make the expression of communities with no influential voice in the media as honest and efficient as possible.

Being a part of the inner workings of *megafone.net* has enriched my journey through life. With Antoni I learned to facilitate group creative processes with good humor, understanding, and generosity because he has always considered participants as people first and foremost. Working at his side has shown me how dealing humanely with people in a project of which one is the leader is a fundamental part of that project's success.

Mery Cuesta is an art critic, exhibition curator, and cartoonist. Bachelor of Fine Art and Master of Communication and Art Criticism from the Universitat de Girona. She is art critic for the *Cultura/s* supplement of *La Vanguardia*, as well as writer and cartoonist on contemporary art and popular culture. In 2002 she was awarded the Espais Prize for Art Criticism, which led to the publication of her first book, an analysis of experimental film produced in 1970s Spain. Her curatorial projects address questions relating to the analysis of audiovisual images and popular culture, and include *Quinquis de los ochenta: cine prensa y calle* (CCCB, La Casa Encendida, and AlhóndigaBilbao), *Cervantes' Left Hand* (Instituto Cervantes, Istanbul) and *Humor Absurdo: una actitud ante la vida en situaciones críticas* (ARTIUM, Vitoria). Besides her radio and television appearances, she has two comics on the market—*Caida y auge de Antxon Amorrortu* and *Istanbul Zombi 2066*—and is currently preparing a third: a comic-essay on the effects of digital culture. She is also the drummer for the punk-rock group *Crapulesque*.

Motoboy Culture and Public Policy: Interfaces of the City of São Paulo

Eliezer Muniz dos Santos

[Originally published in *canal*MOTOBOY*, Spanish Cultural Center in São Paulo, 2007]

Could there really be a *motoboy* culture? Why has it been the subject of various cultural productions in recent years? Are we facing a social phenomenon that has yet to be completely interpreted? Movies, plays, songs, books, soap-opera characters, documentaries, and now... an art exhibition? What is so distinctive about this new class of urban workers that it makes them the subjects and protagonists of daily life in our cities? Nowadays, we can assert that motorcycle couriers or *motoboys* represent important aspects of social coexistence. From their privileged place in traffic they can grasp many of our problems and work to implement public policies that may improve the quality of life in our country's main urban centers. This means that we are facing a new power. The intersection of culture and politics became clearer between May and June 2007 when we held a series of debates and film screenings as part of the exhibition of Antoni Abad's *Motoboys Transmitem de Celulares* ('Motoboys Broadcast From Their Cell Phones') on the 25th anniversary of the Cultural Center in São Paulo.

How should we understand the *motoboys*' position and environment if we are to consider them the protagonists of complex measures to which all of society should give thought? The logic of these messengers' mobility indicates that merely considering a new geometric treatment of streets and avenues is not enough to define the conflict of urban spaces. First, we have to understand what kind of information those messengers offer, and how they carry out their work so that the city itself can evolve. The very existence of these professionals is intrinsically linked to the numerous transformations the city has undergone in becoming more urban, including its traffic jams in the context of rapid global growth. This growth imposes the need for concrete measures for improvement on all of society. In order to apply such improvements in the social realm, it is important to understand how they affect the lives of these people (workers, parents, youths and often inhabitants of the city's sprawling outskirts) who earn their living with motorcycles. We must understand how they organize themselves, how they build strategies that allow them to get the job done and how they create their own identity. Thus, when we take their own lifestyle into account, we discover what we call 'their culture.'

It is also essential for us, as we begin curating the *canal*MOTOBOY* project, that the voices of the professional motorcycle couriers be heard. That their lives be narrated without intermediaries and that even their nickname, *motoboy*, be discussed among them in order to create their own representation. They view themselves, and are viewed by society, in several different ways: as 'bikers,' 'messengers,' 'motoboys,' 'motorists,' 'deliverys,' 'couriers,' and even 'mototaxis,' a service they offer in other regions of Brazil. Pejorative names have also arisen, especially '*cachorro louco*' ('crazy animal'), among others. In many cases, such substitute names hide a form of disdain for these workers, belittling them with stereotypes in the context of their work or even denying the stereotype itself, as

occurred when the city's traffic authorities sought to define them in terms of
the principal characteristics of their services as 'motocargo' ('motorcycle cargo'),
a definition one would apply to a thing rather than a person.

Sociologists remind us that these 'reductions' can be explained as a manner
of defining the Other in a way that keeps him from exercising his right to equal
participation in politics and other areas including his work or other aspects of social
life. The Other is therefore assigned an artificial identity in society. The members of
this community are not really aware of the personal risk they run in their efforts to
recognize themselves and to gain recognition. In order to belong to a social group
(*motoboys*, 'crazy animals,' etc.), they discard their own self-esteem. This is a
characteristic of processes of social stereotyping that generate a negative image
and stigma in relation to oneself and to society in general, and such a problem
cannot be combated without information or class consciousness. In fact, cultural
conflict will be inevitable if this community is to build a positive identity with regard
to its social representation. And perhaps, as a response, it will find the meaning
of expression itself. This, in turn, would be reflected in all areas of everyday life,
including politics, economics, work, leisure, and the family.

In this sense, fostering the intersection of politics and culture was already
part of the process when, for the first time in the history of this professional
category, artist Antoni Abad created a cultural project that offered 12 *motoboys* the
opportunity to explore a form of sociability previously impossible for this group.
Over the course of various months, Abad held weekly meetings with them to discuss
their main problems and to furnish them with cell phones connected to the Internet
so that their voices could be heard instantaneously by the entire community. We
then saw the emergence of an expressive set of codes and signals that may signify
a substantial change not only in the identity of the professionals who belong to this
community, but also with regard to the worldview (*Weltanschauung*) they construct
on the basis of this experience. Instead of merely creating a set of contributions and
digital images in the Internet's virtual world, this project made it possible to carry out
a structural change as the dialog between this category of professionals and overall
society visibly expanded. These motorists' concerns and struggles drew the interest
of a group of university researchers and their institutions, who then helped them to
work on the issues raised by *canal*MOTOBOY*. It also became clear that
the experience of self-representation by these professionals generated its own
dynamic based on a form of sociability that emerges from social networks, partially
through the meetings and debates carried out by the project, but most of all, through
the participants' uploads to *www.zexe.net/SAOPAULO*.

As they realized that this platform was capable of influencing public opinion,
the professional motorists made almost 2,800 uploads of photos, videos, and
sound recordings in just four months. Of these, over 240 were interviews with other
professionals and people who were part of their everyday lives. These bore the tag
FALA ('talk'). Motivated as well by subjects the group itself defined with tags such as
DIA A DIA, TRÂNSITO, ACIDENTE, TRABALHO, FAMÍLIA, REUNIÃO ('day to day',
'traffic', 'accident', 'work', 'family', 'meeting'), and others, they clearly showed that
their participation in this project published on the Internet in real time made them
not only broadcasters, but also active users of an autonomous and independent
communication device that allowed them to fulfill their desire to become the
chroniclers of their own reality. They thus escaped the constraints of stereotypes

projected by the press and other dominant media and created a splendid tool in the struggle to reinvent their own day-to-day existence.

Among other factors, we can see how they have offered a legitimate formative space for the city's cultural life. This is clear from the images in which they gather to discuss the contents of the web page and even the fate of *canal*MOTOBOY*. We discover a city from the vantage point of the motorists and, from a more esthetic standpoint, we notice that the photos begin to reveal their gaze, thus becoming symbolic instruments for investigating that experience: the *motoboy's* way of seeing reflects how he himself is seen.

The *motoboys* have thus created their demands with a clear awareness of the level of complexity with which they must contend in order to resolve their problems, and today there is consensus about the fact that the solutions are also complex (here it is enough to recall official statistics on the high number of fatal accidents in recent years). We have therefore reached the conclusion that, for the time being, there is no guarantee that the administration's initiatives will be successful, as that would require their policies to include genuine class representation.

Clearly, these professionals complain about the lack of an efficient accident prevention program which would include a preventative driving course and professional training—though as yet there are no studies relating motorcycle and occupational accidents—but it is equally clear that the government has also neglected to teach professional motorists the best strategies for acting in the interest of fellow citizens and respecting human life. Here we could mention the practically tribal manner in which they defend themselves and each other in traffic, helping each other when the tragedy of an accident strikes. Their voices should not be silenced, because only they understand that feeling of helplessness as they wait on the hot asphalt for an ambulance to arrive. And those voices shall be listened to by all.

Given the urgency of establishing a dialog between the government and civil society regarding the *motoboy* community, the key objective of our curatorial project is to fill a need—thanks to the execution of the *www.zexe.net/SAOPAULO* project— and to make a place for the demands of this category of motorists in São Paulo's political agenda for the next municipal elections.

We appreciate the great understanding and supportiveness of everyone involved in this project, including new participants in these debates. When we see the need to do justice to these motorists who are risking their lives, we finally give meaning to an art that voices concerns about the quality of life in this city and gives prominence to its citizens through culture.

Eliezer Muniz dos Santos, teacher, writer, and curator, graduated in Philosophy from the University of São Paulo. Neka (as he is nicknamed by the *motoboys*) is a special representative of the community of professional bikers in the city of São Paulo. He has worked as a motorcycle courier for fourteen years (1988–2002). In 2000 he organized the 1st National Forum of Professional Motorcyclists, and he has supported and co-founded several associations and unions for couriers in Brazil. In 2007, Antoni Abad invited him to be Deputy Curator of the exhibition *canal*MOTOBOY* at the Centro Cultural São Paulo. Since then he has been participating in, and collaborating with, this group. He currently teaches philosophy at a public school in the outskirts of São Paulo.

Recalculating the Way: The *Motoboy* and the Political Economy of Affect

Alberto López Cuenca

[Originally published in *canal*MOTOBOY*, Spanish Cultural Center in São Paulo, 2007]

In the now classic compilation of texts *Art after Modernism: Rethinking Representation* (Wallis, 1984), postmodern doubts about representation's role in contemporary artistic practice were forcefully expounded. It seemed that art was no longer required to involve the creation of representations (as kinetic art, performance art, installations, minimalist sculpture and land art had already demonstrated). The new proposal involved generating situations, spaces or experiences. In that sense, the alarm caused by 'Art and Objecthood' was not coincidental. This belligerent text by Michael Fried (1967) accused minimalist sculpture of being theatrical, that is, of losing autonomy by depending on the surrounding space to trigger artistic experience. It seemed that not only was art no longer supposed to be a representation of something; it was even freed of the formal constraints of the artistic object (of painting, sculpture, or video). However, this contextual interweaving of art, the heteronomy that nullified its supposed self-sufficiency, was hardly new: it had already been deployed by the early twentieth-century's so-called historical avant-garde movements. In their day, Dadaists, Surrealists, Constructivists and members of the Bauhaus had undertaken the (artistic?) task of launching new lifestyles or, at the very least, of reshaping existing ones. To achieve this, art could not be conceived or practiced as a merely representational exercise in capturing essences or evoking reality (if, in fact, art was ever only that). Transforming life was not a matter of imitating it by employing esthetic criteria, but rather of delving into the interstices of everyday life and modifying it: in book covers and theater props, advertising and film posters, the design of tea sets and of entire cities.

The idea of art as a transforming action, which we can explain in terms of its performative capacity, was based on multiple premises. Outstanding among these was the modern artist's privileged position from which to understand the world and influence it in symbolic and concrete terms. This was no more and no less than an avant-garde imperative to act upon reality and it has been passed down to contemporary art, although in very different conditions than those originally proposed, especially since the scope of contemporary artistic production brings that very premise into question. The artist's practically omniscient vantage point for understanding and influencing the world is now questioned by his overall transformation into a specialist in the symbolic industry, that is, a producer of luxury items, leisure experiences, or entertainment at biennials, museums, and art centers. With such imposed limits, the work of the artist cannot see beyond its field of expertise, and cannot, therefore, be expected to generate major projects of social transformation.

And yet, scepticism about the artist's privileged position, combined with the conviction that art can still generate sociability, maintains the possibility of deploying strategies for artistic action in the social sphere. They may be less ambitious than those of modernity, but they are also more diverse. This, then, is the backdrop for the development of some of the projects that Antoni Abad has coordinated with communities and cellular technology, projects that overcome the artist's omniscient condition to embrace the performative, non-representational nature of art.

Sociability Networks

Antoni Abad has spent the last four years working with the programmer Eugenio Tisselli to develop a series of works that use cell phones and their ability to transfer information directly via the Internet to form unique cooperative communities. The first of these projects, which I had an opportunity to review, was called *sitio*TAXI*. Carried out in Mexico City over a period of two months in 2004, it allowed a group of 17 taxi drivers to send images, videos, audio, and text files to an open-access web site. With neither editing nor pre-selection, that site collected and updated files sent in real time by members of this urban group. At that time I wrote a brief review of *sitio*TAXI* titled 'El taxista como etnógrafo' ('The Taxi Driver as Ethnographer'). Looking back, I find that I still subscribe to one part of this title, but not to another. 'The Taxi Driver as Ethnographer' satirized Hal Foster's well-known essay, 'The Artist as Ethnographer' (1996), which argues that some contemporary artists have become critical investigators of their own society—and I think I was correct in emphasizing that in *sitio*TAXI* it is not the artist who speaks, but the taxi drivers themselves. Rather than presenting the artist as a privileged voice, it focused on the taxi drivers, allowing them to narrate their experiences and put forward their own stories. I was mistaken, however, in describing the taxi driver as an ethnographer, a mere chronicler of his reality, implying that this project's fundamental effect was the modification of representations or the transformation of our commonplace concept of taxi drivers. It is clear that *sitio*TAXI* employs mechanisms of representation—images, texts, audio, and video recordings—but it does much more than simply 'making the reality of the taxi driver visible' or 'promoting representations absent from traditional media' (though it is certainly true that on the few occasions they do appear there, taxi drivers are generally presented as victims, criminals, or the passing heroes of some rescue operation). In fact, rather than different representations of reality, what *sitio*TAXI* set in motion were mechanisms of sociability, creating social relationships and strategies of subjectivity. In other words, *sitio*TAXI* opened up a space for expression and agency of its participants, beyond its role as a counter-field for representation.

This aspect has become a constant in the works that followed *sitio*TAXI*. For example, the planning and launching of *canal*GITANO*, which took place in Lleida in 2005, involved a series of negotiations and conflicts that do not appear in the online audiovisual material even though they constitute a crucial part of the project. First of all, *canal*GITANO*'s *modus operandi* led participants to question the Gypsy community's traditional separation of men and women, including how and where they are allowed to meet and the nature of their interaction. Moreover, *canal*GITANO* provoked an unusual confrontation with the patriarchs—the community's *de facto* authority figures—after they forbade one of the female participants from continuing to take part in the project. When both she and her mother challenged them, she was readmitted to the project. And the institution of power itself was subjected to scrutiny with the creation of *canal*PATRIARCA*, in which the patriarchs were asked questions such as 'What does it mean to be a

Gypsy?' or 'What does it mean to be a patriarch?' These uncomfortable interviews pressured them to explain themselves and to reflect upon their Gypsy identity— matters taken for granted and thus rarely thought through explicitly.

Over the course of 2006, Antoni Abad set up canal*CENTRAL in San José, Costa Rica. He provided cell phones to members of that city's large community of Nicaraguan immigrants and taught them how to maintain the project's website. There again, the true scope of canal*CENTRAL lay not in the visibility of its web images, but in the underlying series of negotiations with local authorities and institutions. On one hand, the project was hindered by the fact that the cell phones had been imported illegally from Miami and their software was not compatible with Costa Rica's telephone system. This called for the resolution of both technological and legal issues to make them operative. Equally complex was the chore of registering telephones for 22 illegal immigrants in a country where it is an essential requirement to prove legal residency in order to obtain access to mobile telephone services. Not only did canal*CENTRAL make evident the control of communications and the technical and legal conflicts generated by the state monopoly of the communication industry; it also forced a modification or transitory suspension of that control. As a result, a momentary parenthesis was opened for the Nicaraguan community to make itself heard.

In 2006 canal*ACCESSIBLE was launched in Barcelona. Participants drew up a map of architectural elements that reduce urban access for the physically impaired (an alternative cartography in response to the numerous triumphant cartographies of the city that boast of its museums and parks, bars, monuments, and subway stations). Although canal*ACCESSIBLE seemed to be about drawing up a map, it actually provoked responses at both a collective level (some of the handicapped formed special teams to reconnoiter areas of the city that were not originally part of the project) and an institutional level (after the map was reproduced in local media, the city government responded with a map of 'accessible Barcelona'). The project's efforts forced the city government to eliminate many of the architectural obstacles documented by members of canal*ACCESSIBLE. While it was originally conceived as a short-term project, canal*ACCESSIBLE led to the creation of a group of collaborators known as the 'Asociación Accesible' (the 'Access Association'), who have continued to meet and work since the project closed.

Clearly, taking photos and uploading them to the Internet is only one part of these projects, because their goal is not simply to foster the visibility of alternative representations of life (of Gypsies, immigrants, or the handicapped). They also seek to actually generate life through interaction with the environment. As they unfold, these projects reveal all kinds of restrictions, including those imposed by tradition or patriarchal powers, by telecommunication and immigration legislation or by urban architecture. But it is not just a matter of revealing or drawing our gaze to the opaque network that regulates social life (from adolescent relationships to cell-phone use or urban mobility); these projects also create spaces for unexpected or reconfigured social relationships. This is a key issue, as 'the subject' of these projects is not the creation of a manner in which a group can represent itself, but rather the empowerment and production of social relations, that is, the very fabric of collective and individual existence.

The political economy of affect

Political philosopher Michael Hardt—alone, and later with Toni Negri in their polemical book, *Empire*—has described contemporary society's characteristic and predominant spheres of production. For these authors, affect is one of our contemporary economy's fundamental products. As such, it would be part of what they call 'immaterial labor,' that which produces intangible goods such as knowledge, services or communications.

'In short, we can distinguish three types of immaterial labor that drive the service sector at the top of the informational economy. The first is involved in an industrial production that has been informationalized and has incorporated communication technologies in a way that transforms the industrial production process itself. Manufacturing is regarded as a service and the material labor of the production of durable goods mixes with and tends toward immaterial labor. Second is the immaterial labor of analytical and symbolic tasks, which itself breaks down into creative and intelligent manipulation on one hand and routine symbolic tasks on the other. Finally, a third type of immaterial labor involves the production and manipulation of affects and requires (virtual or actual) human contact and proximity. These are the three types of labor that drive the postmodernization or informationalization of the global economy' (Hardt and Negri, 2000).

The immaterial labor of affect is characterized, according to Hardt, as a 'binding element' involved in areas of production such as health care, entertainment and the cultural industries that focus 'on the creation and manipulation of affects'. At differing levels, this affective labor has a role in the entire service sector as an integral part of communication and interaction processes. There, it takes the form of 'in-person services' in institutions ranging from banks to fast-food restaurants. For Hardt, 'this labor is immaterial, even if it is corporeal and affective, in the sense that its products are intangible, a feeling of ease, well-being, satisfaction, excitement, passion—even a sense of connectedness or community'.

This perspective reveals not only the material production of social life—that is, how the system of relations of objects articulates the experience of individuals—but also the most intimate and emotional aspects of the subject. The de-materialized economy produces and identifies sensations, affective states, and desires—that is, modes of subjectivity and subjection. Controlling the production and management of emotional life signifies, in the final analysis, the creation of bonds of submission. If standardized affect is processed as if it were merchandise, then experience is homogenized and economically unproductive attitudes and states are eliminated. So, the affect industry is an integral part of contemporary modes of production, where it serves to foster or favor one set of emotional states and attitudes (well-being, possession, control, satisfaction) while rejecting others (altruistic attitudes, feelings of failure, destitution or uprootedness). Nevertheless, despite being an integral part of modes of production, the affect industry can be challenged by 'anti-capitalist' practices, as Hardt points out.

To say that capital has adopted and extolled affective labor, and that from a capitalist standpoint such labor has proved to be one of the most effective ways of producing value does not imply that, thus tainted, affect is of no use at all to anti-capitalist projects.

In fact, affect is crucial for the activation of spheres of sociability whose goal may not necessarily be the production of capital, hence the current importance of strategies that eschew the standardized production of affect, generating emotional and social life that is not programmed by the dominant modes of production.

canal*MOTOBOY: digital media and the critique of affect

Since May 2007, 12 *motoboys* whose work day takes them through the streets of São Paulo carry cell phones, take photographs, record videos, and upload them directly to a web page. There, they can group their files under keywords of their own choice such as ACIDENTE, PROIBIDO, TRABALHO ('accident,' 'forbidden,' 'work'), generating a flexible, open, and negotiable classification system for the information they gather and offer to website visitors. From its eighteenth-century incarnation in coffee houses, discussion groups, or newspaper pages, the public sphere or social meeting place has shifted to television and computer screens; today's redefined public space is markedly mediated by the symbolic: images, sounds, texts, and multimedia. Nevertheless, while today's public sphere functions as a fundamentally symbolic space or more precisely, a media space, this is not a mere play of inert and fixed signs unrelated to the people they address. Those signs are used as constituent parts of mechanisms of enunciation and are activated by individual speakers, television viewers and other specific users. Clearly, the degree of involvement in the process of producing meaning comes into play here. At certain levels of that process we find ourselves subjected (signified) by its signs while, at others, it is we who signify (subject) the signs. This negotiation with the networks of signification triggers the affective and dialogic constitution of the public sphere, which thus takes form at the same time as the subjects who give it meaning: subjection and subjectivity go hand in hand.

*canal*MOTOBOY* set in motion a mechanism of symbolic production that is crucially one of subjective awareness in the sense that it unleashes a process of agency and enunciation. *canal*MOTOBOY* inaugurates ephemeral moments of defiance and action that do not require an ideal free subject. Instead, they bring out the conflictive and agonistic nature of its participants' daily lives--the eternally unfinished condition, always under negotiation, of the subject. From that standpoint, the community is the sphere of production for bonds that are symbolic but also affective in a process that runs parallel to capitalism's immaterial modes of production. In selecting and sending visual or audio material, in their meetings and discussions about group strategies for continuing their work, they dismantle and redirect the economic functions assigned to affect and signs by the productive framework of advanced capitalism. That is why it must be viewed as a critical exercise in the Foucaultian sense. As the French author put it: 'I would therefore propose, as a very first definition of critique, this general characterization: the art of not being governed quite so much' (Foucault, translated by L. Hochroth & C. Porter, 2007, p.45). In other words, critique, the act of dissenting, is the launching of mechanisms that elude the 'mode of being represented,' that is, of being governed, defined, or supplanted by others. In this case, critique involves criticizing the institution of representation rather than just the object of representation. In a practical sense, it is the criticism of a practice rather than a mere critique of representation. *canal*MOTOBOY*, like the previous projects launched by Antoni Abad, is more than the activation of a network of resistance to media representations of the *motoboy*; it does not simply replace one set of representations with another (a truly sisyphean task given the scale and scope of the media's hegemonic representations of the *motoboy*). Crucially, *canal*MOTOBOY* constitutes the art of being governed in a different way, launching a dynamic of collective elaboration of the group's representation that directly affects the source of production of image and awareness: social and collective practice.

In the same paper Foucault wrote: 'I will say that critique is the movement by which the subject gives himself the right to question truth on its effects of power and question power on its discourses of truth. Well then!: critique will be the art of voluntary insubordination, that of reflected intractability. Critique would essentially insure the desubjugation of the subject in the context of what we could call, in a word, the politics of truth' (p.47).

On one occasion, Antoni Abad recalled a particularly significant comment by one of the patriarchs of the Gypsy community of Lleida: 'The Internet is the devil.' Like anything new or unfamiliar, the Internet is viewed as a threat to stability because it permits actions that fall outside, and cannot be controlled by, established norms of governance. As we mentioned earlier, the young participants in *canal*GITANO* decided to interview the patriarchs, asking them to explain what it means to be a Gypsy, to be a patriarch, and how they define the term '*payo*' (non-gypsy). Thus, *canal*GITANO* became a tool for revealing mechanisms of power and truth and thus confronting them, rendering them visible and vulnerable. The unforeseen use of the electronic media, cell phones, and the Internet, serves to critique (in the Foucaultian sense) established social relations. On another occasion, Antoni Abad referred to his past work as a sculptor to illustrate how his attitude as a sculptor shapes his current work with digital media, expressing his desire to 'shape the medium so that others can use it' and concluding with a question: 'Why should artists have a privileged perspective?'

References

Foster, Hal, 'The Artist as Ethnographer,' in *The Return of the Real: The Avant-Garde at the End of the Century*, Cambridge, Mass. & London: MIT Press, 1996.

Foucault, Michel, 'What is Critique?' in S. Lotringer (ed.), *The Politics of Truth*, Los Angeles: Semiotext(e), 2007.

Fried, Michael, 'Art and Objecthood,' Artforum, no. 5, New York, June 1967.

Hardt, Michael, 'Affective Labor,' Boundary 2, vol. 26, no. 2, Summer 1999.

Hardt, Michael and Antonio Negri, *Empire*, Cambridge, Mass.: Harvard University Press, 2000.

Wallis, Brian (ed.), *Art after Modernism: Rethinking Representation.* New York: The New Museum of Contemporary Art, 1984.

Alberto López Cuenca is Doctor in Philosophy from the Universidad Autónoma de Madrid and Professor of Art Theory and Philosophy at the Universidad de las Américas, Puebla. He is a regular contributor to the cultural supplement of the newspaper *ABC* and the *Revista de Libros*. His work has appeared in international publications such as *Afterall*, *ARTnews*, *Lápiz*, *Curare*, and the *Revista de Occidente*, and he has been guest lecturer at Columbia University in New York and Goldsmiths, University of London, as well as lecturer at the Universidad Autónoma de Madrid.

Smartphone Culture and Mobile Politics, *Avant la Lettre*
Gerard Goggin

Introduction: Abad's invention of smartphone culture… as a force for a better world

The tenth anniversary of Antoni Abad's *megafone.net* allows us to reflect upon the contribution of the artist and this work, to understand a central arena of contemporary society and culture around the world—digital technology and culture. In what follows, I wish to argue that, in particular, Abad has made a highly significant contribution to our understanding of the high watermark of mobile phone and mobile media culture. My contention is that there are two main elements to the potent intervention Abad has given us.

Firstly, as a pioneer in experimental use of cellular mobile phones in art, he was also a trail-blazer in understanding and unfolding the social and technical possibilities of mobiles. In 2004, at a time when technology companies, software developers, and users themselves were collectively struggling to move mobile phones beyond their well-established niche as a voice communications technology (Goggin, 2006), Abad devised ways to make phones multimedia. In doing so, Abad anticipated, and influenced, the shape of 'smartphone culture'—the kinds of meanings, rituals, practices, and affordances (or capabilities) of mobile phones that become well established after 2007, with the arrival of Apple's iPhone, Google's Android Operating System, and the galaxy (to borrow the Samsung marketing phrase) of feature-rich mobile phones, which combined apps, sensors, Global Positioning Satellite (GPS) technology, photos, and videos, with social media, the Internet, and much more (Aguado, Feijóo and Martínez, 2013).

Secondly, Abad's inauguration of a kind of smartphone culture, *avant la lettre*—that is, as an avant-garde figure, and a bricoleur—anticipated, and offered a critique of what has been called 'the phoneur' (Luke, 2005). The smartphone user as phoneur—the subject of smartphone culture—becomes joyfully embroiled in the steadily ubiquitous, 'taken-for-granted', data-intensive new worlds of smartphones, mobile media, and the new ways in which they are anchored in, gather information about, harvest and make use of places and the people, environments, animals, things, and objects that populate them (Wilken & Goggin, 2014). In its first decade, Abad's *megafone.net* has been clear-eyed and steadfast in its vision, of using the mobile phone platform to give voice to the marginalized. As such, his work has been a rare, long-term, evolving endeavour to suggest, and enact, the ways that mobile technology, networks, and software can be a powerfully consequential cultural platform—digitally amplifying resources, ideas, and collectivities for social transformation. Especially notable in this regard has been the attention Abad has paid to disability, and disabled communities, in relation to mobile technology.

Smarter (phone) platforms for cosmopolitan social transformation

Abad's early *megafone.net* projects involved confronting technical as well as esthetic and social challenges in this artwork. Put simply, circa 2004 the mobile phone was still fairly rudimentary in its ability to record, store, and distribute data, texts, images, and sounds. At a moment in 2004, before smartphone culture is fully installed as a socio-technical system in contemporary societies, *megafone.net* shows that it is possible to reconfigure for alternative, artistic, and popular purposes, against the grain of the massive commodified, consumer platform it becomes a few years later.

As well as its abiding interest in technology, what defines *megafone.net* is its preoccupation with inequality, exclusion, and marginalization in our social life and culture. Abad works carefully, methodically, and, above all, respectfully, with a diverse range of communities around the world, to apprehend, appropriate, and, finally, shape the mobile technology platforms in and via which their lives now take place.

Rather than simply celebrating the great salvation or benefit that digital technology may bring, Abad is highly conscious of the awful paradox around mobility in society, and the ambiguous, various meanings of mobile that technology might, or might not, activate for us (Ilcan, 2013). All the geographically diverse, highly differenced, marginalized communities participating in *megafone.net* share something in common: a salient relationship to mobility. They are forced to move through displacement, or seek refuge; they have migrated; their work involves moving around cities (deliveries; driving passengers; picking up clients); they are historically diasporic, fugitive, unwanted populations, spread across many states and societies (in the case of Gypsies).

In the case of people with disabilities, the question of mobility is also of paramount, constitutive importance, in structuring life worlds, life chances, and everyday life. Four of Abad's *megafone.net* projects have concerned themselves with communities of people with disabilities for whom movement, and mobility, is a deeply existential, political, and fundamental issue: people with 'limited mobility' in Barcelona (2006–13), Geneva (2008), and Montreal (2012–13); and blind people and people with visual impairments in Catalunya in the project *The Blind Point of View* (2010). Indeed I first encountered Abad's work through the project *GENÈVE*accessible* (2008), where wheelchair users photographed obstacles in the Swiss city with GPS-equipped portable phones, and uploaded the images and data to the Internet to produce a map of the city's accessibility ('une cartographie de l'accessibilité de la ville': *http://www.megafone.net/geneve/about*).

At this time in 2008, smartphone culture was just coming into full swing, with interest growing in location and mapping technologies. In terms of its technical nous, conceptualization, and political efficacy, this project was really ahead of its time, paving the way for many other activist, DIY (do-it-yourself), user-generated content projects since then. In the field of disability, technology, and accessibility, it was a genuine revelation. Much work in this area is not especially concerned with interrogating technology for its underlying values–and whether it supports, or obstructs, the achievement of social justice and human rights for all, including persons with disability (Ellis & Kent, 2011). Here Abad's work put the politics of movement, and by extension mobile technologies, into circulation, well before people started talking about 'smart cities.'

Social transformations in mobile, digital worlds

Barcelona is known and loved for many reasons. In the technology sector, Barcelona is the famous host city of the annual celebration of the mobile technology industry, Mobile World Congress (formerly known as GSM World). Here the tech industry celebrates their growing market, which in 2014 exceeded 7 billion mobile phone subscribers. Barcelona is also the home of Antoni Abad, who deserves to be much better known for his canny, ethically fertile, culturally innovative contribution to mobile technology, not just for the way in which he shows us how we can do clever things with this epochal, omnipresent form of digital technology. Rather, Abad shows us how we can 'make do' with mobile media in social life. How we can improvise with mobile technology to precipitate a movement towards better worlds. And how we can grasp, and conjure with the deeper cultural meanings, and political implications, of this extraordinary technology; a technology that should enable, rather than limit or curtail, the possibilities of our lives across the many parts of the worlds in which we dwell.

References

Aguado, Juan Miguel; Feijóo, Claudio, and Martínez, Inmaculada J. (eds.), *La comunicación móvil: hacia un nuevo ecosistema digital*, Barcelona: Geodisa, 2013.

De Certeau, Michel, *The Practice of Everyday Life*, trans. Steven Rendall, Berkeley, Calif. & London: University of California Press, 1988.

Ellis, Katie, and Kent, Mike, *Disability and New Media*, New York: Routledge, 2011.

Goggin, Gerard, *Cell Phone Culture*, London: Routledge, 2006.

Ilcan, Suzan (ed.), *Mobilities, Knowledge, and Social Justice*, Montreal: McGill-Queen's University Press, 2013.

Luke, Robert, 'The Phoneur: Mobile Commerce and the Digital Pedagogies of the Wireless Web,' in Peter P. Trifonas (ed.), *Communities of Difference: Culture, Language, Technology*, New York: Palgrave Macmillan, 2005, pp.188–204.

Wilken, Rowan, and Goggin, Gerard (eds.), *Locative Media*, New York: Routledge, 2014.

Gerard Goggin is ARC Future Fellow, and Professor of Media and Communications, at the University of Sydney. He has longstanding interests in the social and cultural aspects of mobile technology, as well as disability. His books include: *Disability and the Media* (to be released in 2015; with Katie Ellis), *Routledge Companion to Mobile Media* (2014, with Larissa Hjorth), *Locative Media* (2014, with Rowan Wilken), *Global Mobile Media* (2010), *Cell Phone Culture* (2006), and, with Christopher Newell, *Digital Disability* (2003).

The Artist as Ignorant Schoolmaster: The Collectivization of the Artistic Voice

Pablo La Parra Pérez

> Collective understanding of emancipation is not the comprehension of a total process of subjection. It is the collectivization of capacities invested in scenes of dissensus.
>
> _Jacques Rancière[1]

> Look, I drive my taxi more than twelve hours a day, stuck in this hellish traffic, but this project made me remember that imagination still exists.
>
> _Don Facundo, participant in *megafone.net*[2]

My intention in this brief text is to define Antoni Abad's project, *megafone.net*, as a form of political art. My main reference will be certain ideas drawn from the work of Jacques Rancière, beginning fundamentally with that philosopher's early 1970s criticism of the idea that the intellectual's political responsibility consists of exposing the laws of oppression and guiding the oppressed towards their liberation. Rancière rummaged through the archives of the workers' movement in search of examples that would question this 'theoretical heroism' based on the distinction between thinkers and doers.[3] In that process, he encountered the work of the revolutionary pedagogue Joseph Jacotot (1770–1840), which offered him an alternative model to the scheme that presupposes a fundamental inequality between the lucidity of the intellectual and the ignorance of the oppressed. Rancière called him the 'ignorant schoolmaster,' because rather than instructing his students, Jacotot put his efforts into providing them with the means to generate their own forms of knowledge. The logic of emancipation: 'that every common person might conceive his human dignity, take the measure of his intellectual capacity, and decide how to use it [...] whoever emancipates doesn't have to worry about what the emancipated person learns.'[4]

Rancière's recent interest in the relation between art and politics is no more and no less than a development of this problem. In the final analysis, the image of the intellectual at the vanguard of political action is mirrored by countless esthetic practices based on the idea that the artist's commitment consists of producing politically enlightening messages capable of redeeming a presumably alienated viewer. It is no coincidence that *megafone.net*'s starting point was precisely a (self-)critical revision of that logic. According to Abad, his project is motivated by a growing disillusionment with the idea of the artist as a privileged interpreter

---

1. Jacques Rancière, *The Emancipated Spectator*, trans. G. Elliott, London & New York: Verso, 2009, p.49.
2. Quoted in Eugenio Tisselli, 'Digital Networks and Social Innovation: Strategies of the Imagination,' in Helmut Anheier and Yudhishthir Raj Isar (eds.), *The Cultures and Globalization Series*, vol. III, London: SAGE, 2010.
3. Jacques Rancière, *Althusser's Lesson*, trans. G. Battista, London: Continuum, 2011.
4. Jacques Rancière, *The Ignorant Schoolmaster*, trans. K. Ross, Stanford: Stanford University Press, 1991.

of society.[5] So, *megafone.net* is first a renunciation of the 'committed artist's' conventional role as spokesperson. It is an unforeseen change of direction, literally a reassignment of funds: rather than drawing on the symbolic capital built up through his career as an individual artist, Abad uses it as the catalyst for a process of collective production of meaning.[6] So, from the standpoint of the artist as ignorant schoolmaster, Abad does not consider himself authorized to speak in the name of the oppressed or to exercise the hypothetical right, often evoked by certain types of public art, to empower or dignify them. Like Jacotot, those would only be his starting points. Having accepted the capacity and dignity of the communities, the artist need only facilitate a decentralized medium for their self-expression. In fact, the requirement that the participants be able to publish their contents without any outside editing or interference was the objective with which Abad and programmer Eugenio Tisselli conceived and shaped the *megafone.net* platform from its very first trial runs in 2003.

For a variety of reasons, the groups of participants in *megafone.net* come from outside the accepted community. They are groups that have rarely found autonomous spaces for expression outside their under- or overexposure in the mainstream media.[7] One had best choose one's words carefully when describing Abad's meeting with these groups. It would be an error, for example, to state that the artist has 'given them a voice.' Such an act would be impossible unless one believed the shopworn idea of a messianic artist stepping down from his pedestal to aid the dispossessed. There is no such thing. And yet, there are unintelligible voices, (mis) perceived as background noise. Artistotle distinguished between 'voice' (*phone*: the animal-like noise that can only transmit a basic sentiment of pleasure or suffering) and 'word' (*logos*: the reflexive judgment of the common, which any citizen has the right to exercise).[8] Throughout history, the political exclusion of certain communities has been based on stripping them of their signs of politicization, that is, of their imagination beyond the community that wields the *logos*.[9] The fact that *megafone.net* is built through assembly meeting and the shared construction of discourse by those communities signifies the irruption of a *logos* (discernment, subjectivity, awareness) where only *phone* (incapacity, passivity, disconnectedness) was expected. As Rancière affirmed when he described the conditions of possibility for an alternative critical art, *megafone.net* intervenes politically in reality by manifesting the capacity for speech and judgment that belongs to those whom society has pushed out to its passive fringes.[10]

It is not a matter of 'building the awareness' of an ideal viewer: the primary recipients of this manifestation are the participants themselves. They become communities of narrators interacting with their surroundings and 'creating for themselves a body dedicated to something other than oppression.' Thus, each of

5. Antoni Abad interviewed by Romina Oliverio: 'Megafone–Amplifying Voices via a Communal Mobile Phone,' *Rising Voices*, 2011 (<https://rising.globalvoicesonline.org/blog/2011/02/16/case-study-megafone-net-%E2%80%93-amplifying-voices-via-a-communal-mobile-phone/>).
6. Antoni Abad interviewed by Vinicius Spricigo in Various Authors, *canal*MOTOBOY*. São Paulo: Centro Cultural de España-AECI, 2007, pp.46–47.
7. Georges Didi-Huberman, 'Exponer a los sin nombre' in Juan Barja and César Rendueles (eds.), *Mundo escrito. 13 derivas desde Walter Benjamin*. Madrid: Círculo de Bellas Artes, 2013, pp.17 31.
8. Aristotle, *Politics*, I, 1523a11 ff.
9. Jacques Rancière, *Aux bords du politique*, Paris: Gallimard, 1998, p.243.
10. Jacques Rancière, *The Emancipated Spectator*, 2009.

megafone.net's projects is a collection of scenes of dissent. A group of Mexico City taxi drivers interrupt their work day to ask people around them what their dream profession would be. Young Gypsy women from Lleida question their environment's reigning social and gender hierarchies. Sex workers in Madrid represent themselves, offering an image that extends beyond the perception of them as objects of sexual consumerism. Groups of people with physical disabilities in Barcelona, Geneva, and Montreal draw up maps that criticize their cities in real time. Ex-guerillas no longer involved in armed struggle and peasants displaced by the conflict in Colombia sit at the same table and begin to work together in Manizales. *Motoboys* from São Paulo shed their criminalization by the media to demand their rights as workers and their own forms of cultural expression. Young Sahrawis transmit words and images from a refugee camp in the Algerian *hamada*. What these scenes share is that, in all of them, no one is doing *what he or she is supposed to be doing*. Each word or image published on *megafone.net* is a common-sense answer calling for an adjustment of functions, spaces and behavior—an adjustment that surpasses what Plato called *sophrosyne*: social harmony based on a logic according to which each citizen must find a job that corresponds to his or her nature, remaining fixed in the place where they work and involving themselves exclusively in responsibilities that are in keeping with their condition.[11]

These small counterpoints to the *status quo* that pepper *megafone.net*'s publications contain a fundamental political promise: the universally exercisable capacity to impugn the limits of what exists and to participate collectively in the reconfiguration of the shared sphere—definitive proof that the line separating incapable from capable, impossible from possible, is no more unassailable than the words and images that sustain it.

11. *Cf.* Jacques Rancière, *La Mésentente. Politique et Philosophie*, Paris: Galilée, 1995, p.147.

Pablo La Parra Pérez is an art historian currently pursuing a doctorate at New York University, where he is researching the relations between cultural practice and social movements in the Spanish state. He has published in the reviews *Sociologías* and *Journal of Spanish Cultural Studies*.

Mapping Architectural Able-ism
Kimberly Sawchuk

Imagine yourself in a wheelchair, if you are not already in one. Where would you live? Work? Go to school? Meet friends for a coffee, a meal, or a pint? How would you negotiate the icy streets of a Montreal winter? How would you navigate your city? Could you go to a movie theater with your friends?

The built environment of the city is one that does not allow for easy access to public life for those who are in wheelchairs or crutches, or rely on a walker. The obstacles built into architecture found within urban space, that deny those with disabilities access to public transportation systems, reveal the systemic forms of discrimination and the one-size fits all, 'normalized body' that much public space assumes. These are forms of differential mobilities that expose the social and political injustices built into urban environments. Our environment is predicated on what we might understand as architectural able-ism.

As Liz Ferrier and Vivienne Muller write: 'The able-ist perspective produces disability in terms of lack and deviance from the human norm [...] This able-ist production of disability—with its sense of lack and revulsion for the aberrant body/ mind—is a powerful undercurrent informing our understanding of human agency.' (2008: p.2) While there are a range of positions on the relationship between disability and impairment from within critical disability studies, what is undeniable is this: as societies we need to understand how impairment can lead to *disablement* in specific social content and find ways to dis-able able-ist cities through an identification of 'the socio-spatial forces' at work that produce 'material lived and imagined differences' between the abled and the disabled (Crooks and Chouinard, 2006: p.346). This is precisely the contribution of Antoni Abad's *MONTRÉAL*in/accessible*. By putting cell phones into the hands of those who experience, each and every day, the myriad of obstacles that prohibit both movement through and access to public space, a collective portrait, a dynamic group map, is built of the devastating effects of architectural able-ism.

Architectural able-ism is one of the ways a built environment is produced and re-produced to give preference to bodily norms that create hierarchies of corporeal differences, so that those with disabilities are understood as *ipso facto* existing in a 'diminished state of being' (Campbell, 2001: p.44). This is able-ism. What able-ism thus presumes is that *disability* is inherently an undesirable condition that must be overcome, most often through medical treatment to correct. Able-ism, as Fiona Kumari Campbell suggests, means that having a disability is a failing rather than a consequence of human diversity such as race, ethnicity, gender, or sexual orientation. From an able-ist perspective, those with a 'disability' can never quite 'measure up' to the normative yet power fiction of the fully abled body. As Crooks and Chouinard argue, if able-bodiedness is presumed as the norm then those with disabilities are marginalized and marked as inevitably other (2006: p.20).

Architectural able-ism, structured into our built environments, influences our everyday lives and creates differential access to spaces and places for some. While over 200,000 people are estimated to be living with a physical disability in the city of

Montreal, for instance, the relative inaccessibility of cultural centers, movie theaters, galleries, libraries, bars, cafés, terraces, and restaurants renders those with mobility impairments absent and invisible. Just as city streets in North America have been built to favor the smooth circulation of automobile traffic through our streets and round our buildings, they are also structured to favor those on foot, rather than those in wheelchairs.

What becomes crucial is to understand how media might be used to map the extent—the breadth depth and scope—of architectural able-ism. This is precisely the point of *MONTRÉAL*in/accessible* and also *GENÈVE*accessible* and *canal*ACCESSIBLE*, three projects of Antoni Abad on *megafone.net*. In them participants in wheelchairs, or on crutches, use cell phones to photograph the myriad of ways the built environment sustains the marginalization and exclusion from public space. For those who are involved in *megafone.net*, the project provides a way of seeing and a tool to assist in dismantling disabling cities.

Using the *megafone* software, participants in the project come together to produce a dynamic map of the machinations of architectural able-ism: the steps, stairs, city sidewalks, the incivilities that impede access to civic life. What we see is a location-based taxonomy of obstacles, barriers, and 'incivilities' as well as points of accessibility: stairs to subways; cars parked on sidewalks; terraces with no ramps; cash machines that are too high. What is mapped is not how unique this system is—what is mapped is its recurrent pervasiveness. What becomes clear is this: cities and towns in many parts of the world, including North America, are badly adapted to accommodate those who are impaired.

The *megafone* map documents the extent of architectural able-ism. Mapped are traces of the trajectories of participants, and their experience of their neighborhood, a 'textured weave of connections' that constitute the morphological features that become the built environment, differentially experienced by some (Bissell, 2009).

From this point of view, understanding disability as social and material process calls forth the need to cultivate in the words of Fiona Kumari Campbell 'disability imaginaries' that 'think/speak/gesture and feel different landscapes not just for being-in-the-world, but on the conduction of perception, mobilities and temporalities' (2008: p.9). *megafone.net* is a tool that enables a different disability imaginary to emerge through the collective efforts of its participants. Produced is a collectively created image of the places, spaces and routes that are accessible and inaccessible. Using media in this way produces a means to advocate for awareness and change of how cities structure access (or not) to public space. In this way *megafone.net* is more than an art project: it is a clarion call for change.

References

Bissell, D., 'Conceptualising differently-mobile passengers: geographies of everyday encumbrance in the railway station,' in *Social & Cultural Geography,* 10 (2), 2009, pp.173–95.
Campbell, F.A.K., 'Inciting Legal Fictions: Disability's Date with Ontology and the Ableist Body of Law,' in *Griffith Law Review*, 10 (1), 2001, pp.42–62.
Campbell, F.A.K., 'Refusing Able(ness): A Preliminary Conversation about Ableism', *M/C Journal*, 11 (3), 2008: http://journal.media-culture.org.au/index.php/mcjournal/article/viewArticle/46 [accessed February 2013].

Chouinard, V., 'Legal Peripheries: Struggles over Disabled Canadians' Places in Law, Society and Space,' in *The Canadian Geographer*, 45 (1), 2001, pp.187–92.

Cresswell, T., *On the Move: Mobility in the Modern Western World*, New York and London: Routledge, 2006.

Crooks, V.A., and Chouinard, V. (2006) 'An embodied geography of disablement: chronically ill women's struggles for enabling spaces of health care and daily life,' in *Health & Place*, 12 (3), 2006, pp.345–52.

Ferrier, L., and Muller V., 'Disabling Able', *M/C Journal*, 11 (3), 2008: http://journal.media-culture.org.au/index.php/mcjournal/article/viewArticle/58 [accessed February 2013]

Imrie, R., 'Ableist Geographies, Disablist Spaces: Towards a Reconstruction of Golledge's "Geography and the Disabled",' in *Transactions of the Institute of British Geographers*, New Series, 21 (2), 1996, pp.397–403.

Kimberly Sawchuk is professor in the Department of Communication Studies, Concordia University, Montreal. She holds a Concordia University Research Chair in Mobile Media Studies where she co-directs the Mobile Media Lab (with Owen Chapman), *www.mobilities.ca*. Her writings on mobile media, technology, and society have appeared in numerous journals, collections, and anthologies including *MedieKultur, Body and Society, the Canadian Journal of Communication* and *Wi: Journal of Mobile Media*.

Chronology

canal*MOTOBOY
Motorcycle messengers
São Paulo, Brazil
2007–14

BARCELONA*accessible
People with limited mobility
Barcelona, Spain
2006/13

canal*GITANO
Young Gypsies
León, Spain
2005

sitio*TAXI
Taxi drivers
Mexico City, Mexico
2004–05/14

2004
2005
2006
2007
2008

canal*GITANO
Young Gypsies
Lleida, Spain
2005

canal*INVISIBLE
Sex workers
Madrid, Spain
2005

GENÈVE*accessible
People with limited mobility
Geneva, Switzerland
2008

canal*CENTRAL
Nicaraguan immigrants
San José, Costa Rica
2006–07

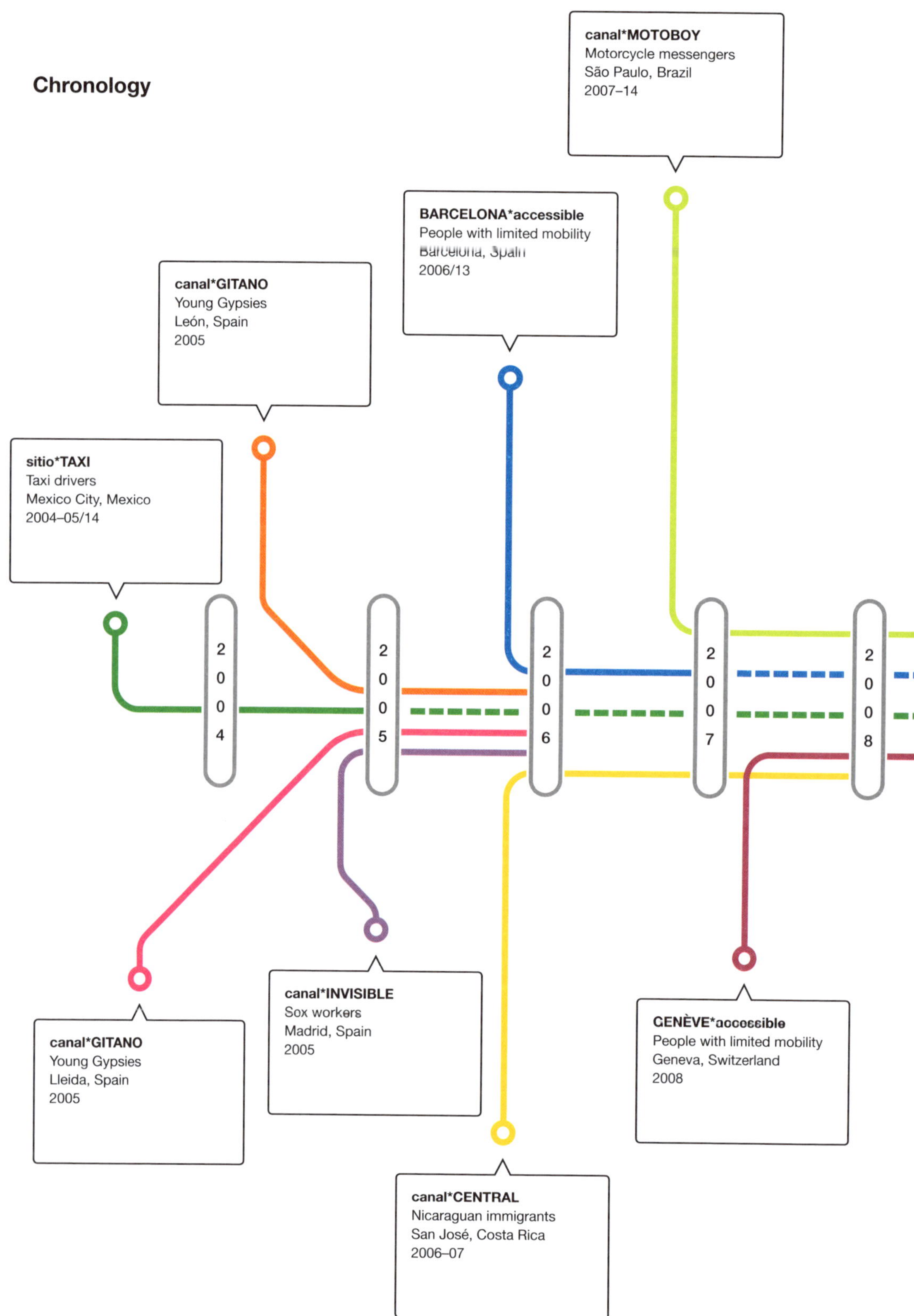

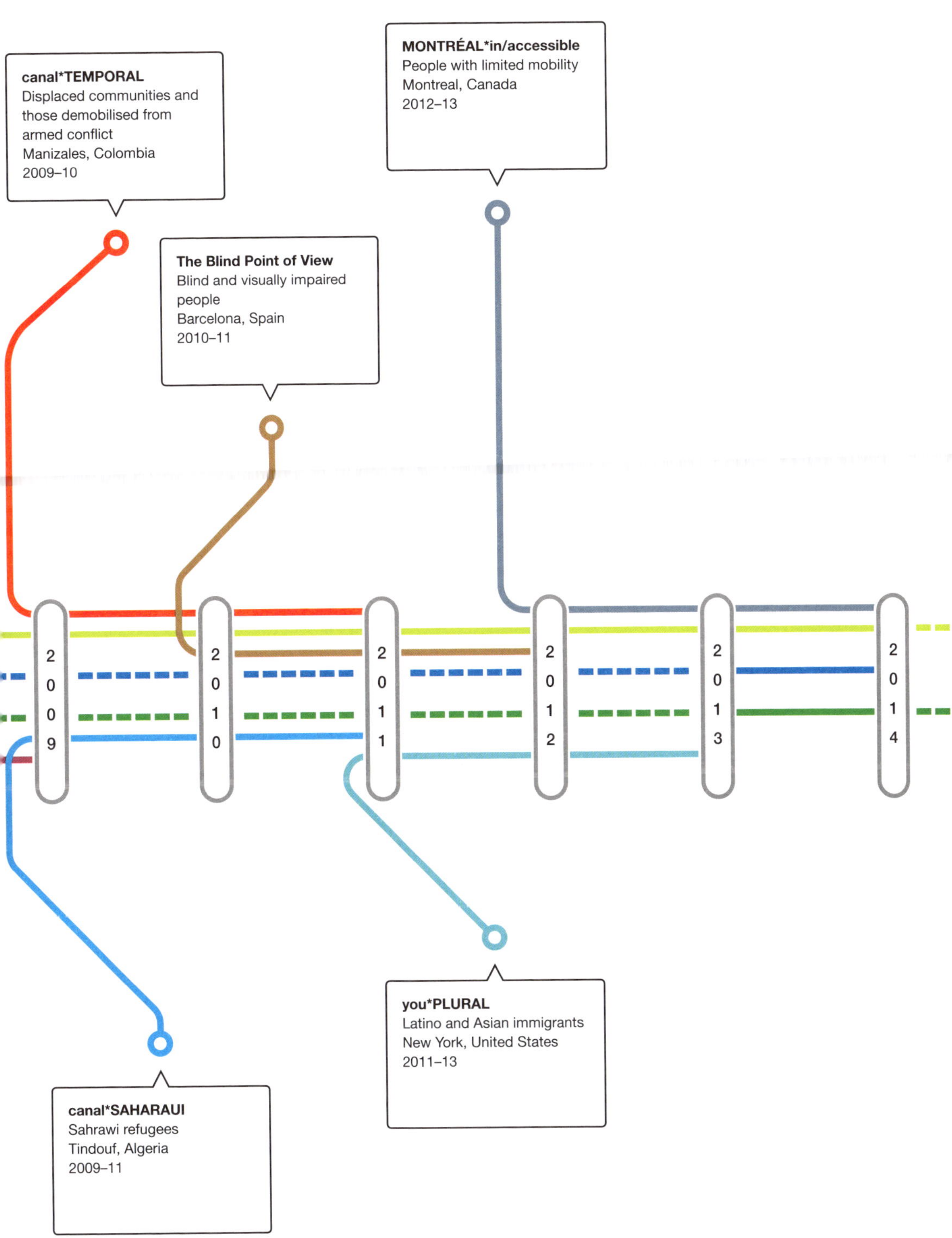

canal*TEMPORAL
Displaced communities and those demobilised from armed conflict
Manizales, Colombia
2009–10

The Blind Point of View
Blind and visually impaired people
Barcelona, Spain
2010–11

MONTRÉAL*in/accessible
People with limited mobility
Montreal, Canada
2012–13

canal*SAHARAUI
Sahrawi refugees
Tindouf, Algeria
2009–11

you*PLURAL
Latino and Asian immigrants
New York, United States
2011–13

2009
2010
2011
2012
2013
2014

accidente adulto amigos AMPARO anciano animales aniversario de independencia Aparadores Arbol artes Artesania Artesanias asociación atardecer Atrio Avión bar Basura boda burocracia calle casa Centro comercial CHAMBA chicharrón circo colectivo comer comercio comida compañeros comprar conferencia corrupción De donde sacaron escolares? deporte descansar descanso desplazarse discriminacion doméstico Domingo edificio el tiempo Entre amigos entrevista escuela estar solo ESTRELLA estudiar Exposición familia femenino fotos fraude Genero gestiones granja grito hogar Hospedaje hospital imprudente Irresponsabilidad Josefa Ortiz joven Lectura maiz mascota Mascotas masculino mercado MISCELANEA mobiliario movilidad MUJERESenRUTA museo música Nacimiento niños ocio ofrenda paisaje PANORAMA Papel picado parque Piñata Piñatasa policía prensa PRIEBA Promesa de campaña Pruebas publicando Puentes radio Renacimiento restaurante RETROVISOR reunión SABADO salud se complica todo Seguridad SENADO servicio sin censura SITIOS sonora Sr.Miguel Angel Mancera TALACHAS TARJETON taxi*COCODRILO taxi*DON FACUNDO taxi*GERARDO taxi*JOSE taxi*MARCOS taxi*MIGUEL taxi*PEDRO taxi*ROSAMARIA tecnología TECOLOTE Tendido telefonico Terapias trabajar trabajo costumbres tradicion tradiciones transportes UAM UAM Lerma ULISES vehículo venta viajar

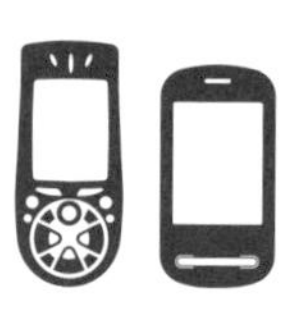

sitio*TAXI
Taxi drivers
Mexico City, Mexico
2004–05/14

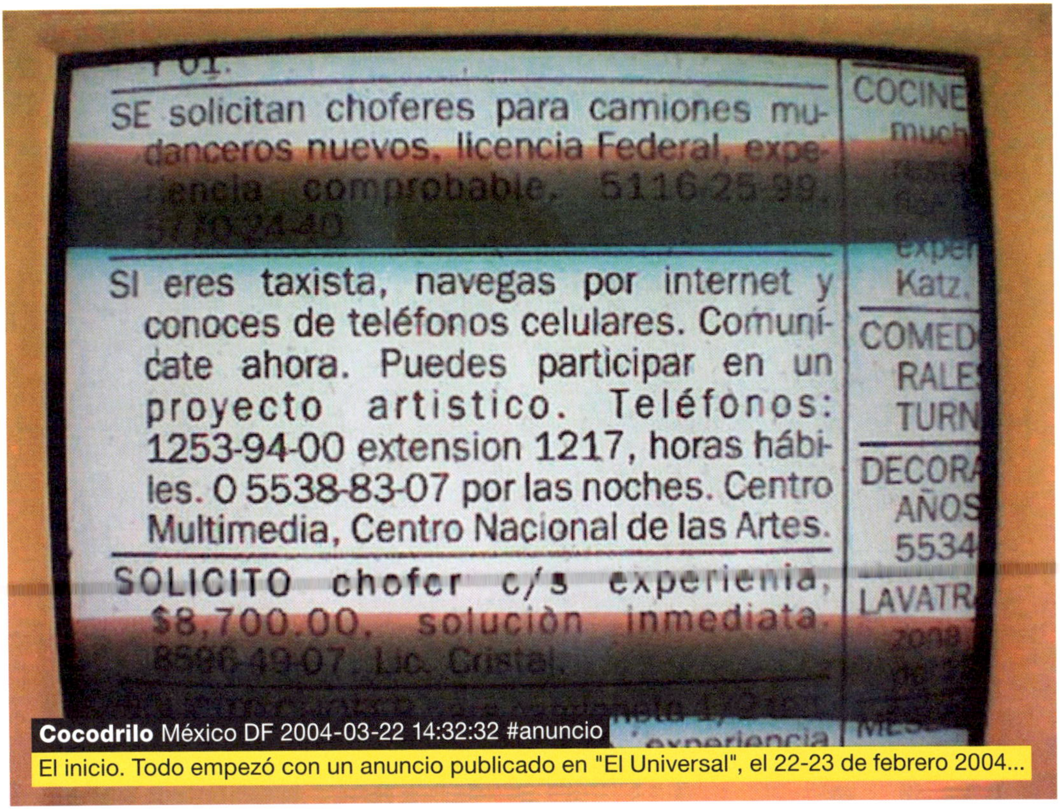

SE solicitan choferes para camiones mu-
danceros nuevos, licencia Federal, expe-
riencia comprobable. 5116-25-99.

SI eres taxista, navegas por internet y
conoces de teléfonos celulares. Comuní-
cate ahora. Puedes participar en un
proyecto artistico. Teléfonos:
1253-94-00 extension 1217, horas hábi-
les. O 5538-83-07 por las noches. Centro
Multimedia, Centro Nacional de las Artes.

SOLICITO chofer c/s experienia,
$8,700.00, solución inmediata.
8896-49-07. Lic. Cristal.

Cocodrilo México DF 2004-03-22 14:32:32 #anuncio
El inicio. Todo empezó con un anuncio publicado en "El Universal", el 22-23 de febrero 2004...

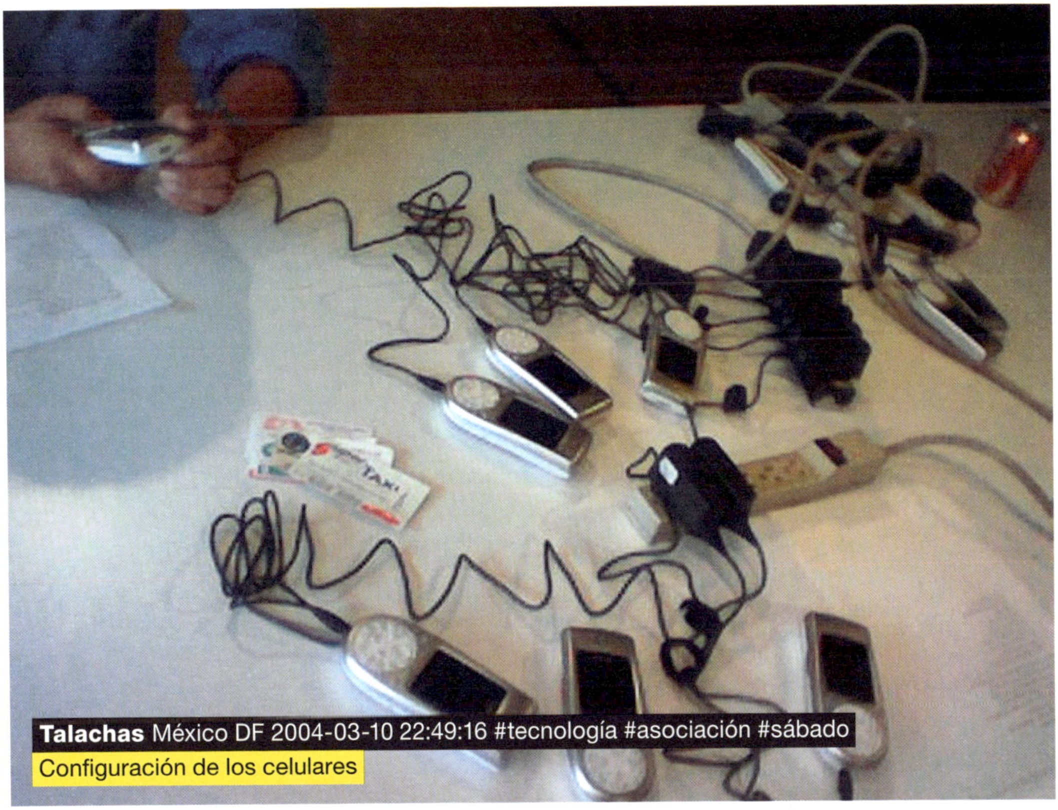

Talachas México DF 2004-03-10 22:49:16 #tecnología #asociación #sábado
Configuración de los celulares

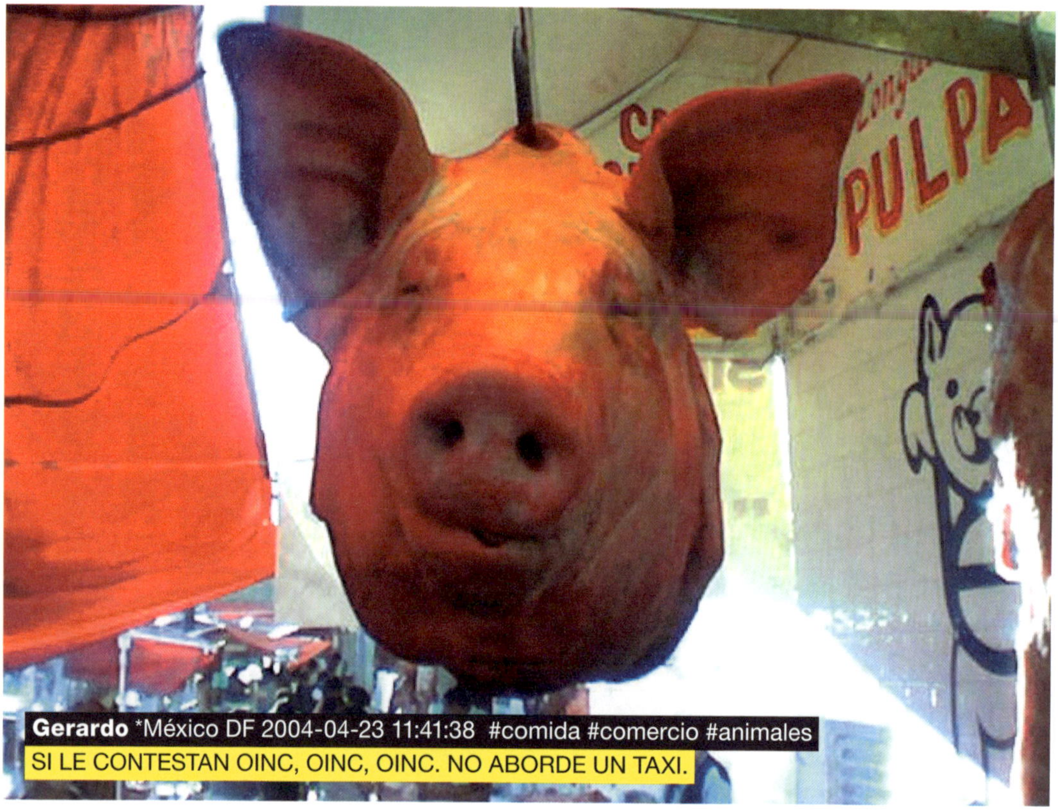

Gerardo *México DF 2004-04-23 11:41:38 #comida #comercio #animales
SI LE CONTESTAN OINC, OINC, OINC. NO ABORDE UN TAXI.

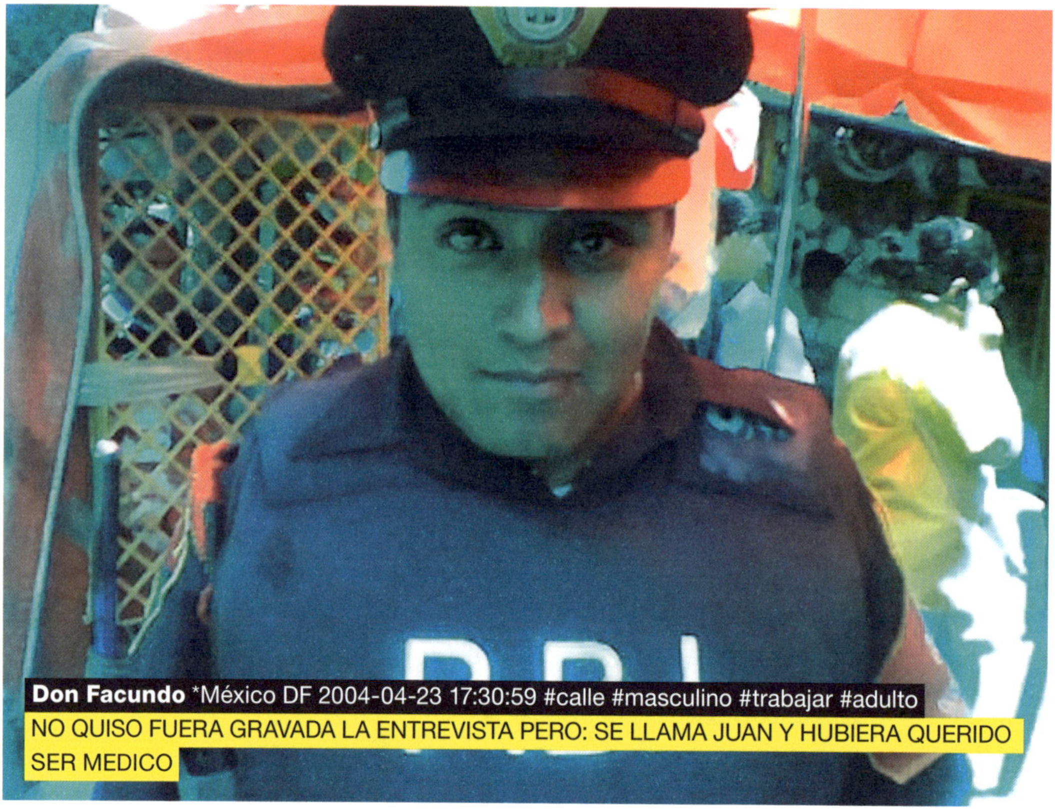

Don Facundo *México DF 2004-04-23 17:30:59 #calle #masculino #trabajar #adulto
NO QUISO FUERA GRAVADA LA ENTREVISTA PERO: SE LLAMA JUAN Y HUBIERA QUERIDO SER MEDICO

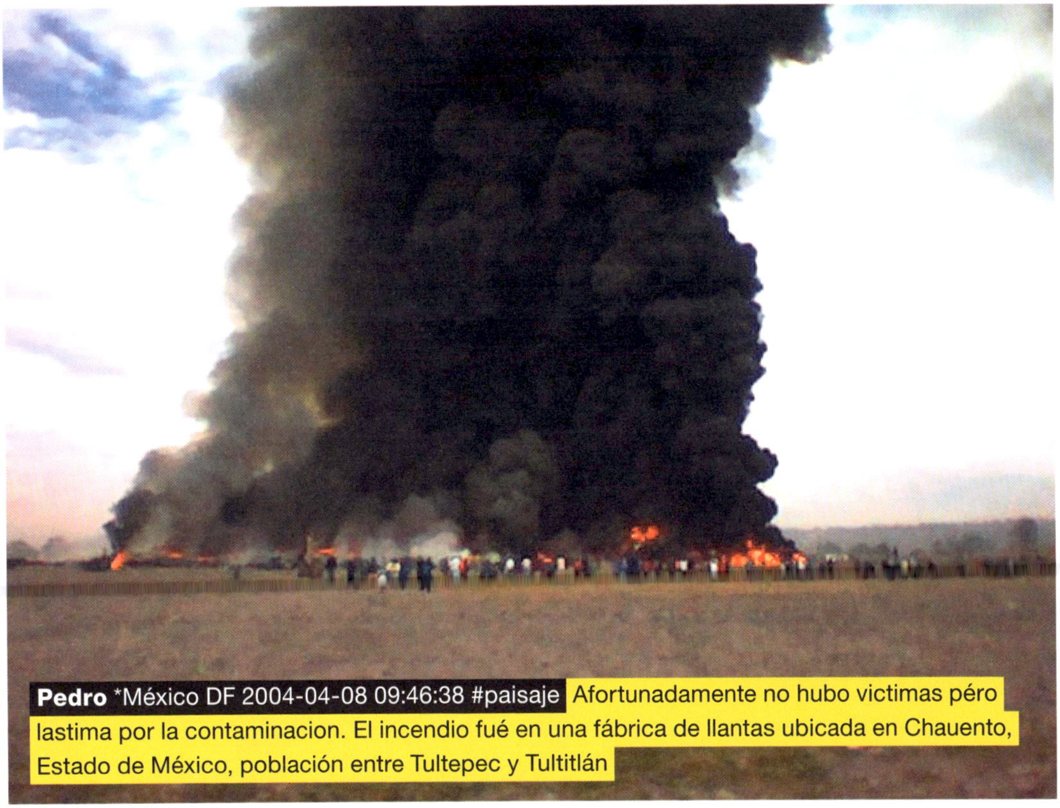

Pedro *México DF 2004-04-08 09:46:38 #paisaje Afortunadamente no hubo victimas péro lastima por la contaminacion. El incendio fué en una fábrica de llantas ubicada en Chauento, Estado de México, población entre Tultepec y Tultitlán

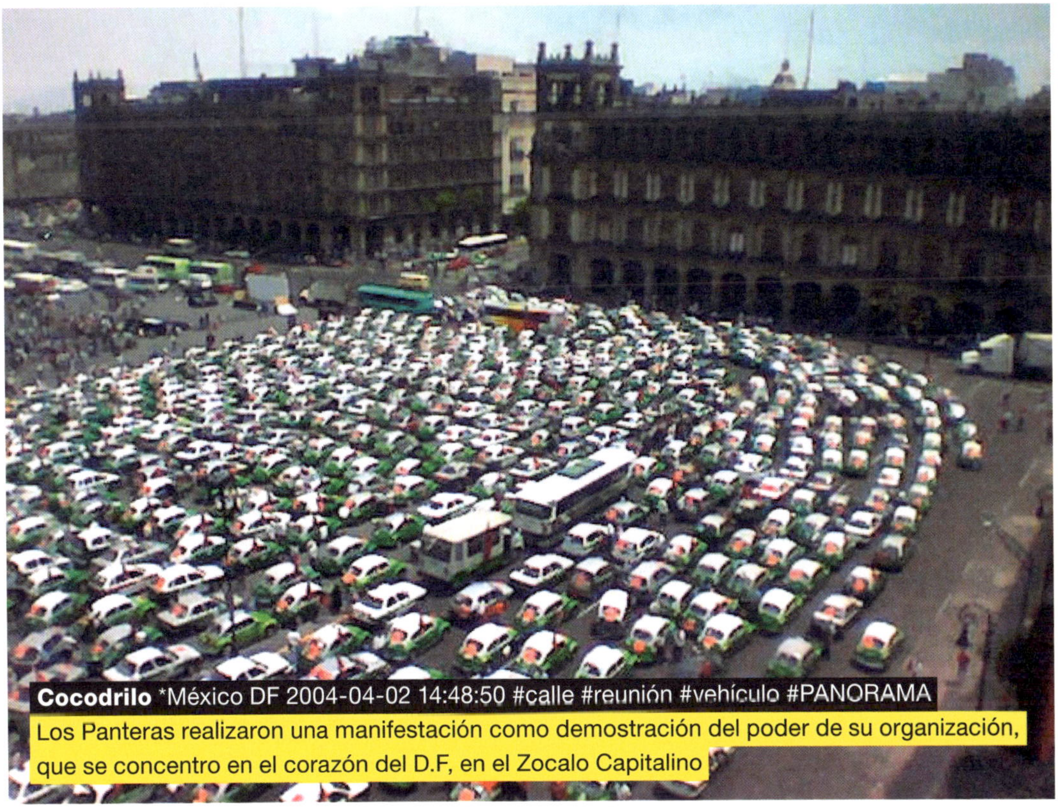

Cocodrilo *México DF 2004-04-02 14:48:50 #calle #reunión #vehículo #PANORAMA Los Panteras realizaron una manifestación como demostración del poder de su organización, que se concentro en el corazón del D.F, en el Zocalo Capitalino

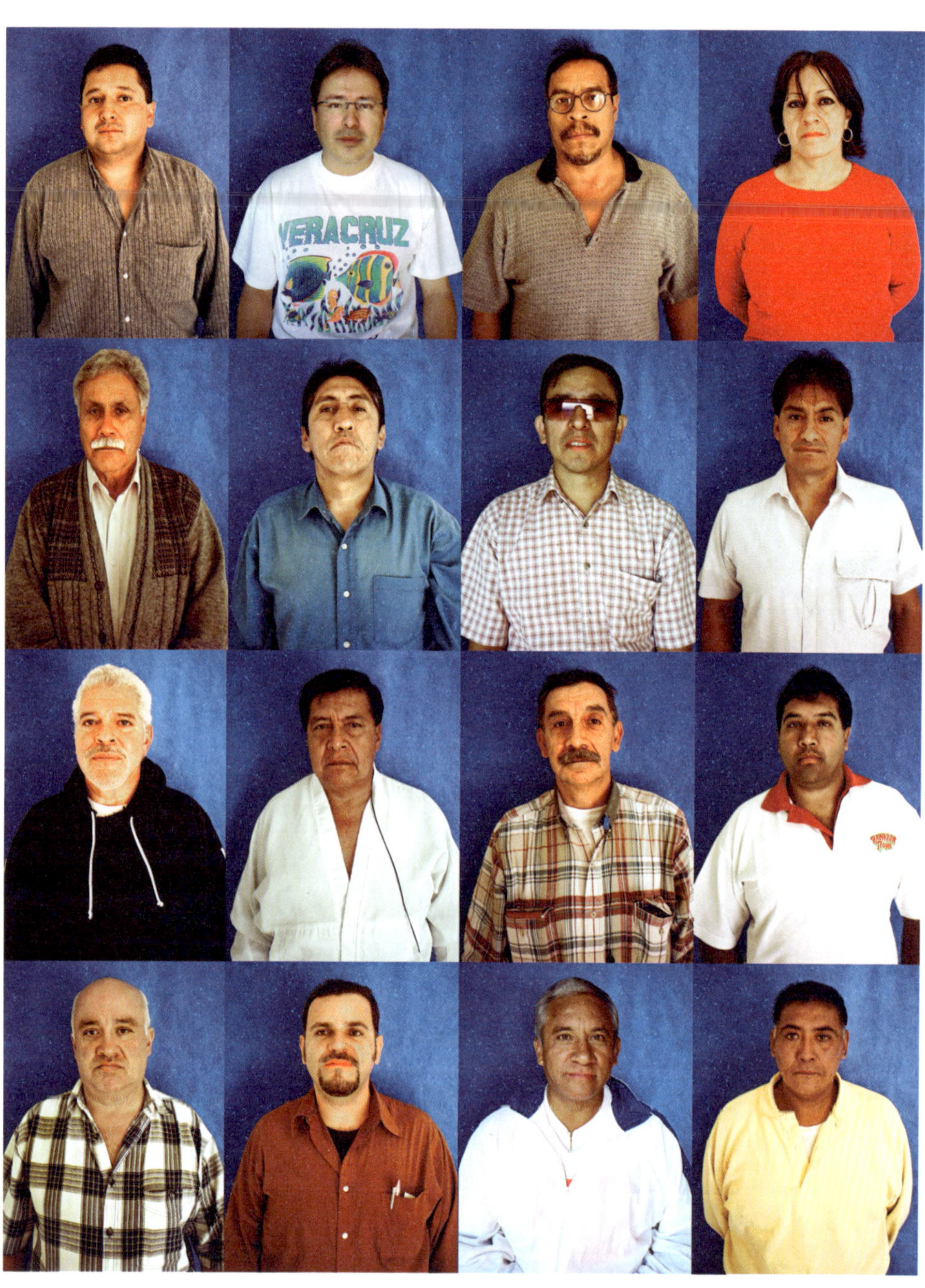

Taxi drivers participating in the project *sitio*TAXI*

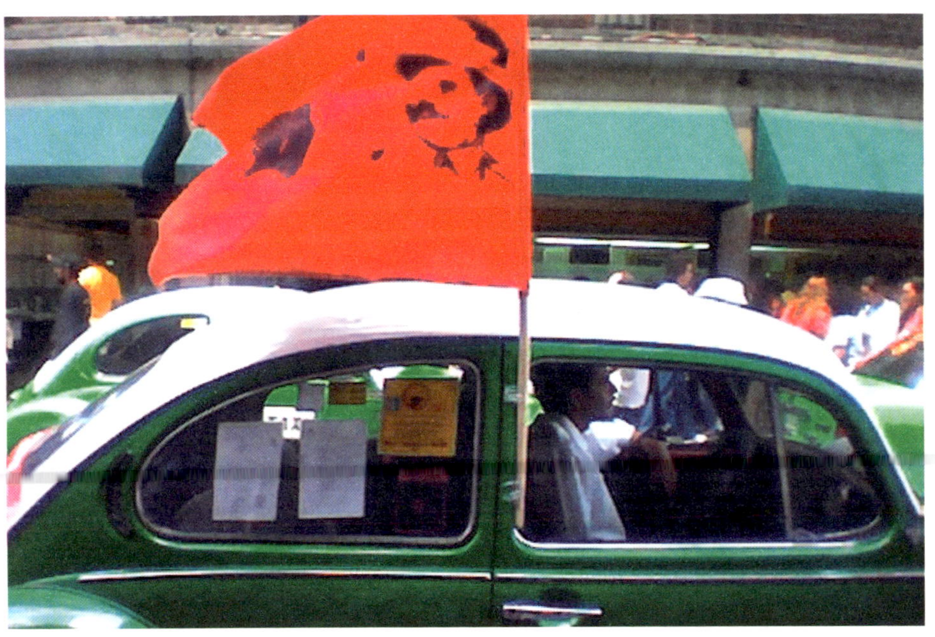

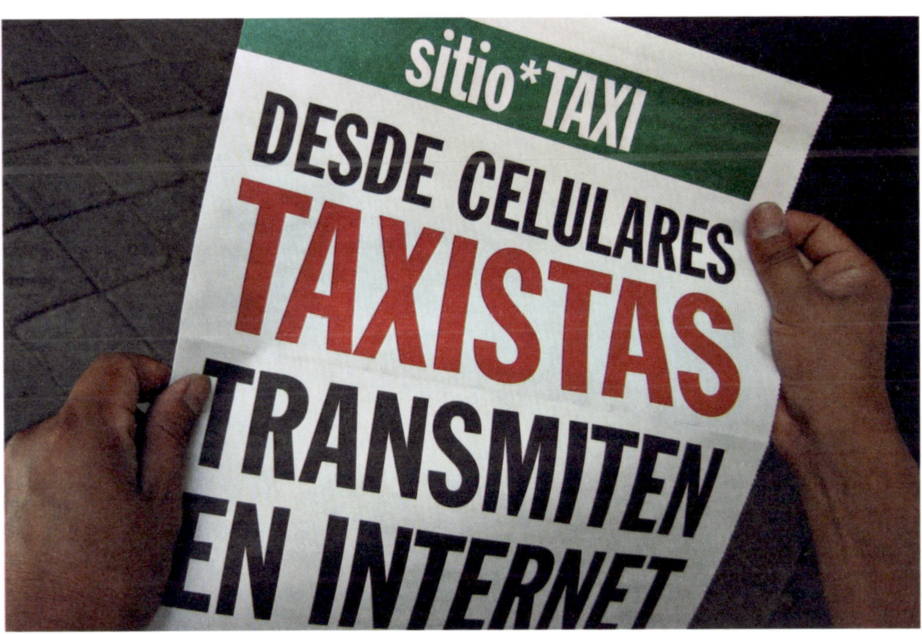

Publication in news sheet format for the project *sitio*TAXI*

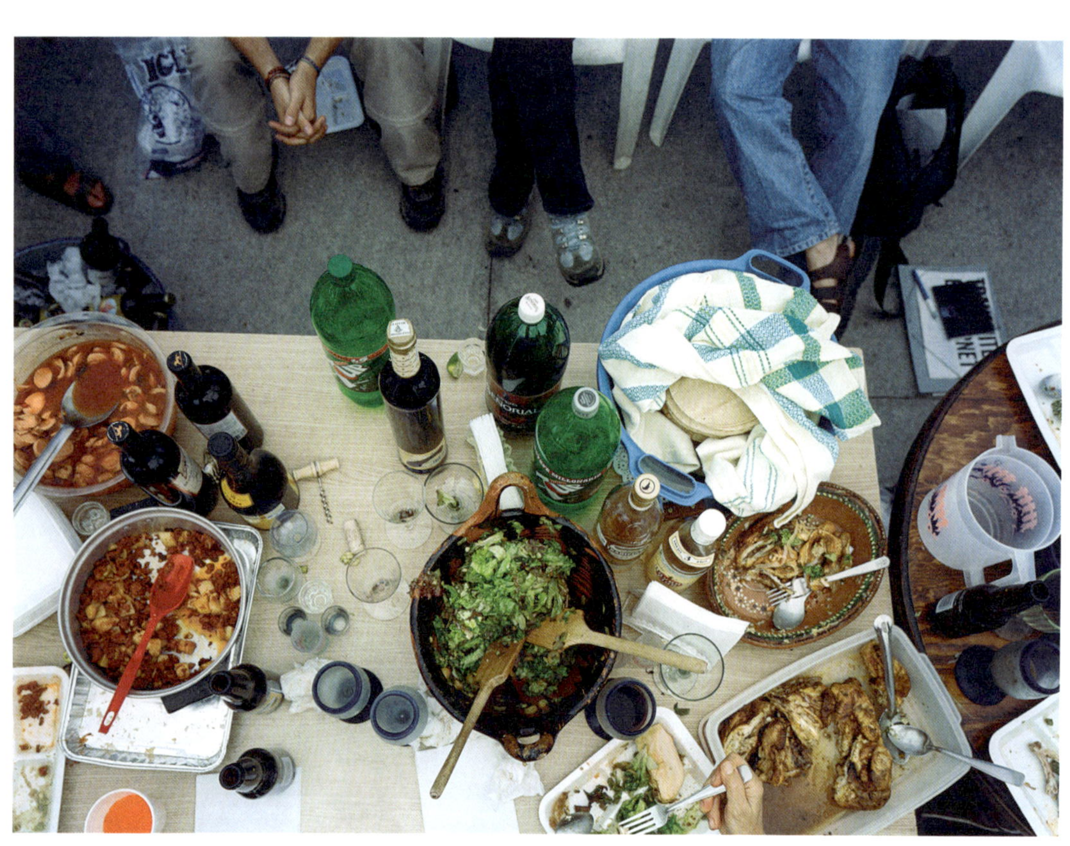

Potluck lunch at the home of don Facundo (Sunday, April 18, 2004)

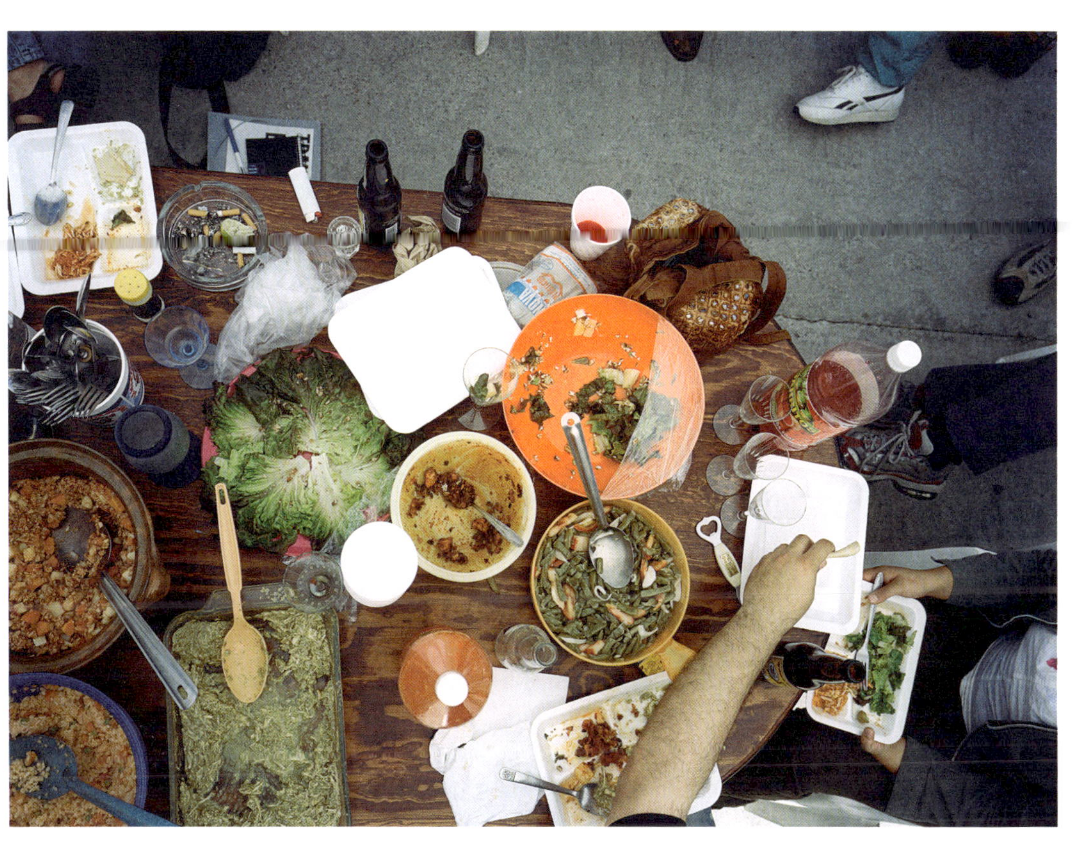

adult animals
asociació bar boda burocracia carrer comerç
companys comprar CULTO
CURRO descansar
desplaçar-se domèstic edifici esport estar
sol estudiar familia feina femenino fotos
gestions infantil jove llar MARIOLA
masculí menjar MERCAU mobiliari movilidad
música obj.casa oci paisatge PÁJARO
parc PATRIARCA PLA RASPALL restaurant
reunió ROMA salut servei SÍMBOL tecnologia
transports treballar vehicle vell viatjar

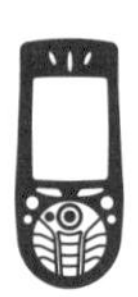

canal*GITANO
Young Gypsies
Lleida, Spain
2005

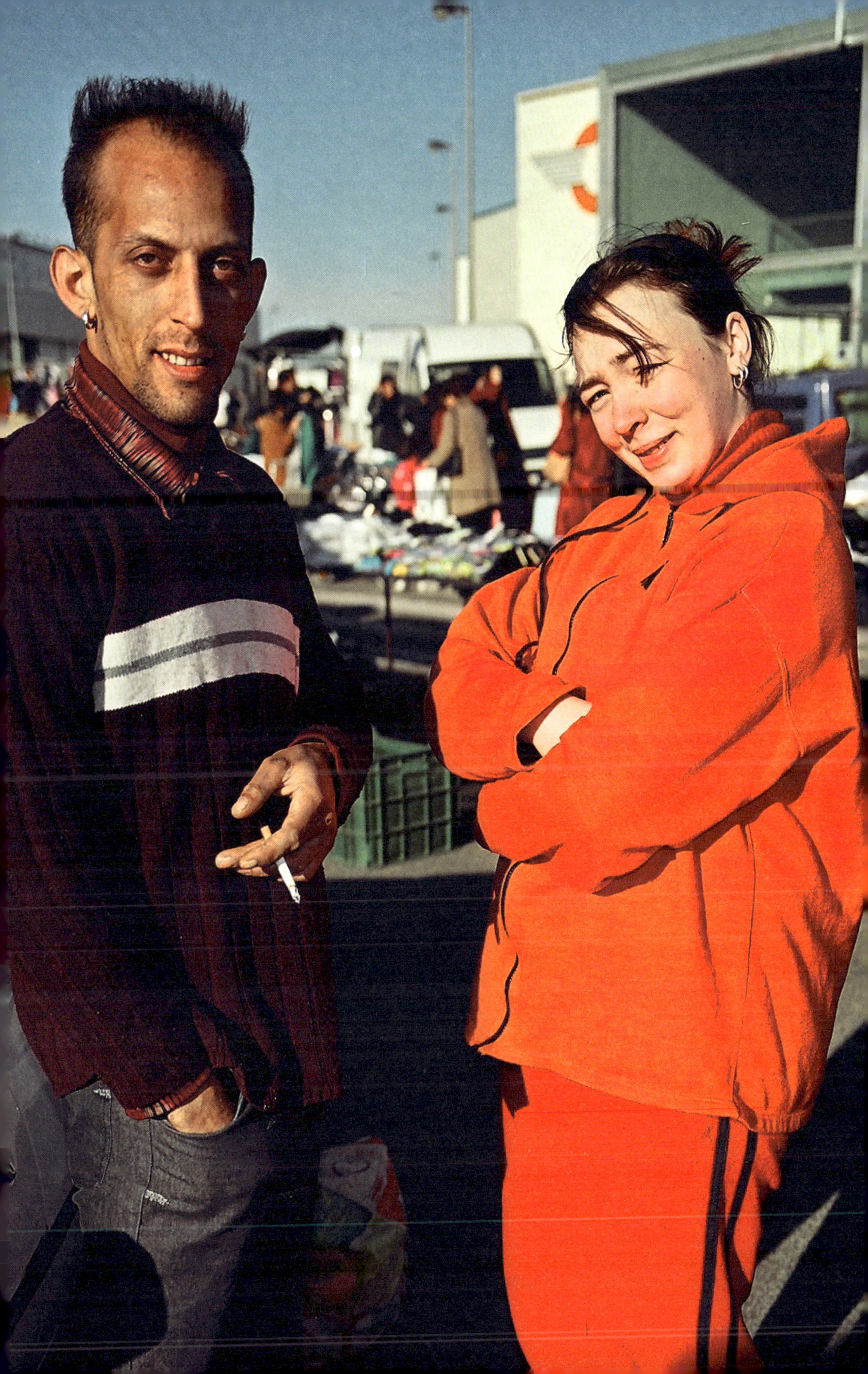

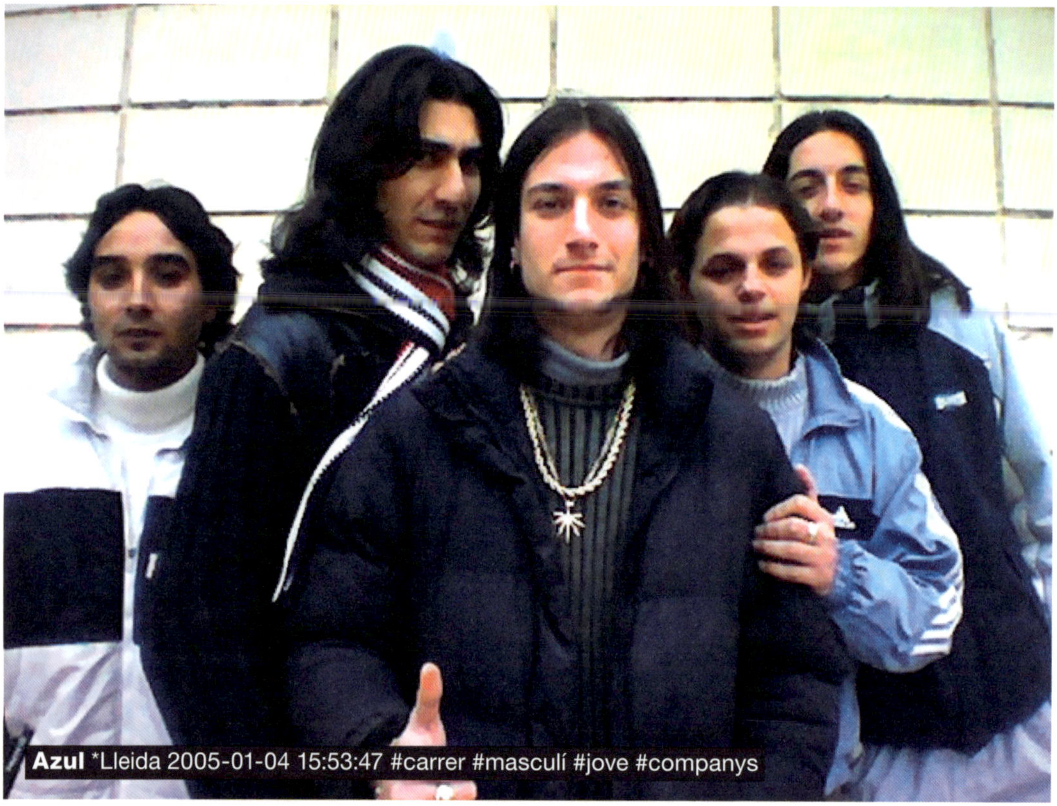

Azul *Lleida 2005-01-04 15:53:47 #carrer #masculí #jove #companys

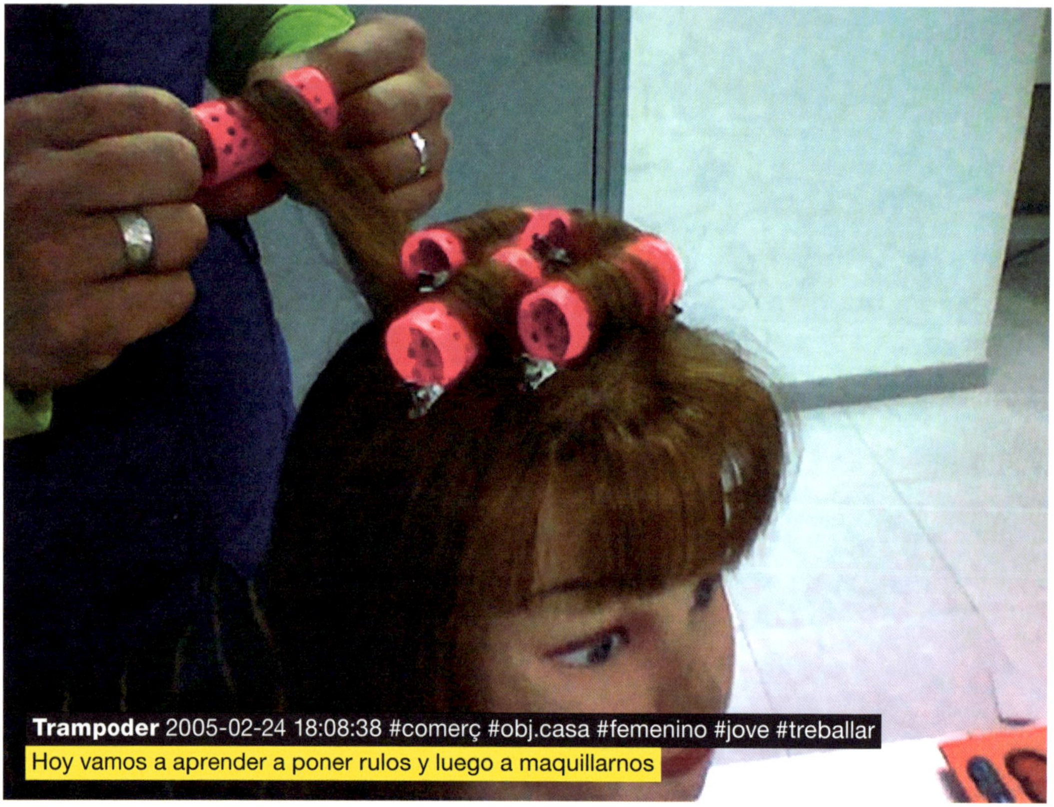

Trampoder 2005-02-24 18:08:38 #comerç #obj.casa #femenino #jove #treballar
Hoy vamos a aprender a poner rulos y luego a maquillarnos

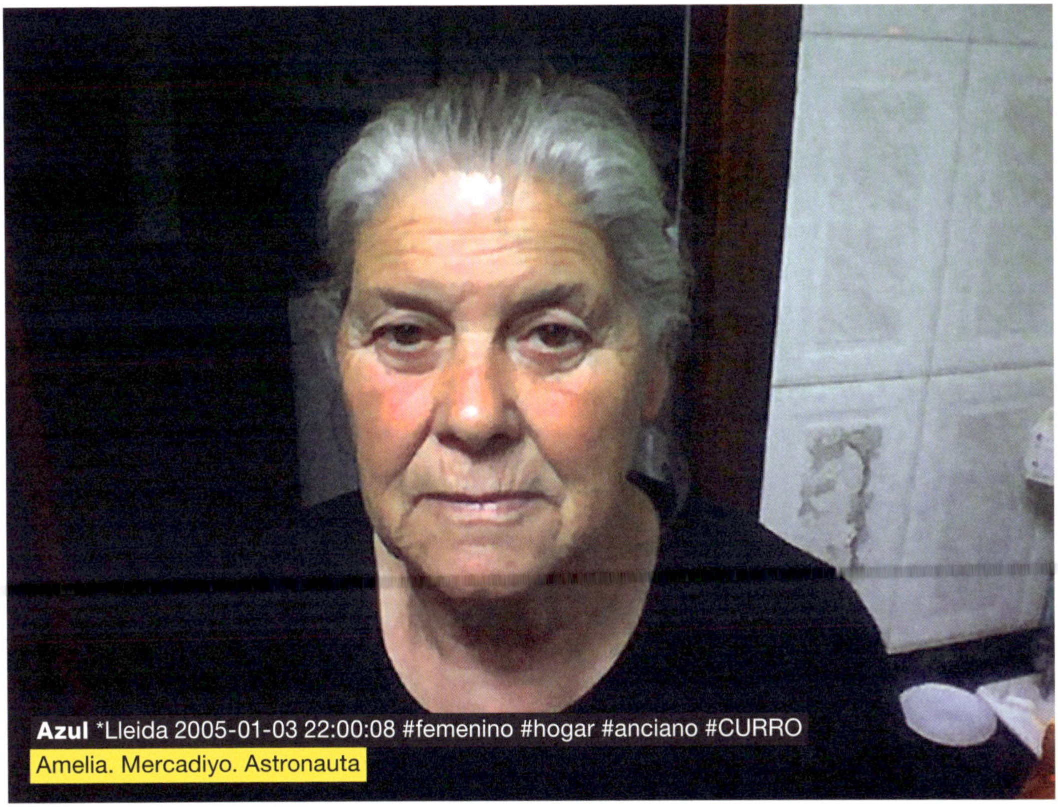

Azul *Lleida 2005-01-03 22:00:08 #femenino #hogar #anciano #CURRO

Amelia. Mercadiyo. Astronauta

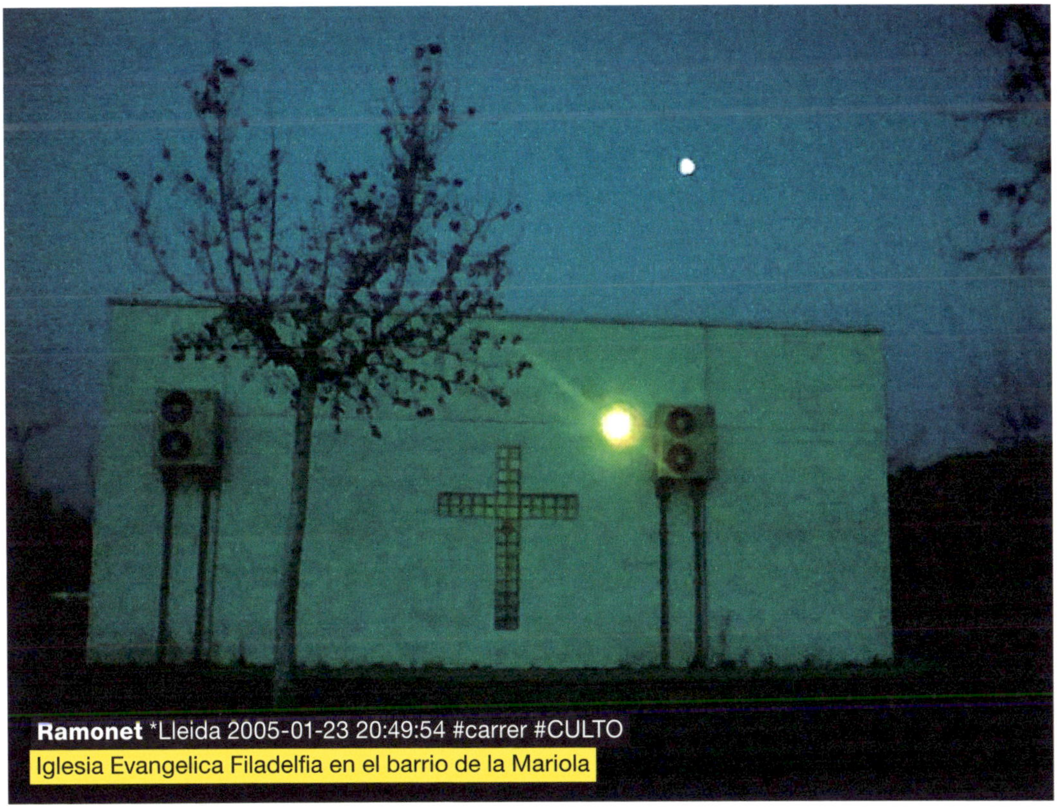

Ramonet *Lleida 2005-01-23 20:49:54 #carrer #CULTO

Iglesia Evangelica Filadelfia en el barrio de la Mariola

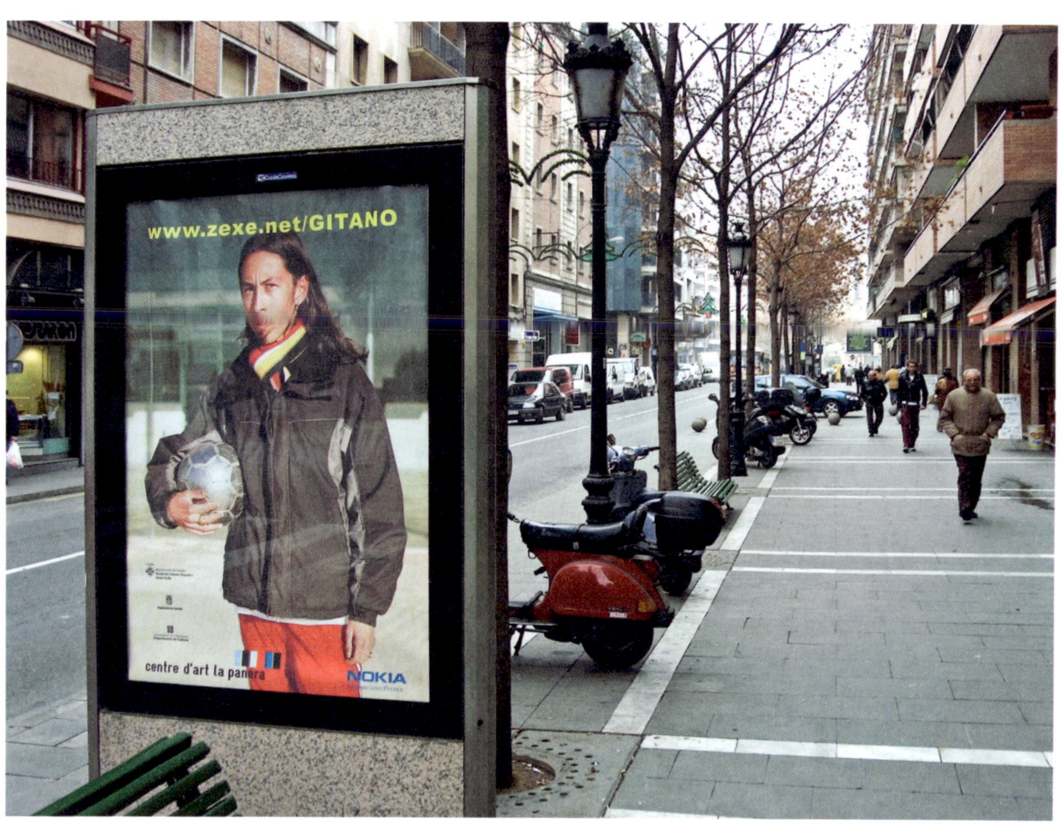

Advertisement and meeting table for *canal*GITANO* at the Centre d'Art la Panera

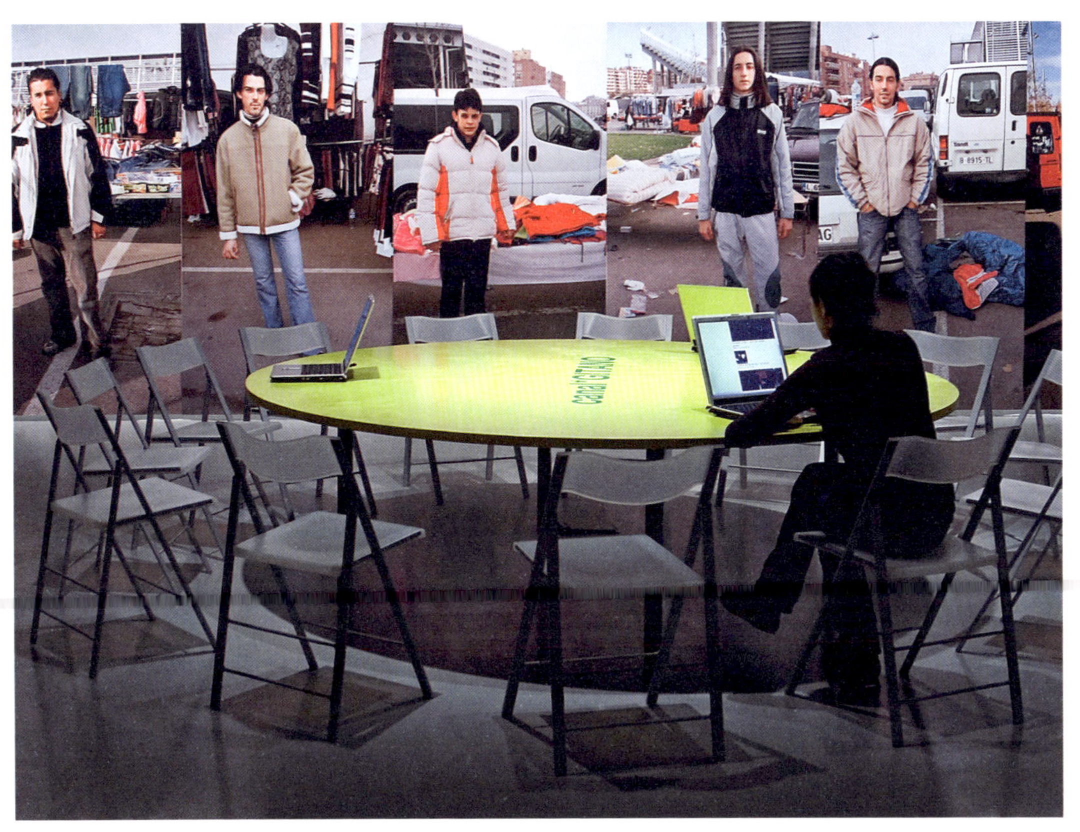

adulto anciano animales asociación
bar BARRIO boda burocracia calle
casa comer comercio comida
compañeros comprar COSTUMBRE
deporte descansar desplazarse
DISTINTO doméstico edificio
entrevista estar solo estudiar familia
femenino formación fotos
gestiones hogar IGUAL joven
masculino mobiliario movilidad música
niños ocio paisaje parque restaurante
reunión salud servicio tecnología trabajar
trabajo transportes vehículo viajar

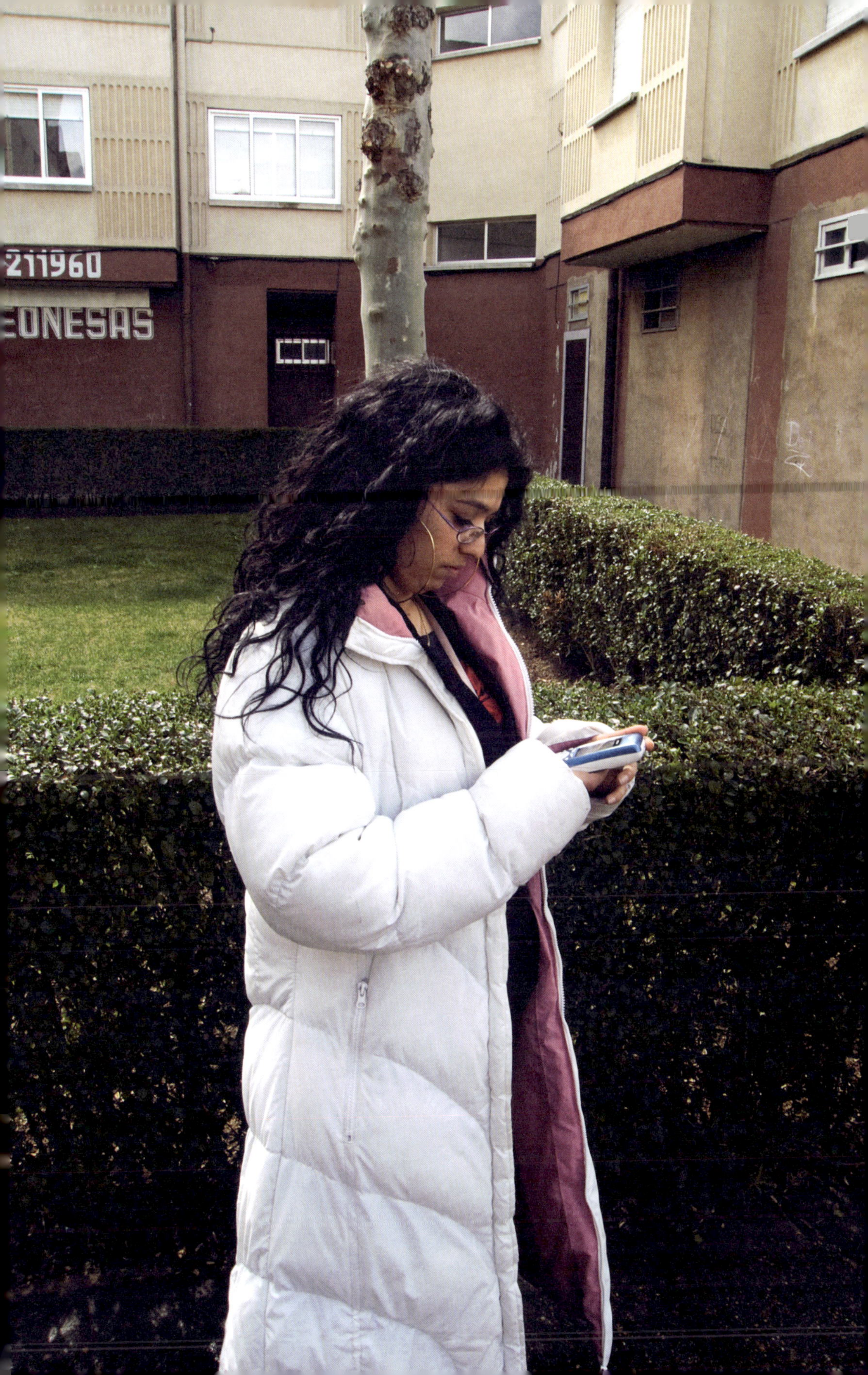

211960
EONESAS

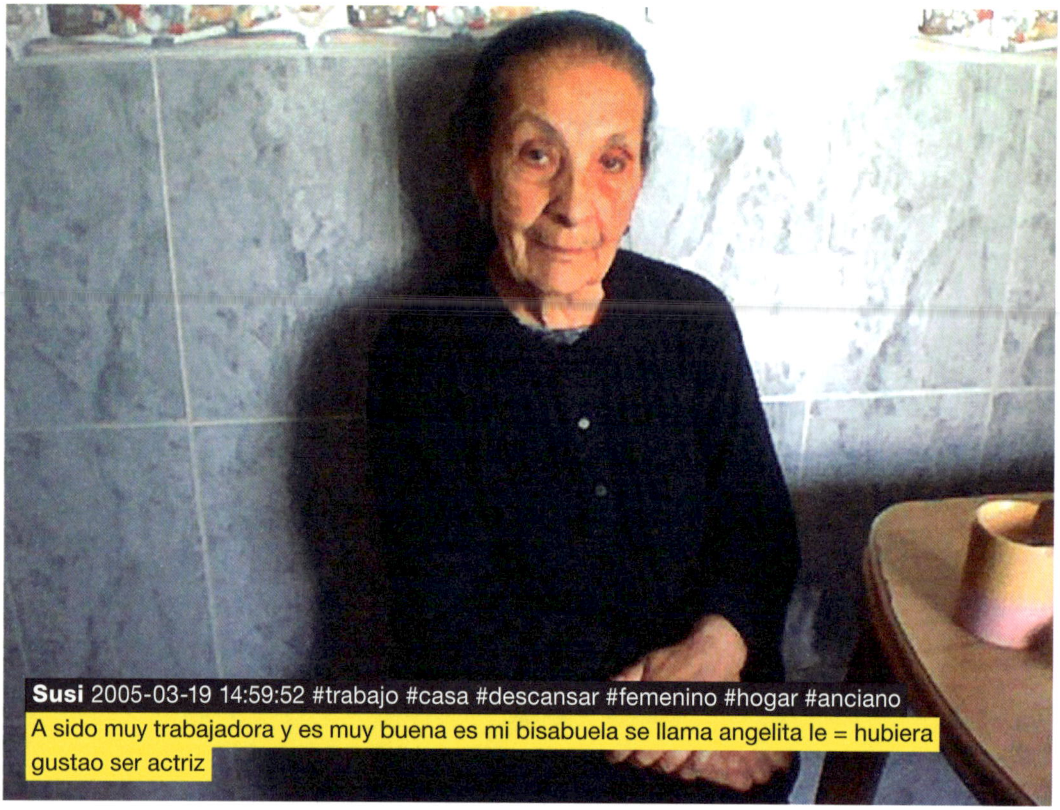

Susi 2005-03-19 14:59:52 #trabajo #casa #descansar #femenino #hogar #anciano
A sido muy trabajadora y es muy buena es mi bisabuela se llama angelita le = hubiera gustao ser actriz

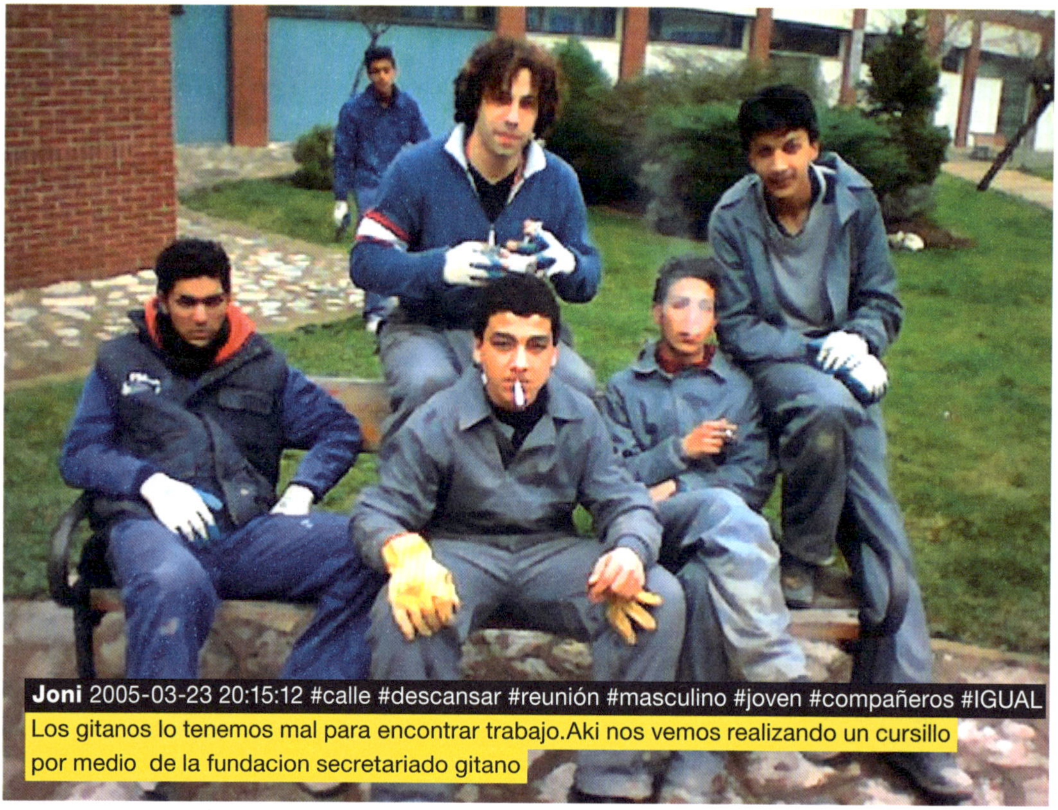

Joni 2005-03-23 20:15:12 #calle #descansar #reunión #masculino #joven #compañeros #IGUAL
Los gitanos lo tenemos mal para encontrar trabajo.Aki nos vemos realizando un cursillo por medio de la fundacion secretariado gitano

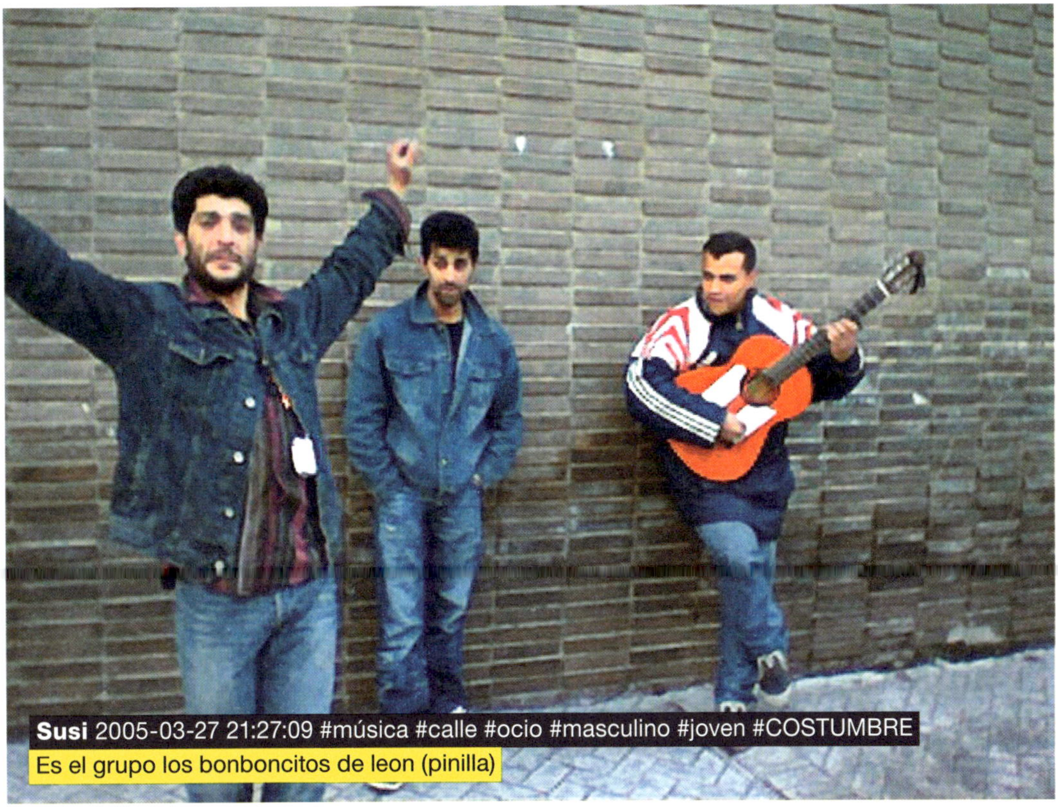

Susi 2005-03-27 21:27:09 #música #calle #ocio #masculino #joven #COSTUMBRE
Es el grupo los bonboncitos de leon (pinilla)

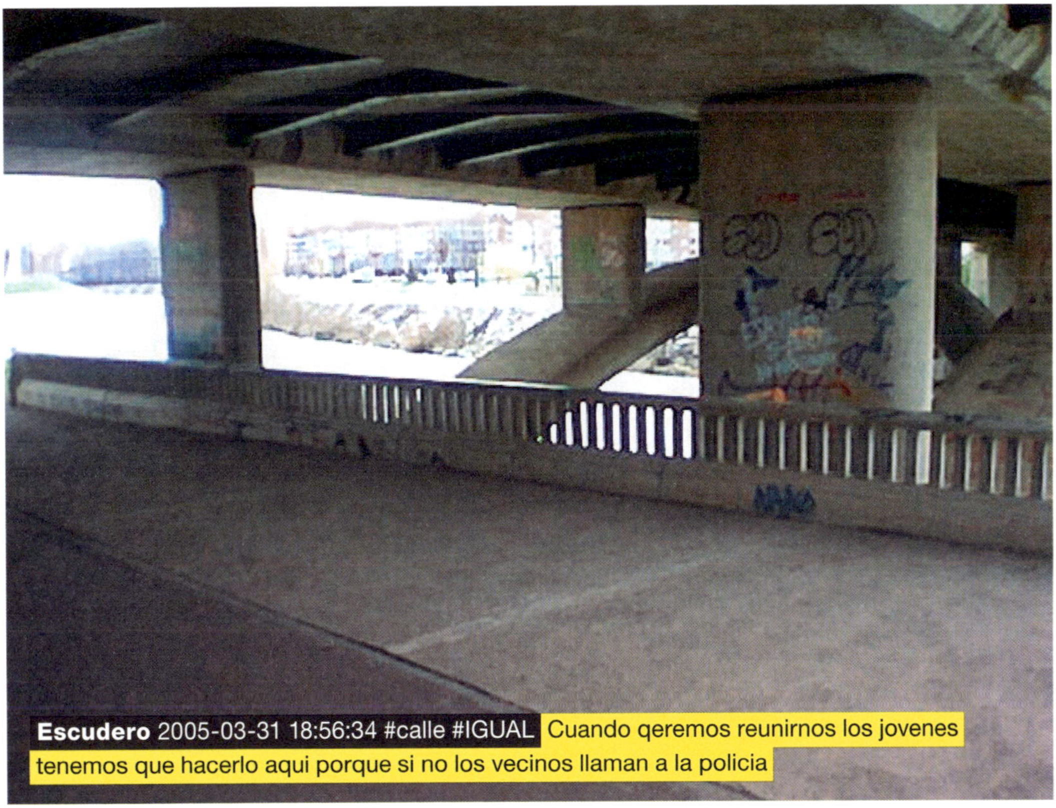

Escudero 2005-03-31 18:56:34 #calle #IGUAL Cuando qeremos reunirnos los jovenes
tenemos que hacerlo aqui porque si no los vecinos llaman a la policia

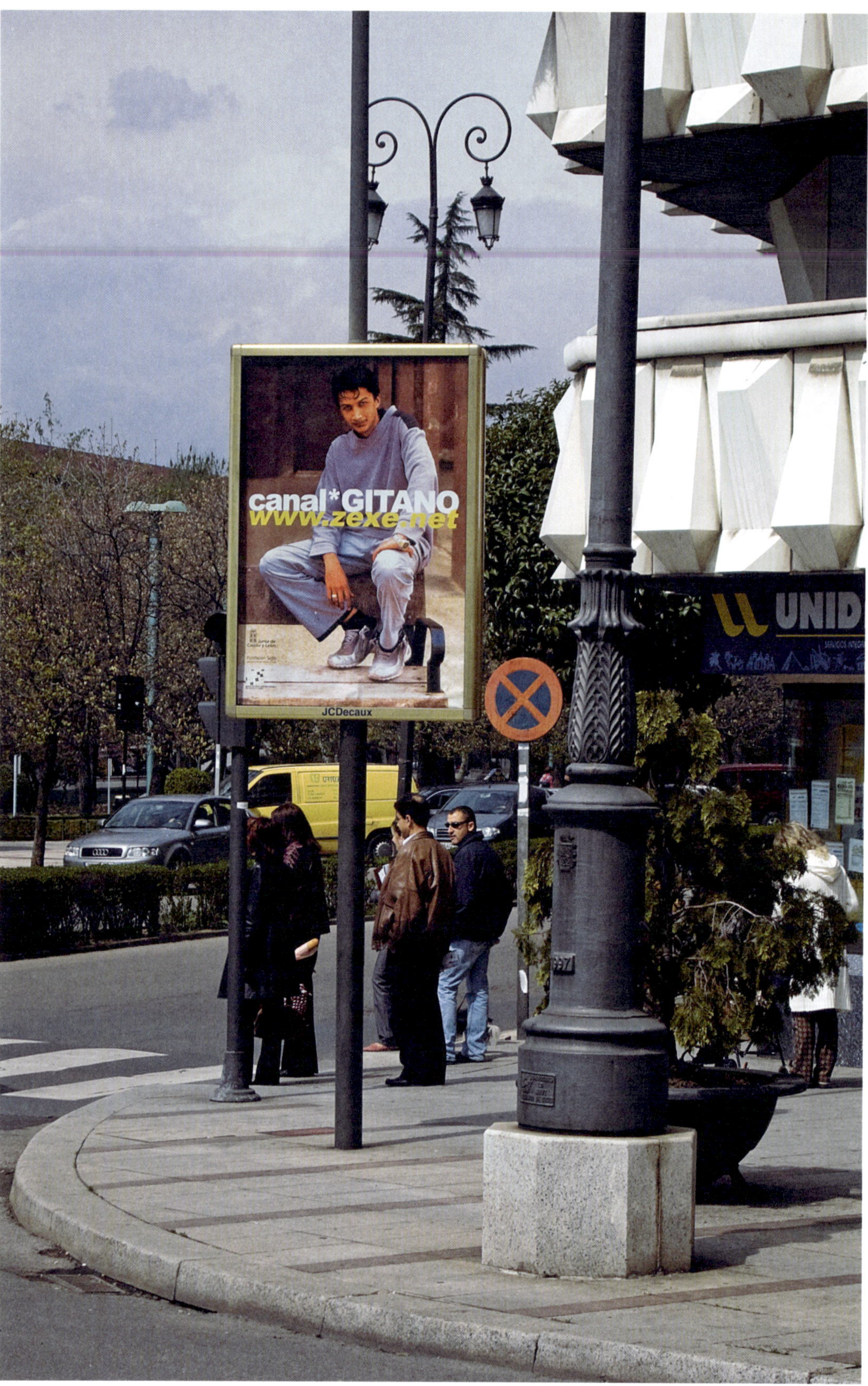

canal*GITANO
www.zexe.net
Junta de Castilla y León
Fundación Secretariado
JCDecaux
UNID

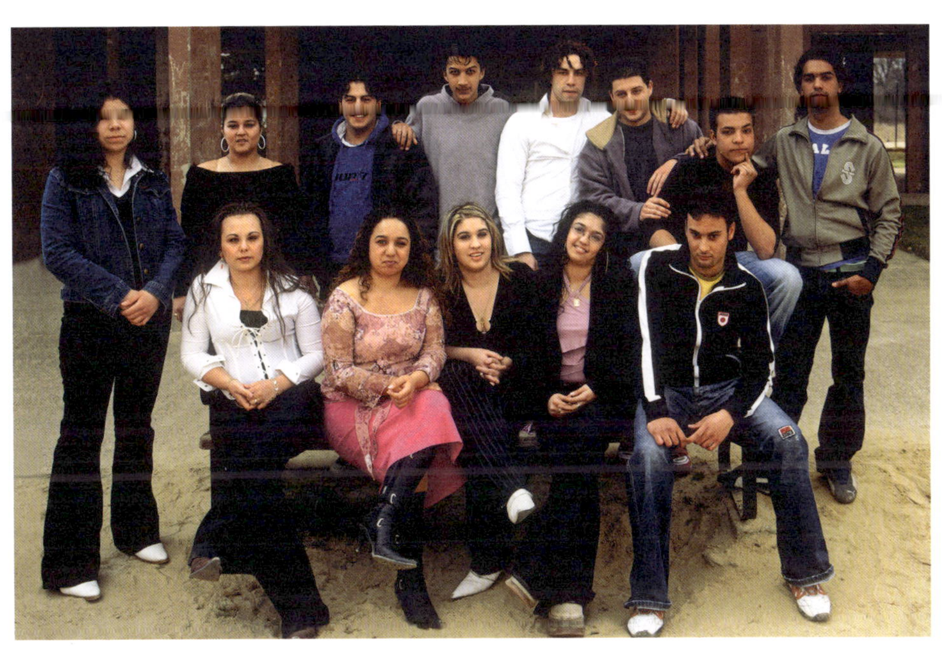

Advertisement and participants in *canal*GITANO*

adulto anciano animales asociación
bar burocracia calle casa comer
comercio comida compañeros
comprar deporte descansar desplazarse
edificio estar solo ESTILO familia
femenino fotos gestiones hogar
joven masculino MENÚ
MISCELANEA mobiliario movilidad música
niños ocio ORGULLO paisaje PAPELES
parque PROFESIONAL
restaurante reunión salud servicio
tecnología trabajar trabajo
transportes vehículo viajar

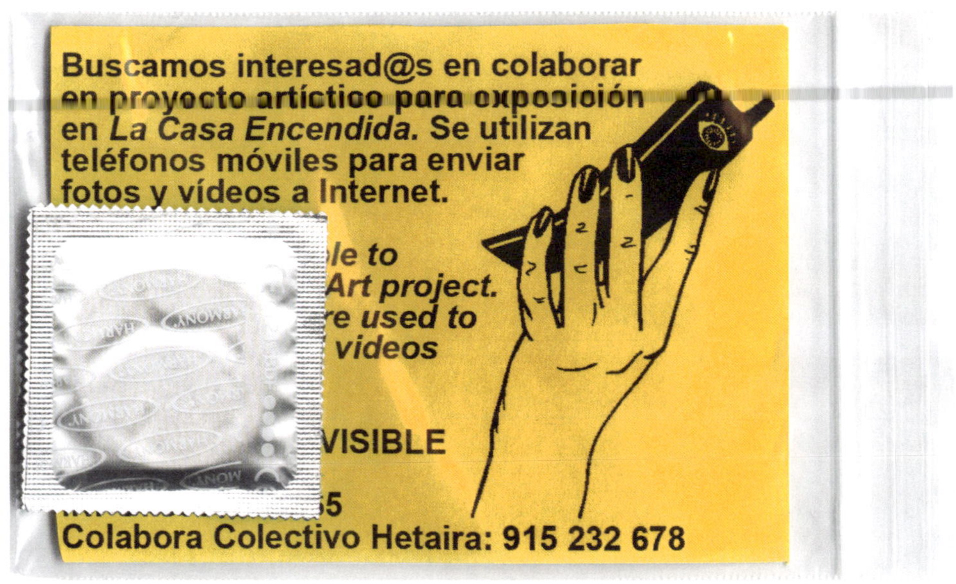

Call for participants in the project *canal*INVISIBLE* included in one of the kits handed out to sex workers by the Hetaira association

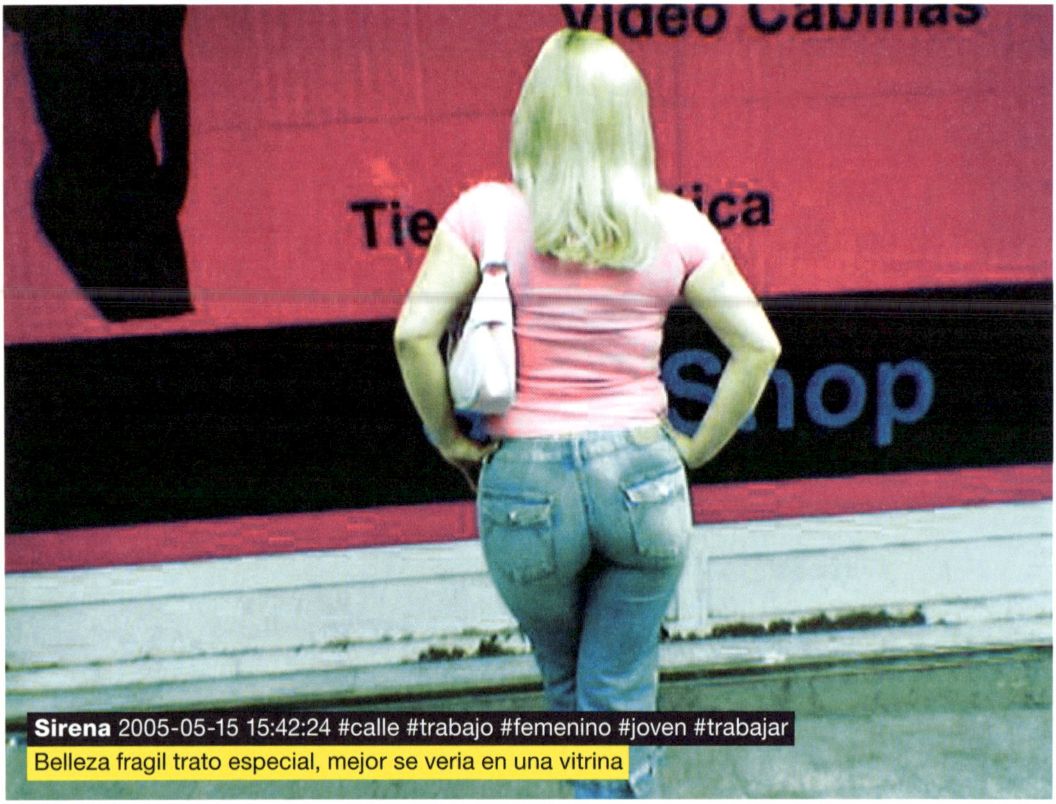

Sirena 2005-05-15 15:42:24 #calle #trabajo #femenino #joven #trabajar
Belleza fragil trato especial, mejor se veria en una vitrina

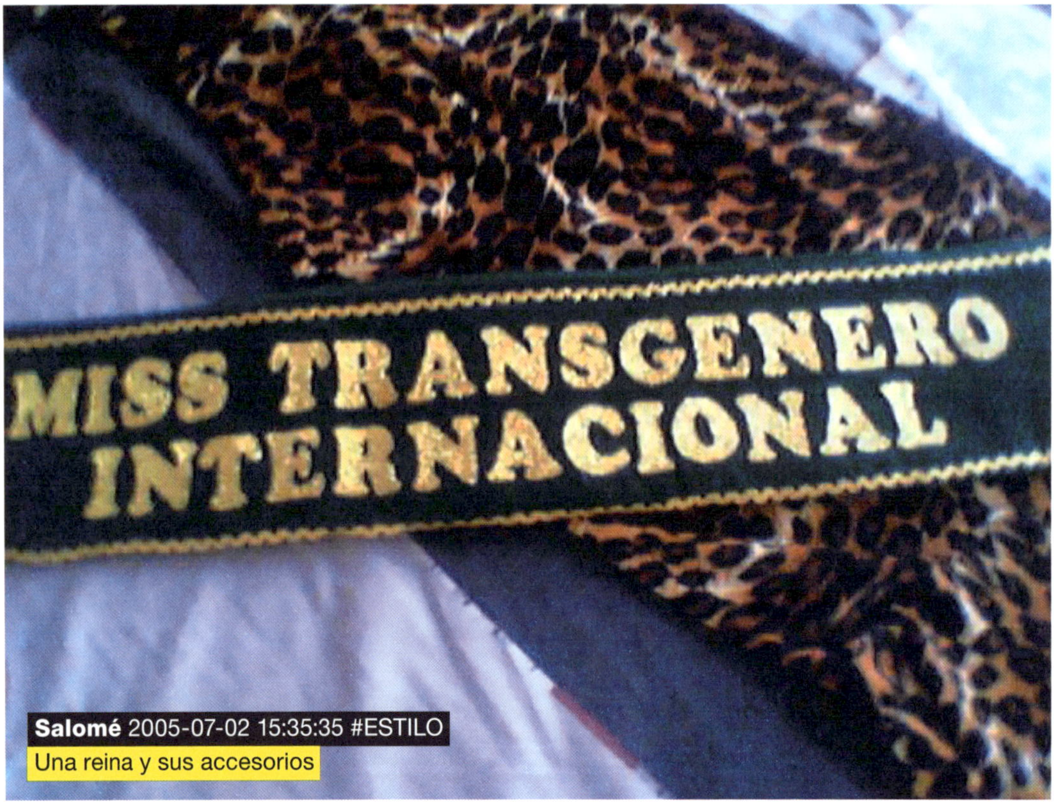

Salomé 2005-07-02 15:35:35 #ESTILO
Una reina y sus accesorios

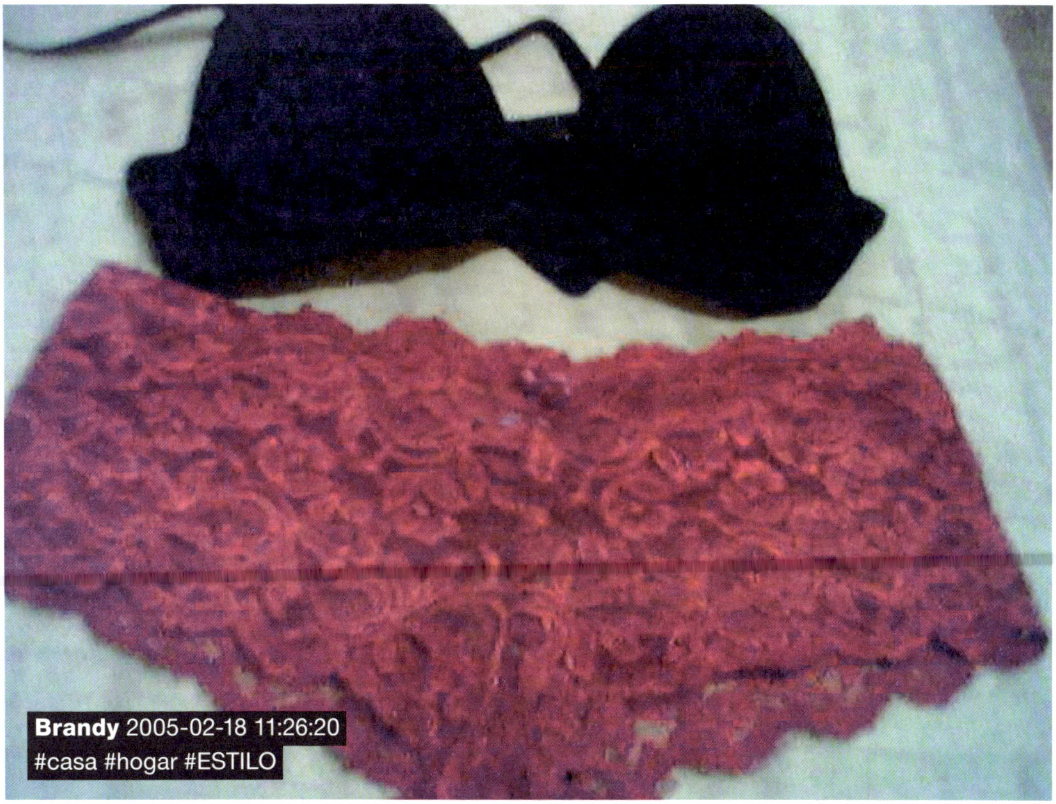

Brandy 2005-02-18 11:26:20
#casa #hogar #ESTILO

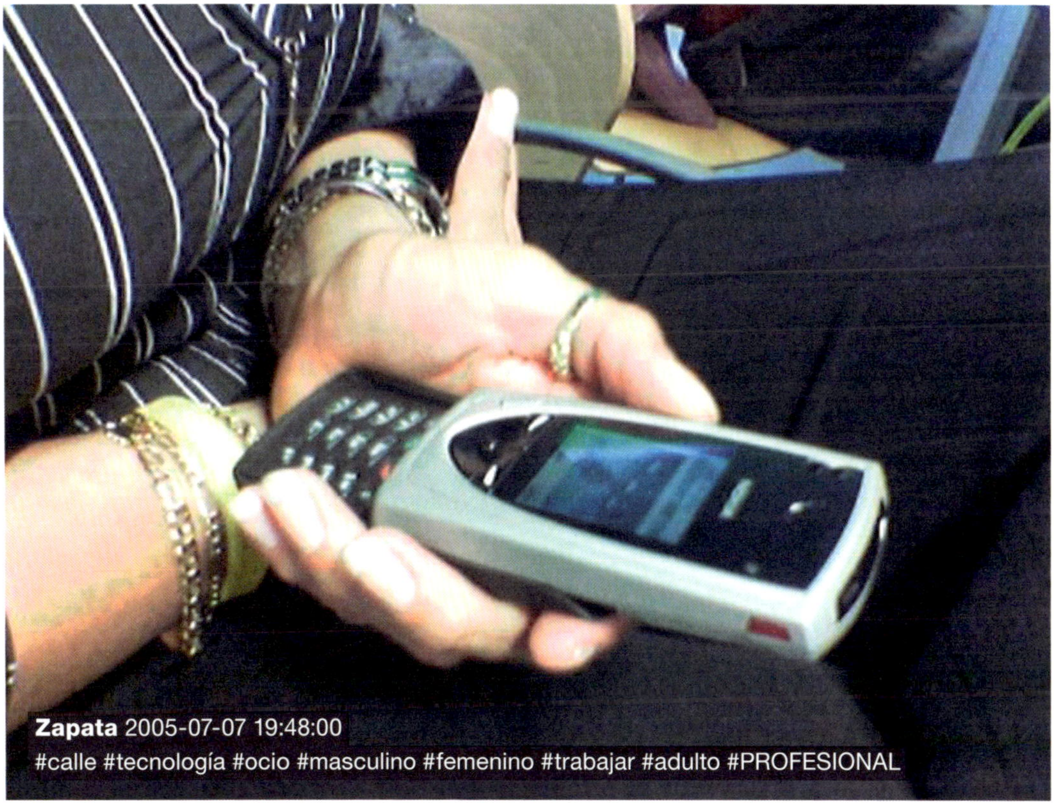

Zapata 2005-07-07 19:48:00
#calle #tecnología #ocio #masculino #femenino #trabajar #adulto #PROFESIONAL

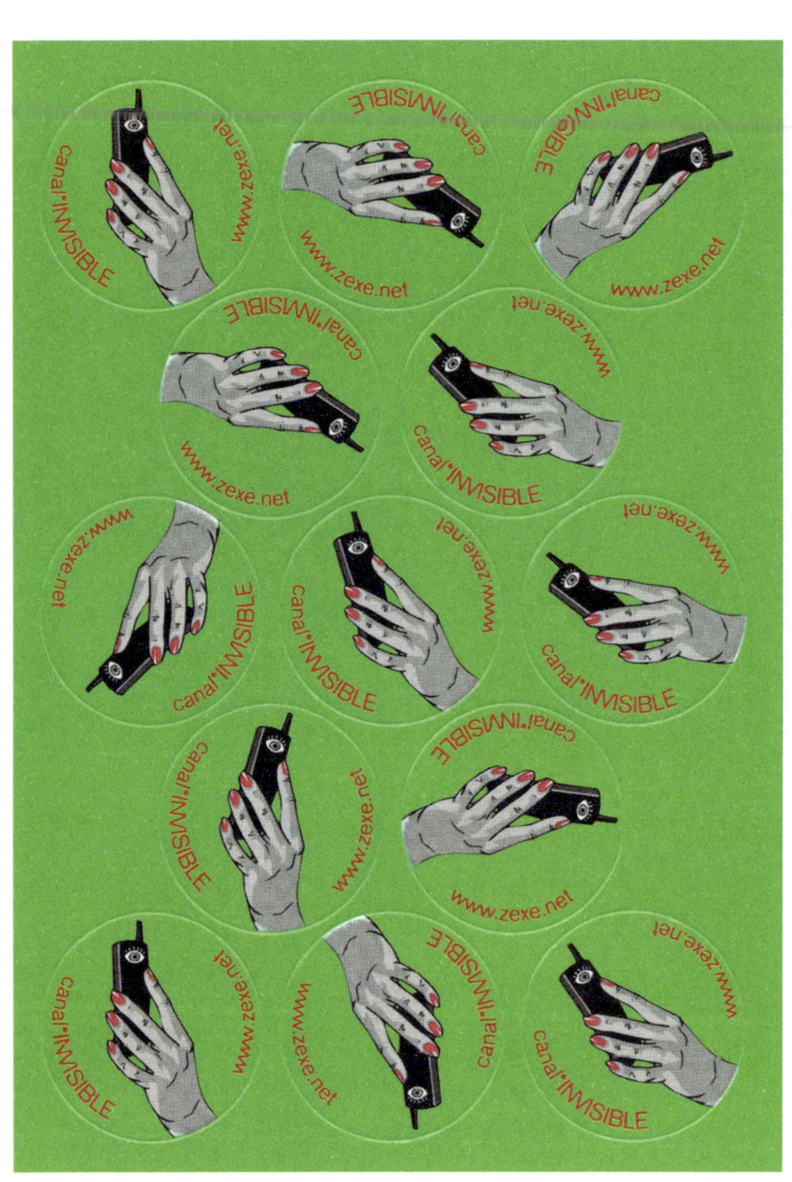

Stickers promoting the project *canal*INVISIBLE*

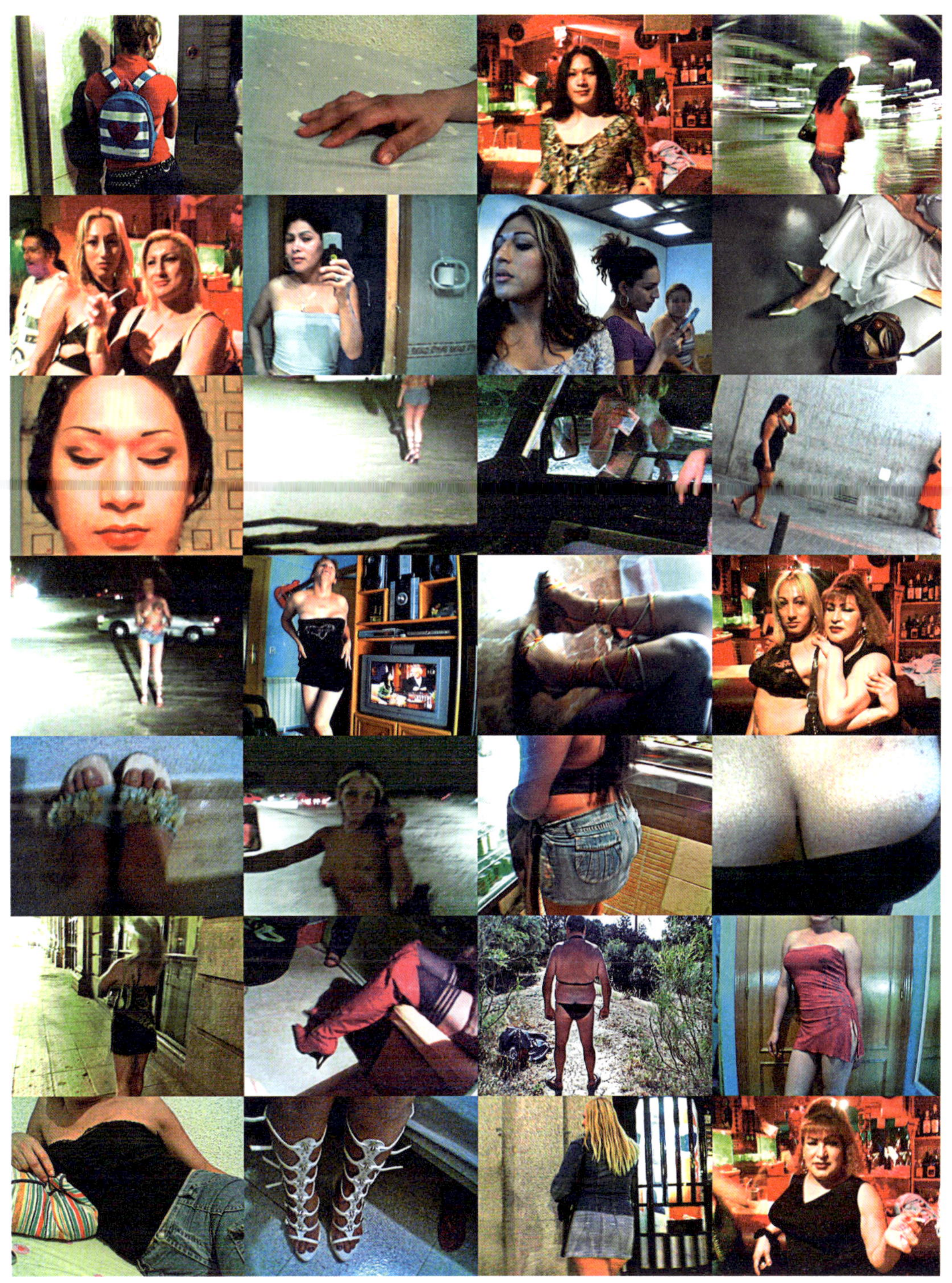

Selection of images published by participants in the project *canal*INVISIBLE*

aberracions adult animals asociació bar bravo!
burocracia carrer comerç
companys comprar cronica descansar
desplaçar-se desviaments dia a dia
DOCUMENTAL domèstic edifici
escales esport estar sol familia feina
femenino fotos gairebé... gestions graons
IDEAL incívics infantil inviables jove
lavabos llar masculí menjar menjar
mobiliari mobiliari urbà MÓN motos movilidad
obj.casa oci parc paviments perill
restaurant reunió salut servei tecnologia temporals
transports treballar vehicle vell viatjar zoo

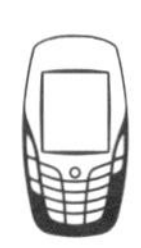

BARCELONA*accessible
People with limited mobility
Barcelona, Spain
2006/13

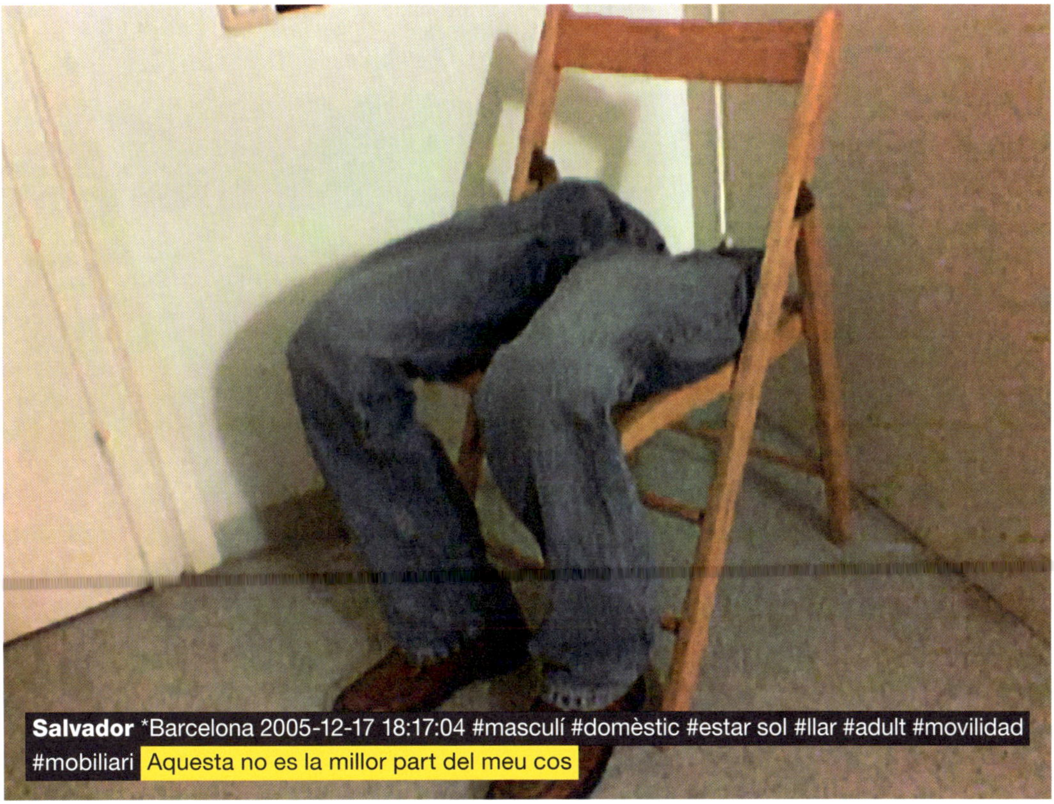

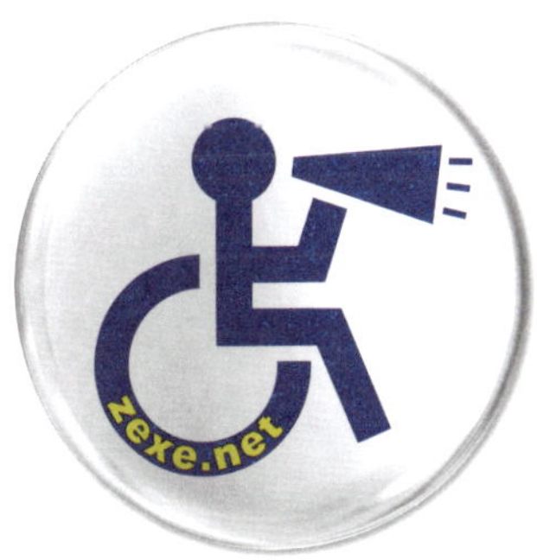

Badge promoting the project canal*ACCESSIBLE

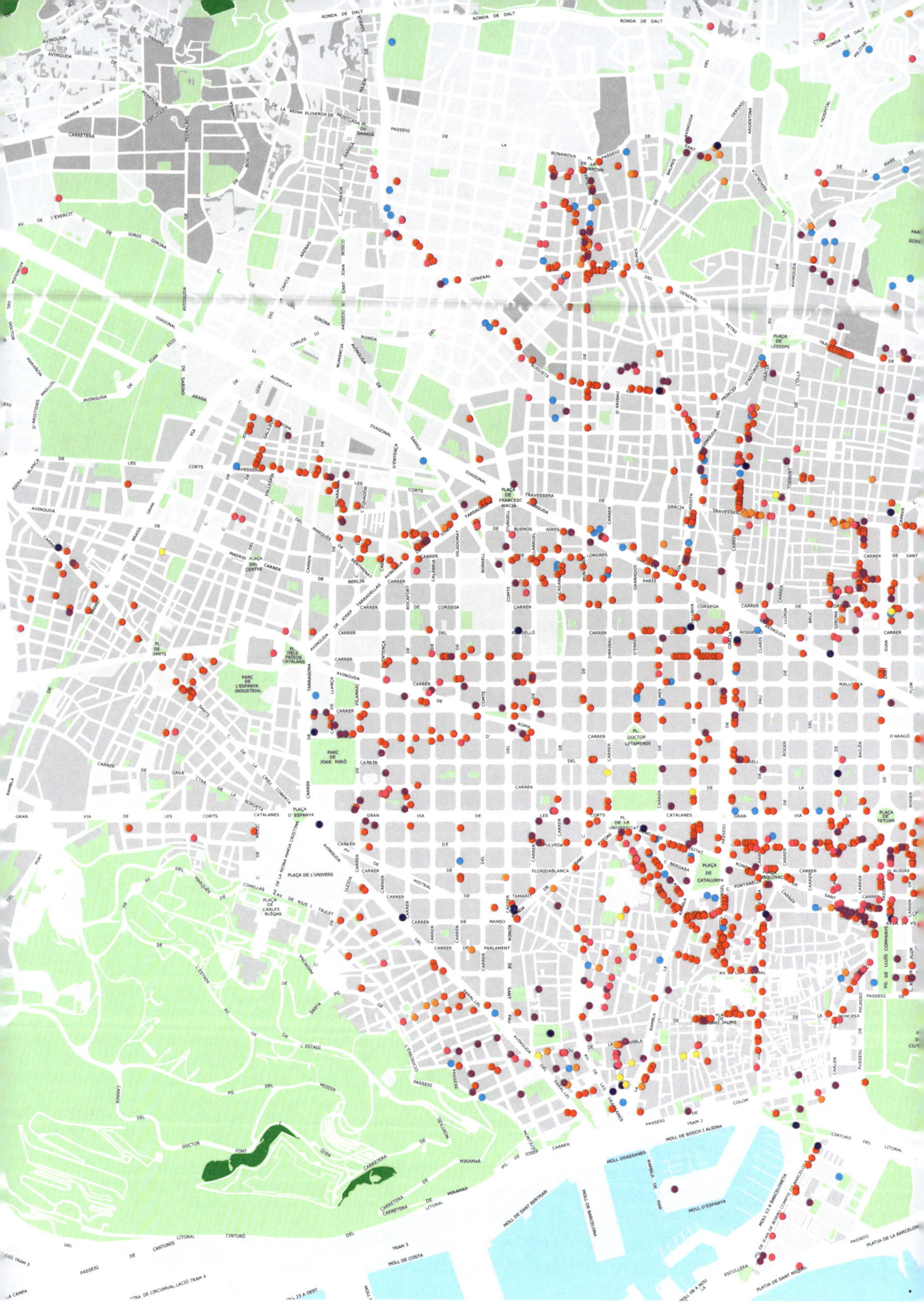

Overall view of the collective mapping of Barcelona

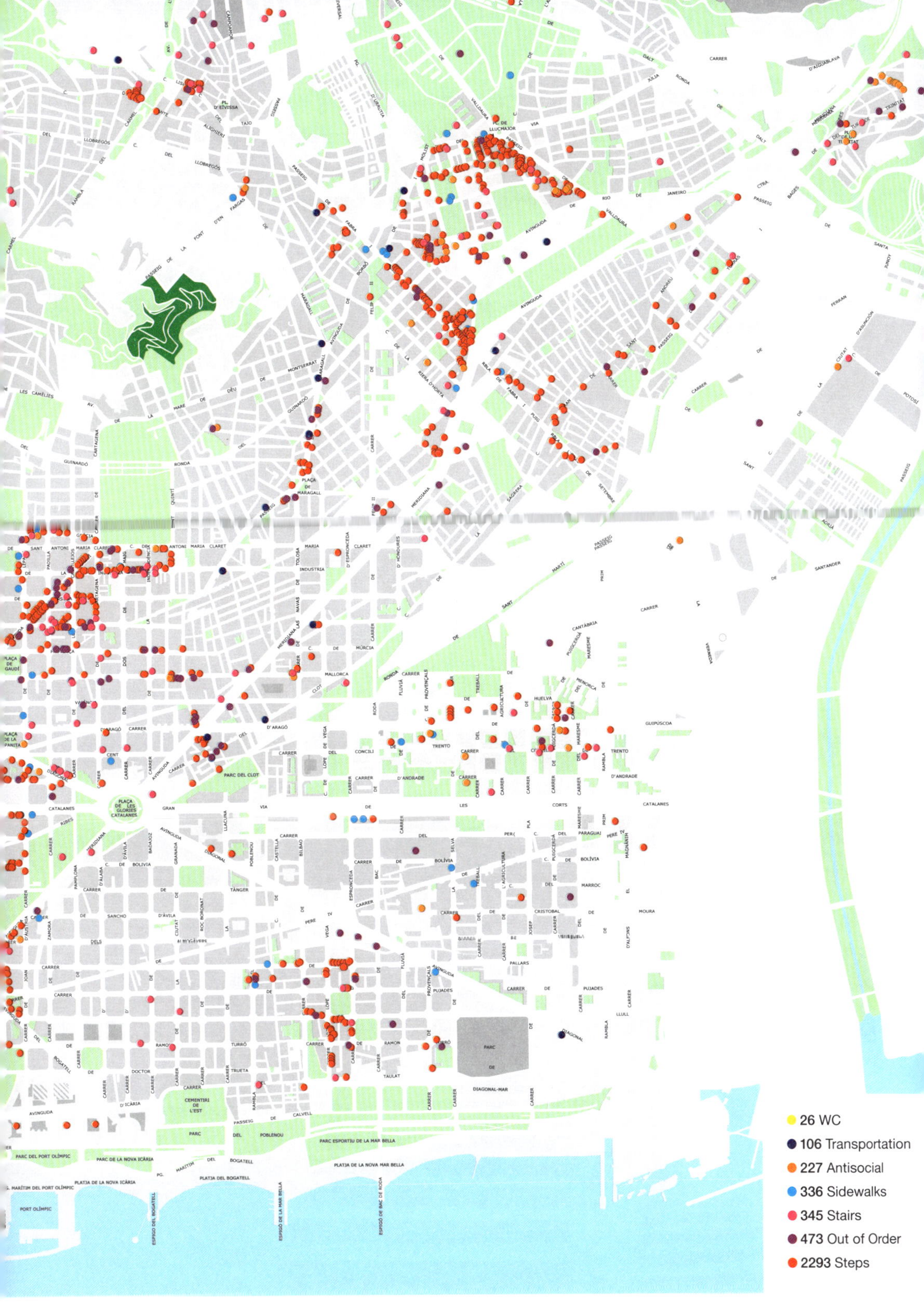

26 WC
106 Transportation
227 Antisocial
336 Sidewalks
345 Stairs
473 Out of Order
2293 Steps

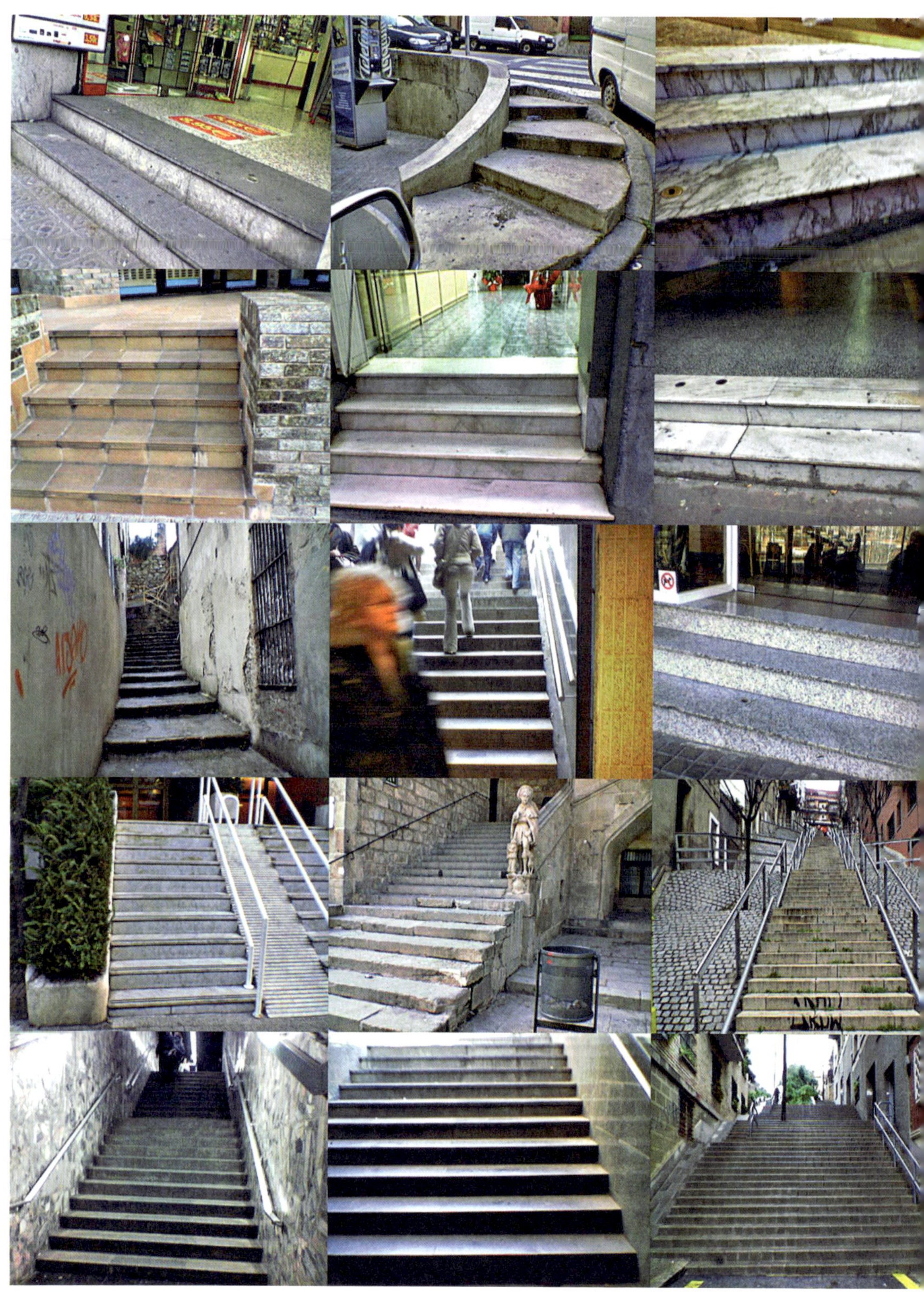

Selection of images of steps published by participants in the project *BARCELONA*accessible*

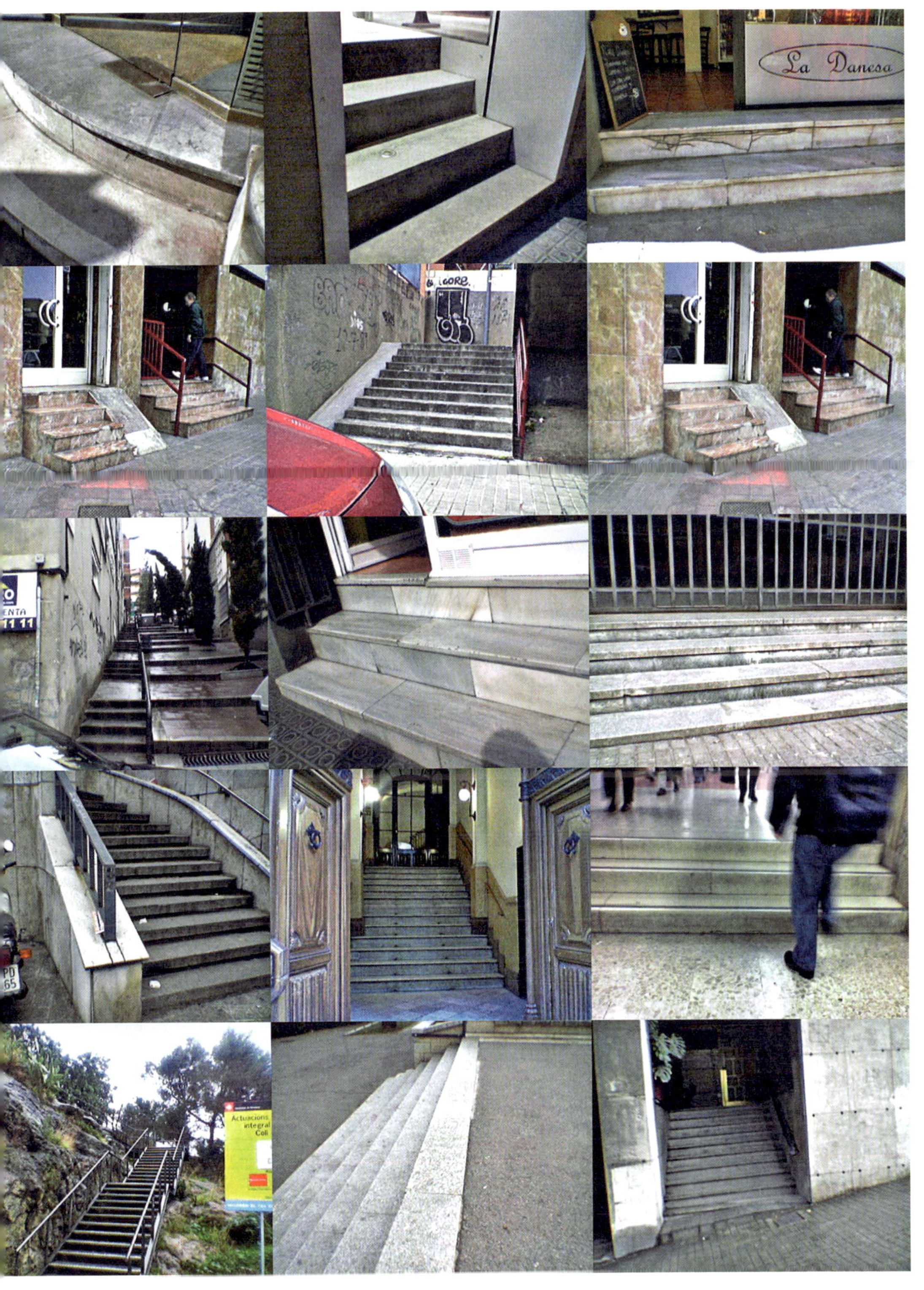

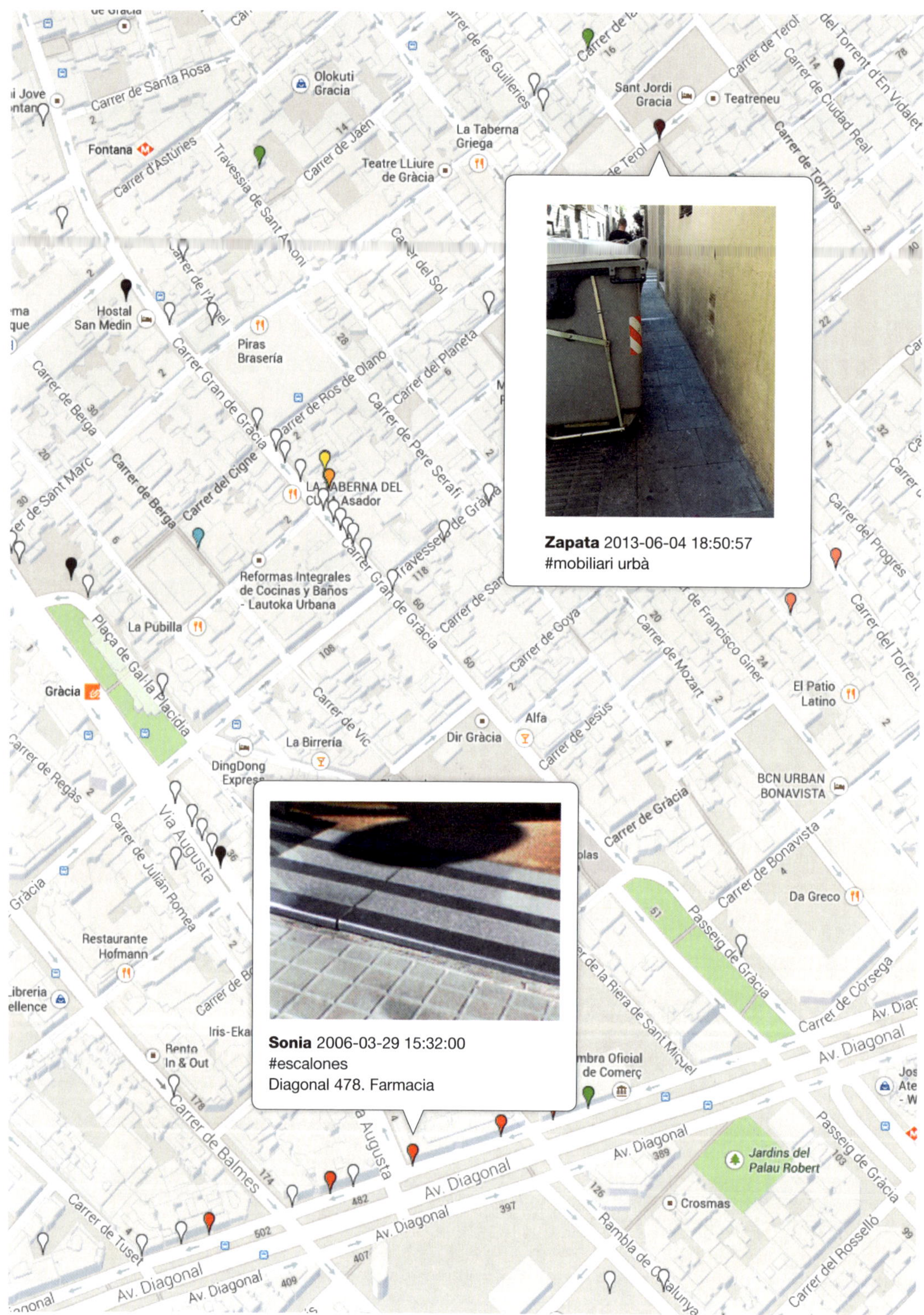

Details of a collective mapping of Barcelona

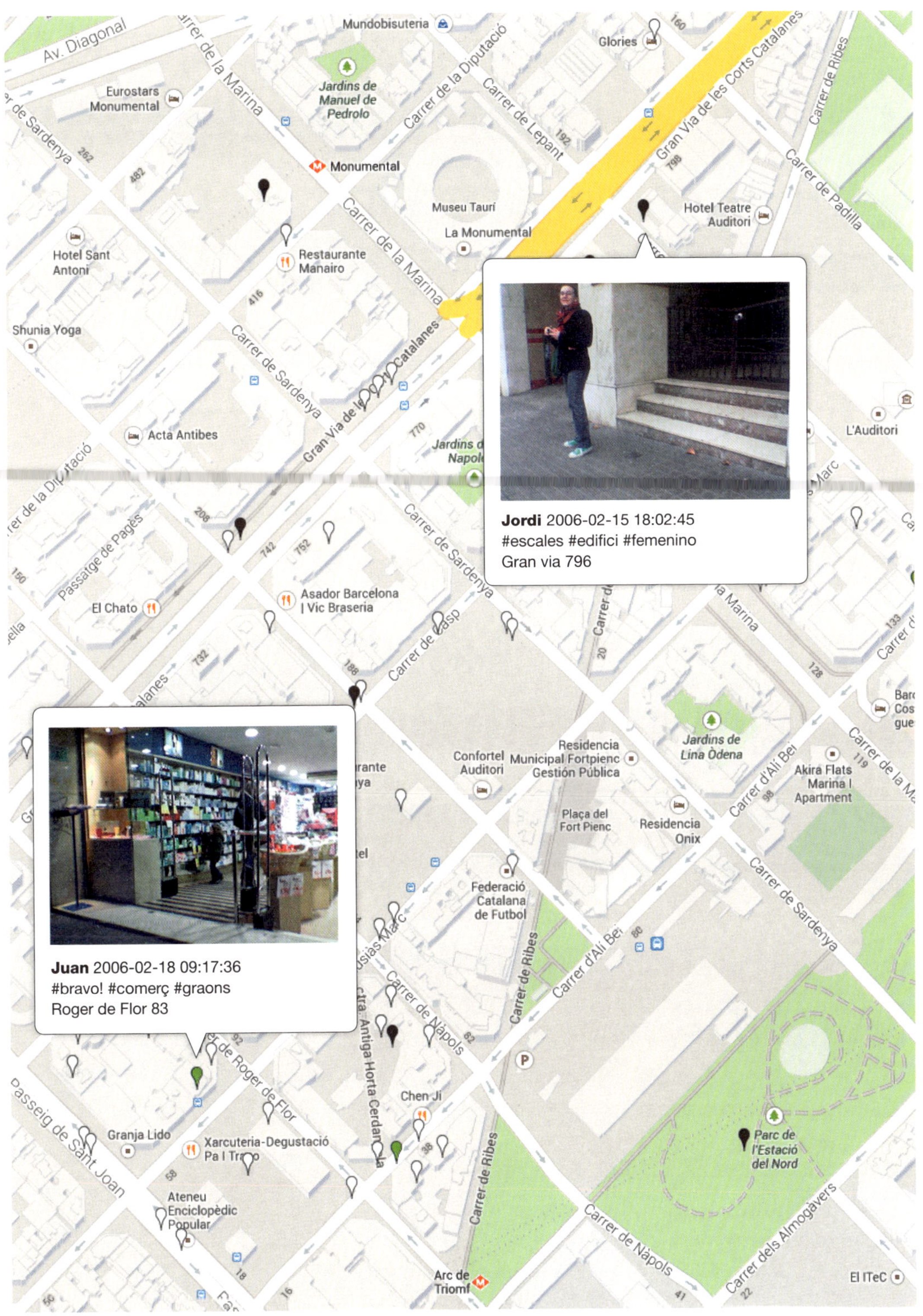

Jordi 2006-02-15 18:02:45
#escales #edifici #femenino
Gran via 796

Juan 2006-02-18 09:17:36
#bravo! #comerç #graons
Roger de Flor 83

adulto anciano animales asociación BACANAL bar burocracia calle casa comer comercio comida compañeros comprar COMUNAL deporte descansar desplazarse doméstico edificio estar solo estudiar familia femenino fotos gestiones hogar joven MARIMBA masculino mobiliario movilidad música niños ocio paisaje PAPELES parque PEGUE restaurante reunión salud servicio tecnología TICONICA trabajar trabajo transportes vehículo viajar VIVIENDA

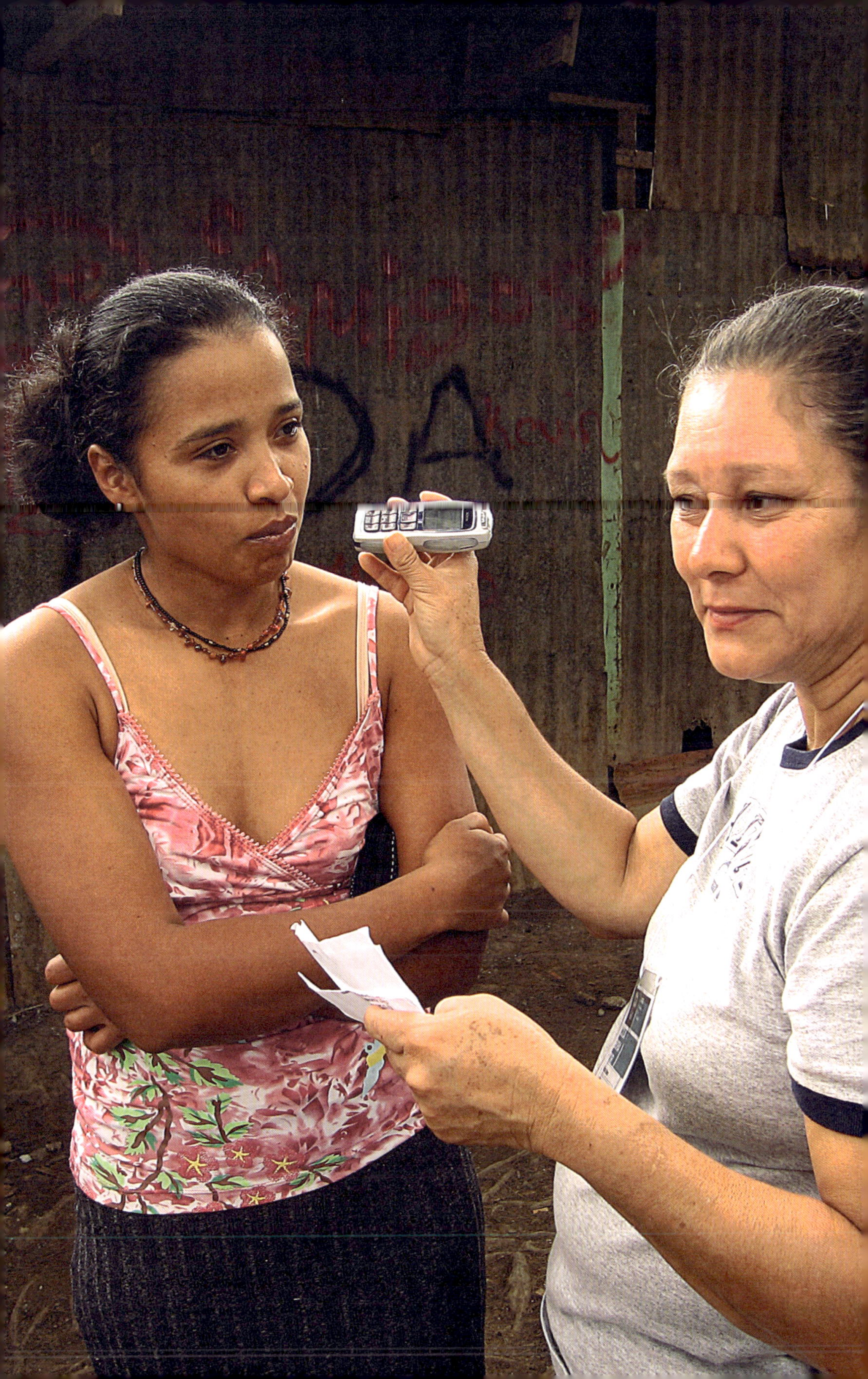

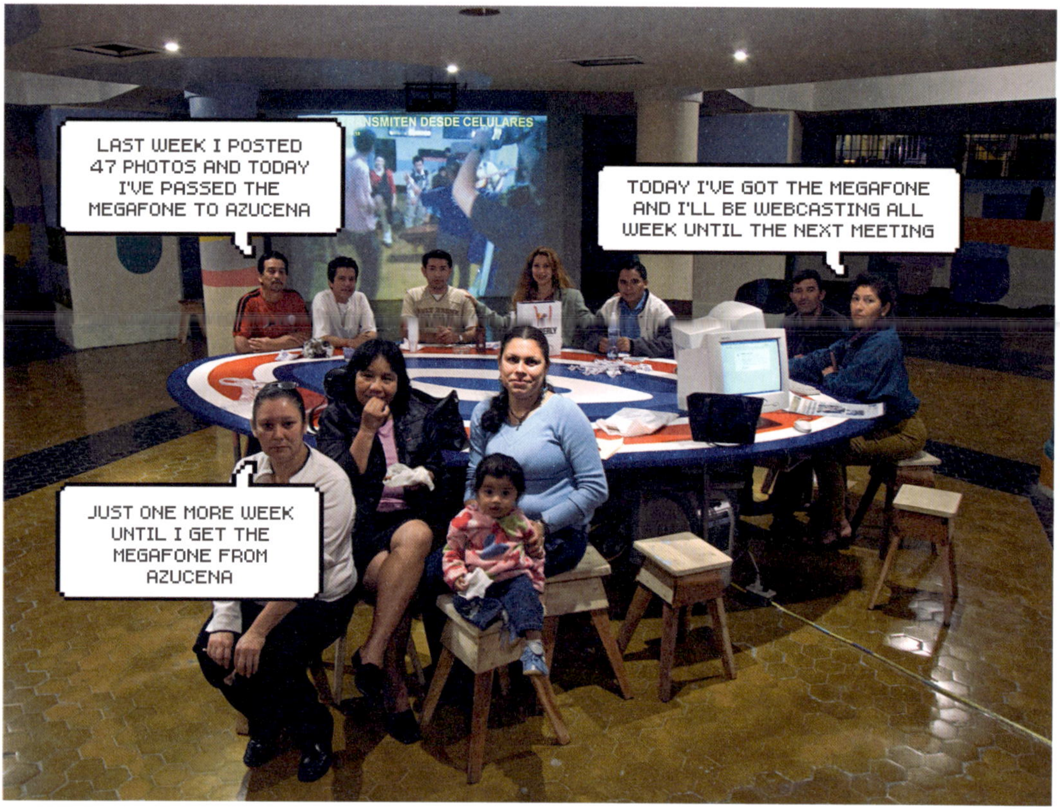

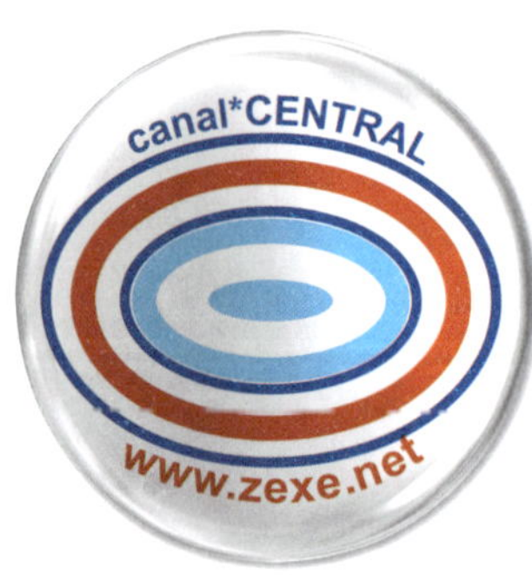

How cell phones are rotated periodically among participants in the project canal*CENTRAL

Badge made to promote the project canal*CENTRAL

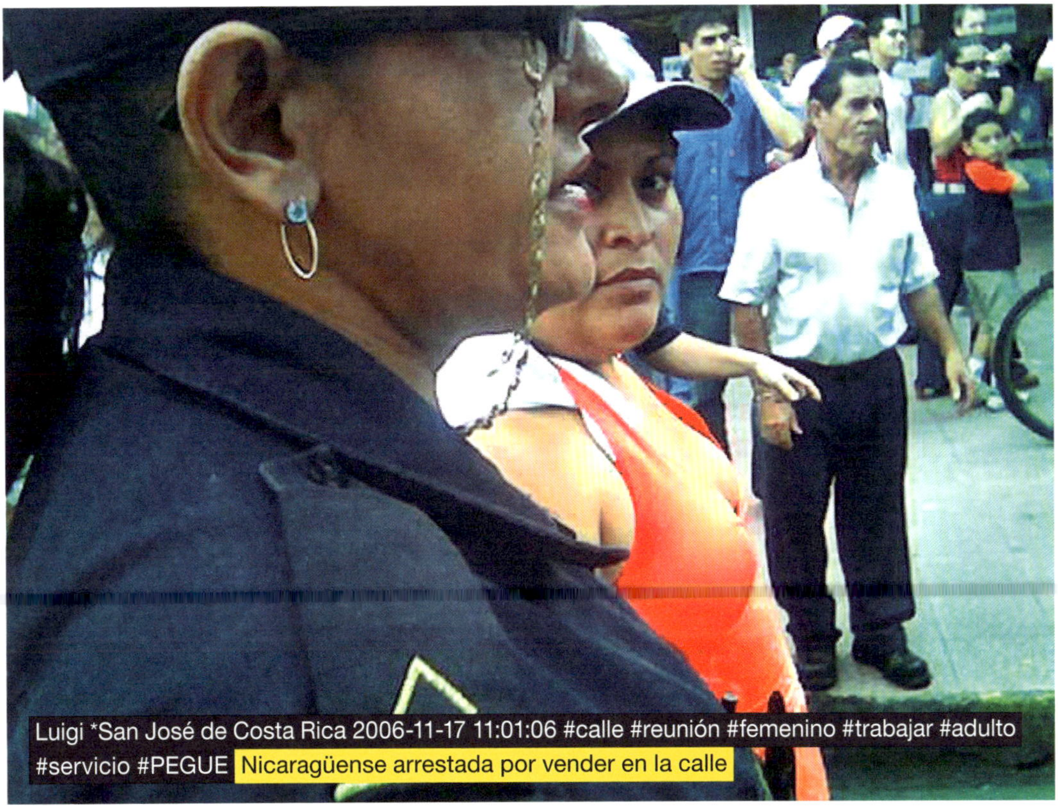

Luigi *San José de Costa Rica 2006-11-17 11:01:06 #calle #reunión #femenino #trabajar #adulto #servicio #PEGUE Nicaragüense arrestada por vender en la calle

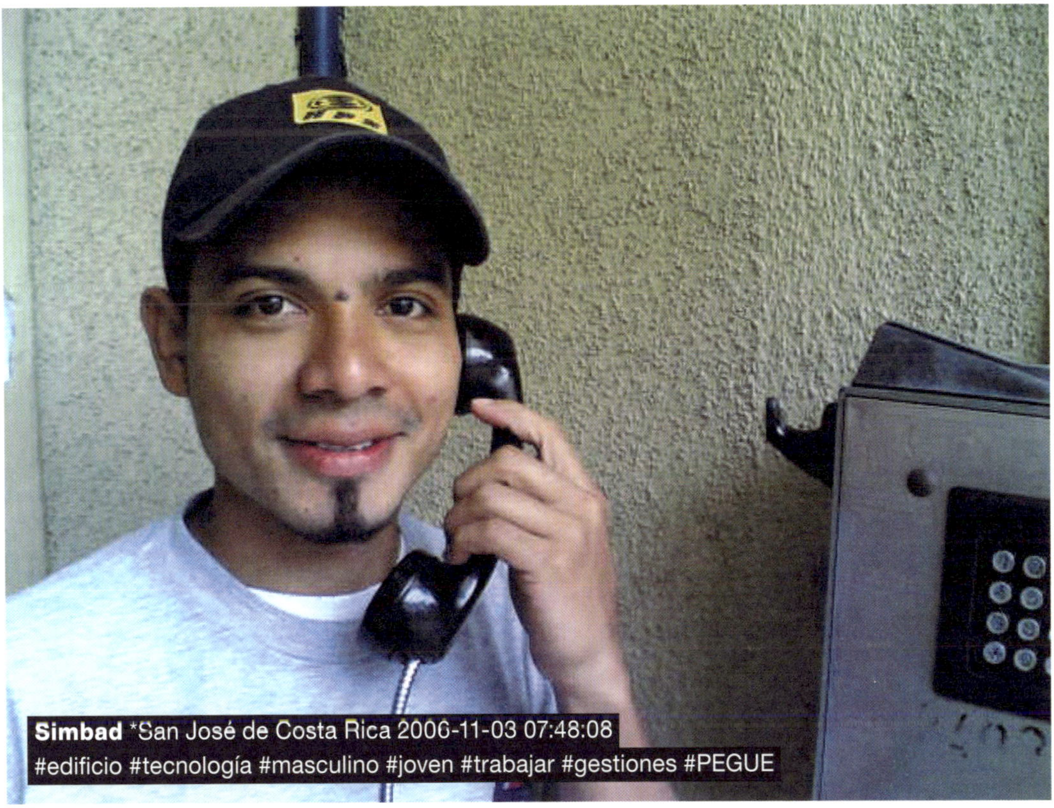

Simbad *San José de Costa Rica 2006-11-03 07:48:08 #edificio #tecnología #masculino #joven #trabajar #gestiones #PEGUE

Y en el río San Juan nos damos las manos

Calderón *San José de Costa Rica 2006-11-11 11:29:12
#TICONICA

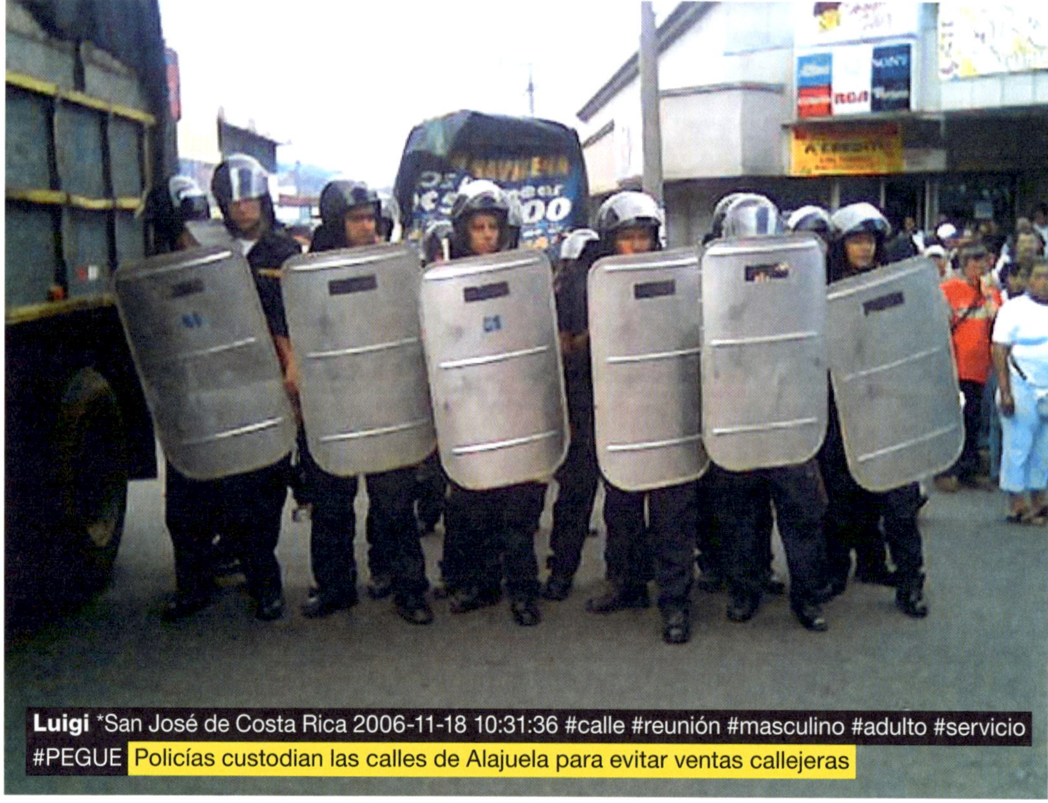

Luigi *San José de Costa Rica 2006-11-18 10:31:36 #calle #reunión #masculino #adulto #servicio
#PEGUE Policías custodian las calles de Alajuela para evitar ventas callejeras

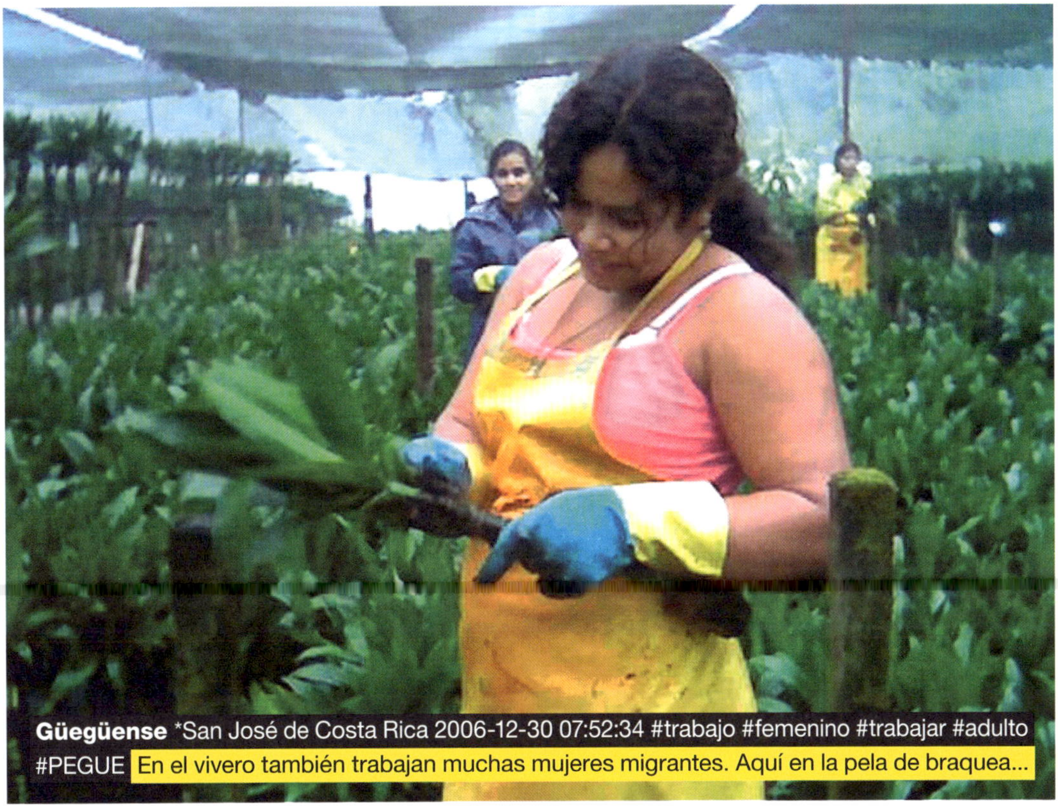

Güegüense *San José de Costa Rica 2006-12-30 07:52:34 #trabajo #femenino #trabajar #adulto
#PEGUE En el vivero también trabajan muchas mujeres migrantes. Aquí en la pela de braquea...

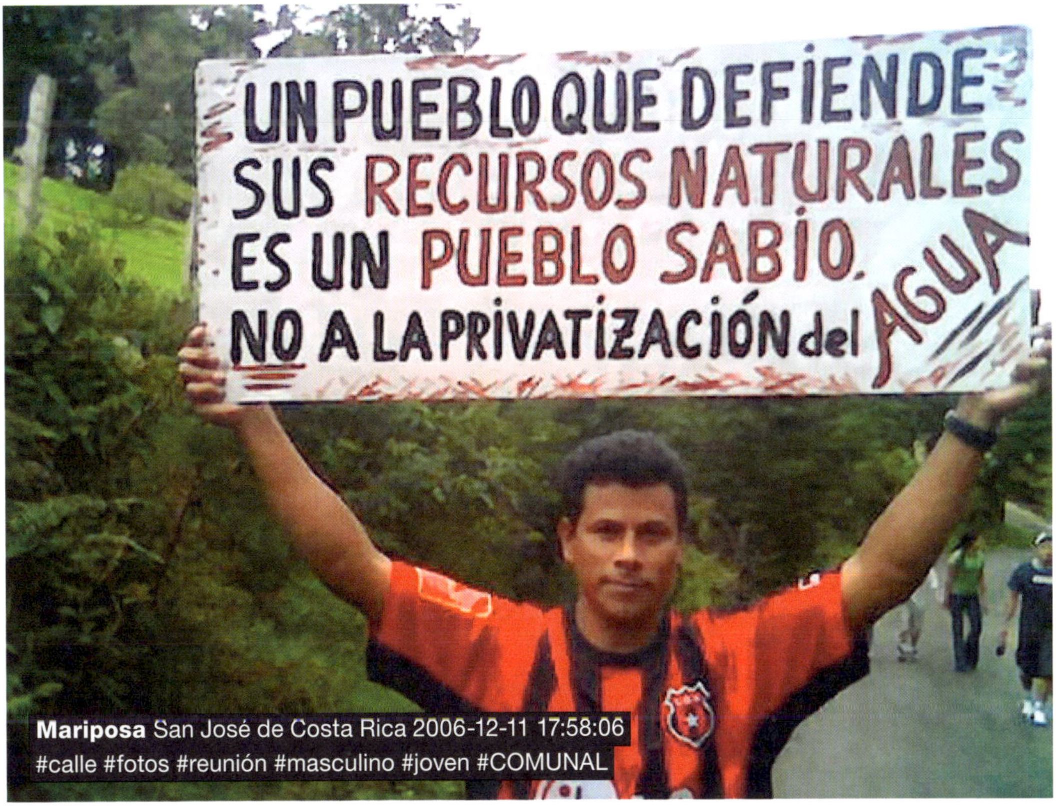

UN PUEBLO QUE DEFIENDE
SUS RECURSOS NATURALES
ES UN PUEBLO SABIO.
NO A LA PRIVATIZACIÓN del AGUA
Mariposa San José de Costa Rica 2006-12-11 17:58:06
#calle #fotos #reunión #masculino #joven #COMUNAL

acidentes adesivo ae aero porto agua ajuda alimentaçao almoço alvará amigas amigos amor animais aniversario antiguidade arte na rua artes associação atenção aviao aviso bairros bancos bar baú beleza bh bicicleta bingos blitz bombeiros buracos cadeirantes camara campus canal*motoboy capacete carnaval carros cartas casas catalogo coop celulares centro cultural chuvas cidade cidade limpa cinema comando comunidade conflito confraternização corredores cracolandia crianças cruzamento culinaria cultura custos debate descanso desperdicio desrespeito dia a dia dia a dia discriminação diversão duas rodas educação elevadores empresas entrevista escola esportes estacionamentos estradas eu eventos exposição faixa faixa preferencial fala familha familia favela fé feira feriado férias ferramentas festas festival fim de tarde floress fotos galera gasolina greve igrejas imprudência incendio injustiça inprudencia irmaos isa jornal lazer leis liberdade livro lixo lojas luta luxo machucado madalena manifestação manutenção maquinas marginal minha vida mobilifest monumento moradia moradores da rua motoboys motofaixa motogirl motoqueiros motos motovia music natal natureza noite noite sp noticia oficinas óleo onibus paisagem paixao panoramica papa paris passeio pedestres periferia perigo pixação placas pneu polícia poluição prejuizo prêmio proibido prova radares raridade refeição religião reportagem resgate reunião reunião rio de janeiro rio tiete ronaldo rotina samba são paulo saude seguranças seminário serviços sinalização sindicato sindimoto sonhos sujeira teatro tendal teste torcida trabalho trampo transito transporte tv usp vagas vergonha viagens vida

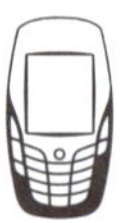

canal*MOTOBOY
Motorcycle messengers
São Paulo, Brazil
2007–14

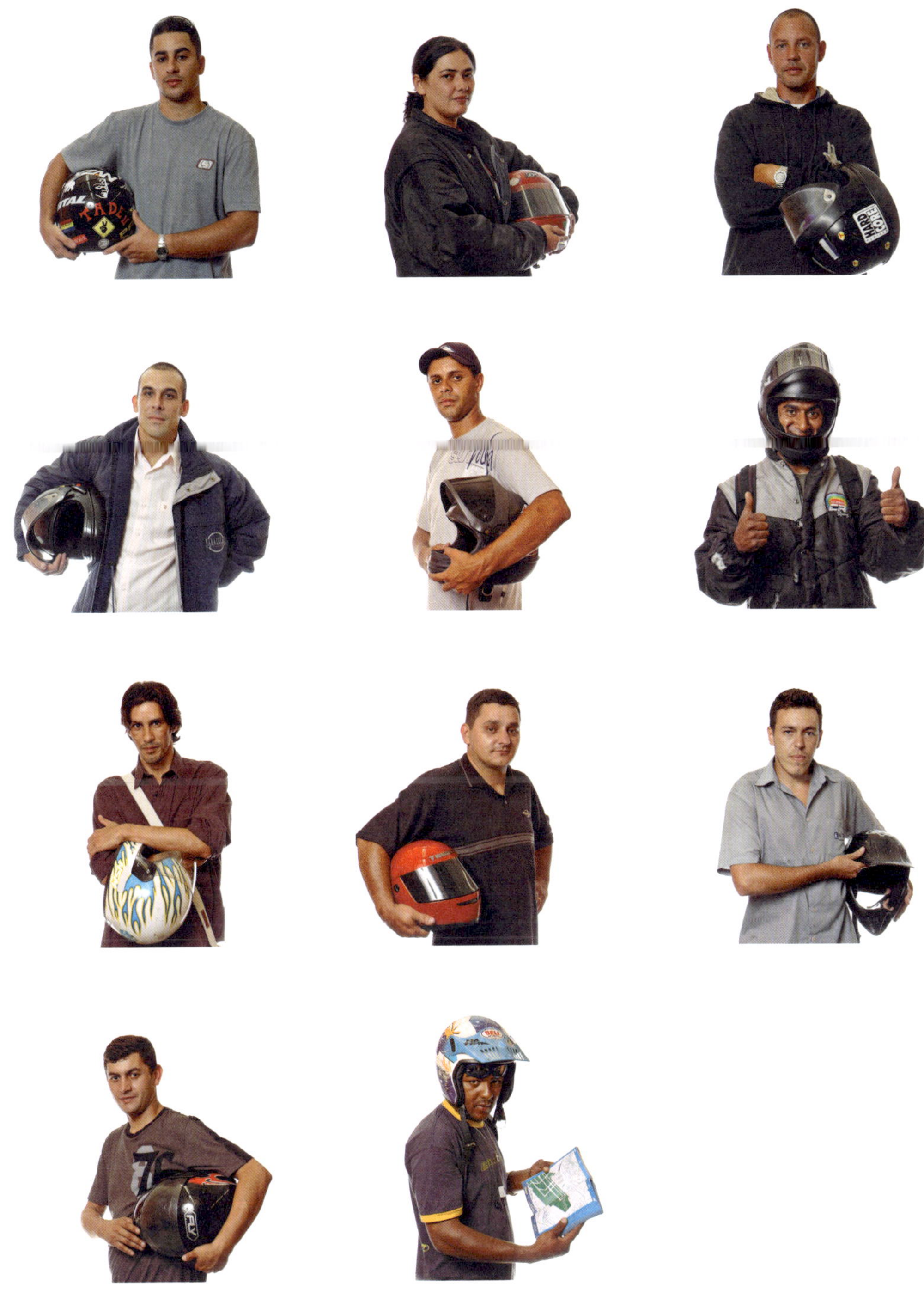

Participants in *canal*MOTOBOY*

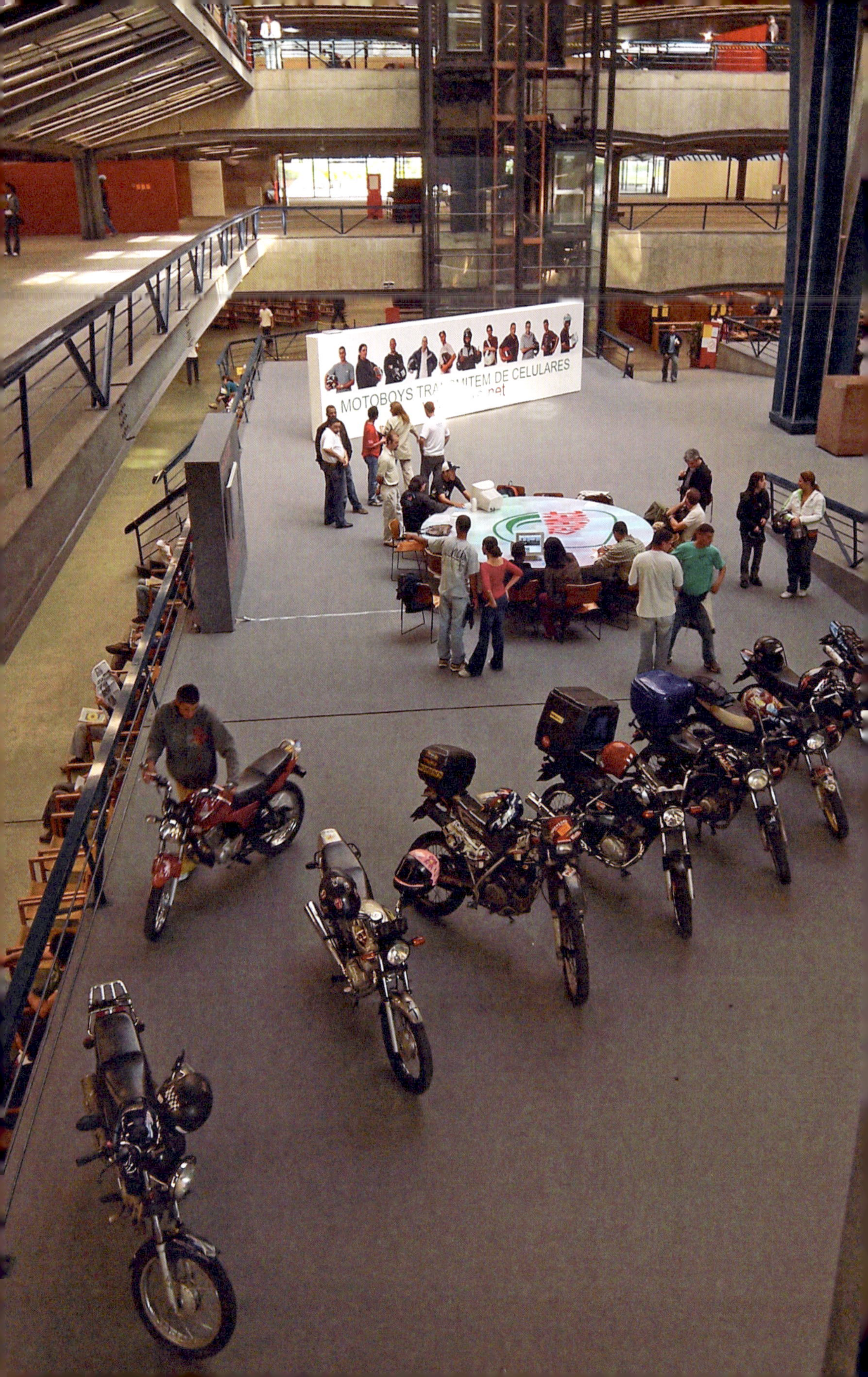

MOTOBOYS TRANSMITEM DE CELULARES
.net

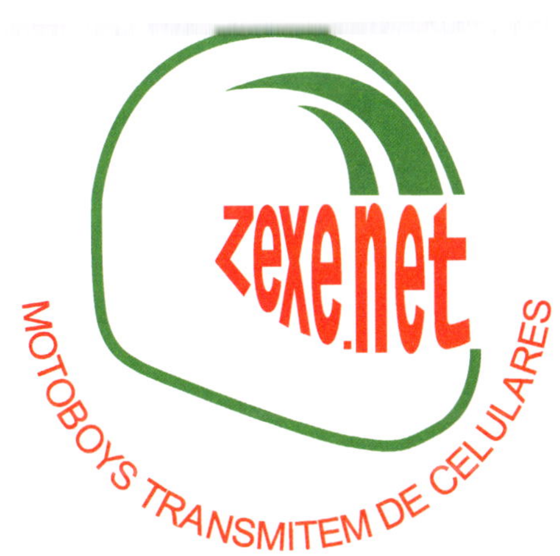

Presentation and logo of *canal*MOTOBOY* at the Cultural Center in São Paulo (2007)

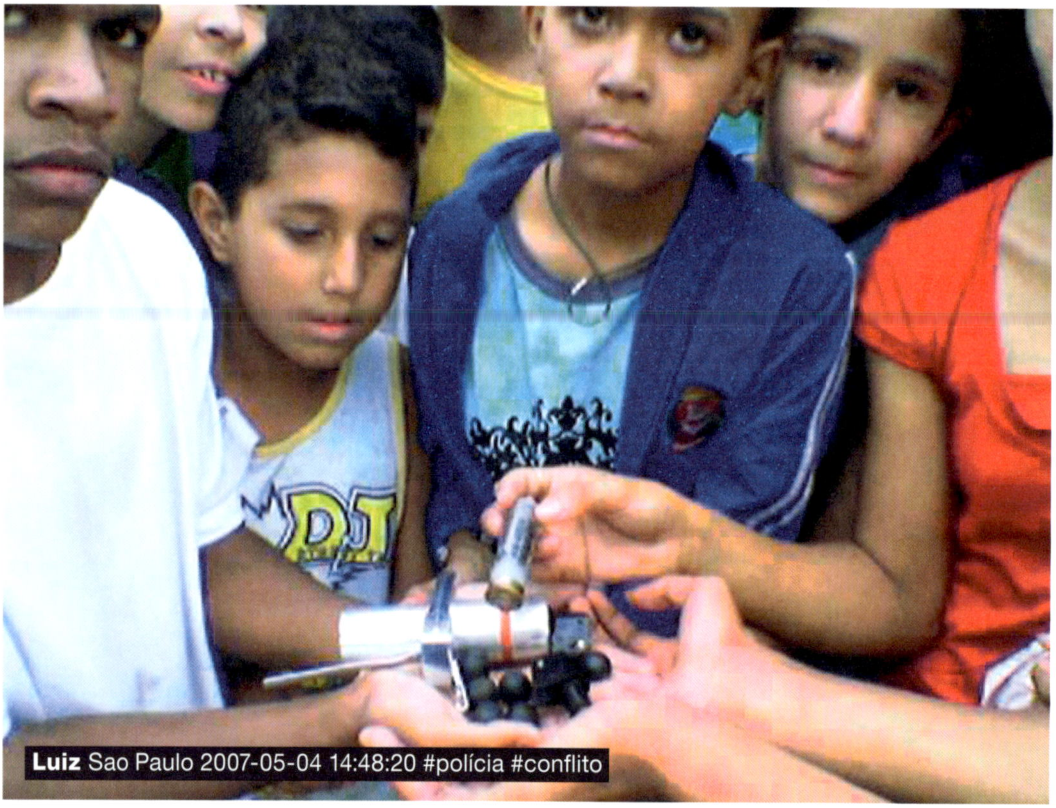

Luiz Sao Paulo 2007-05-04 14:48:20 #polícia #conflito

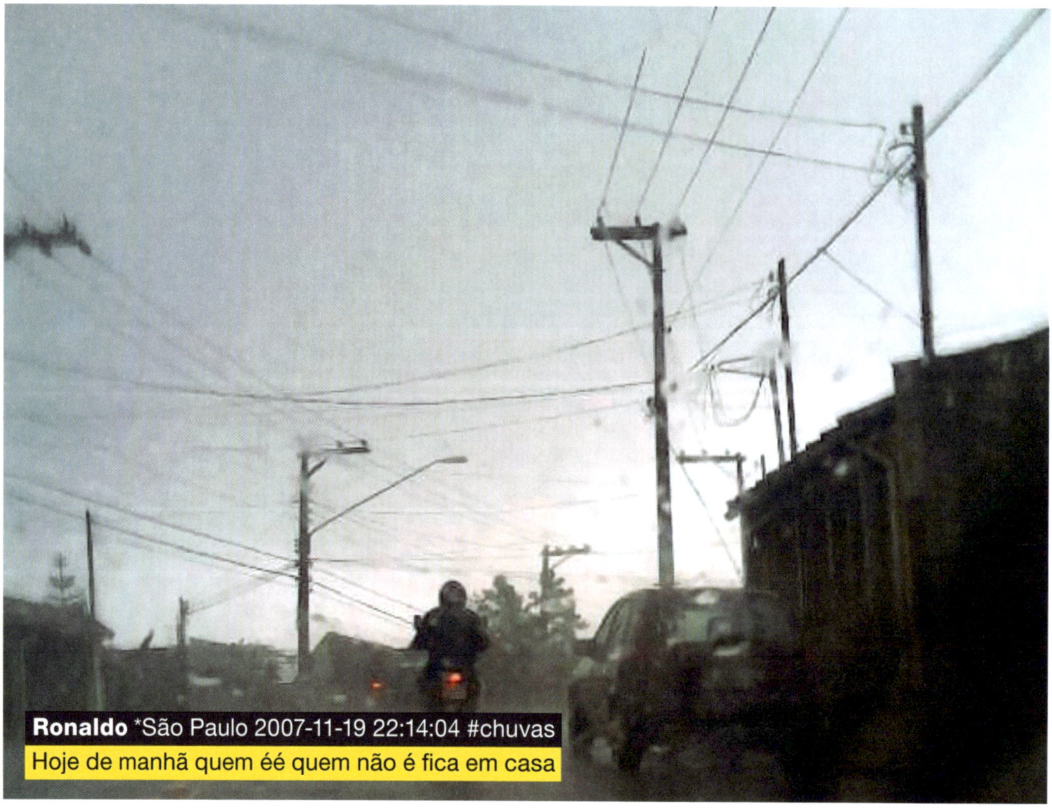

Ronaldo *São Paulo 2007-11-19 22:14:04 #chuvas
Hoje de manhã quem éé quem não é fica em casa

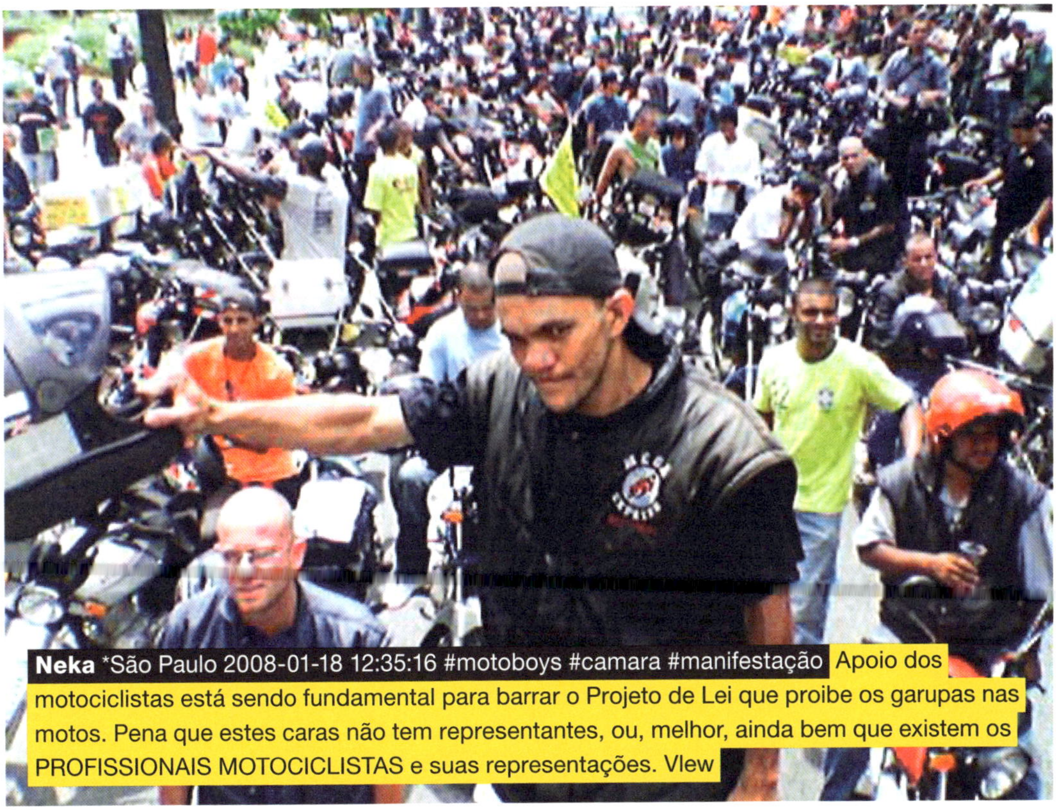

Neka *São Paulo 2008-01-18 12:35:16 #motoboys #camara #manifestação Apoio dos motociclistas está sendo fundamental para barrar o Projeto de Lei que proibe os garupas nas motos. Pena que estes caras não tem representantes, ou, melhor, ainda bem que existem os PROFISSIONAIS MOTOCICLISTAS e suas representações. Vlew

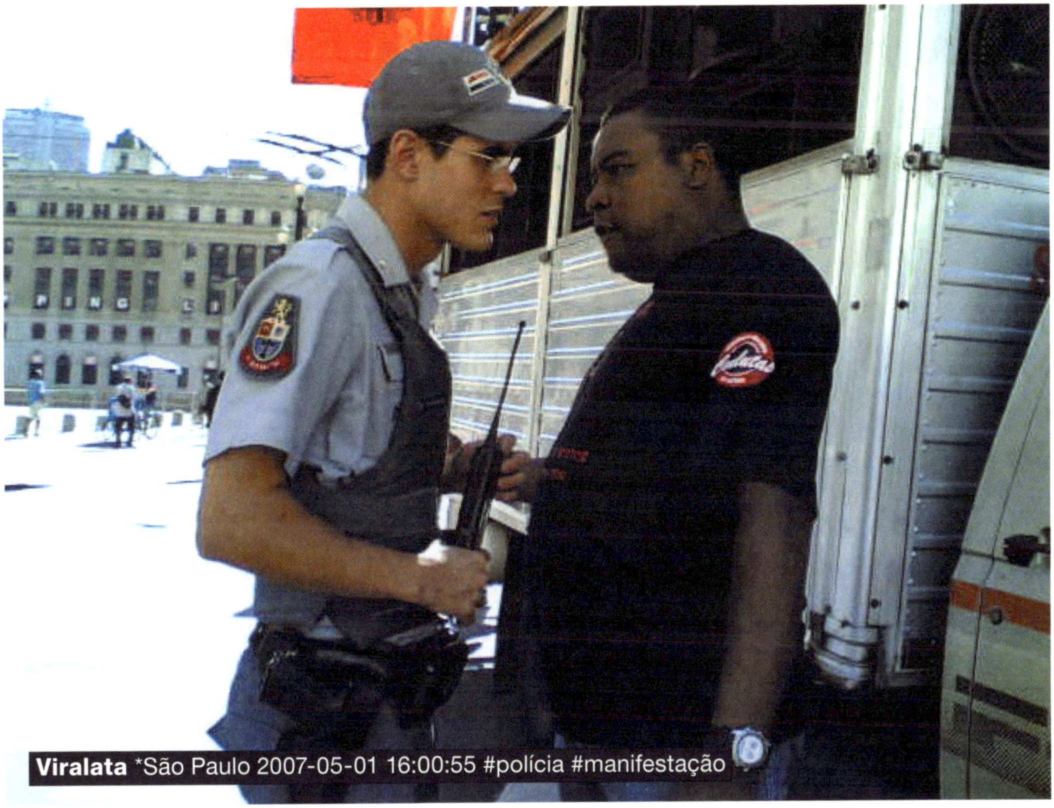

Viralata *São Paulo 2007-05-01 16:00:55 #polícia #manifestação

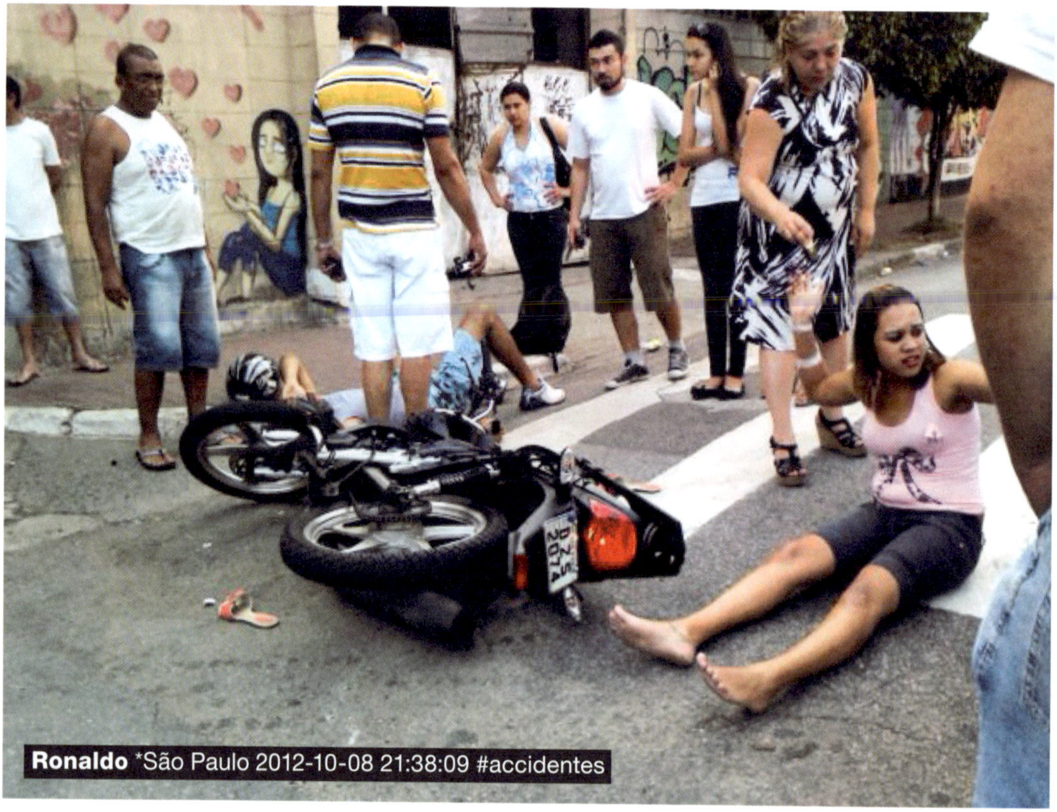

Ronaldo *São Paulo 2012-10-08 21:38:09 #accidentes

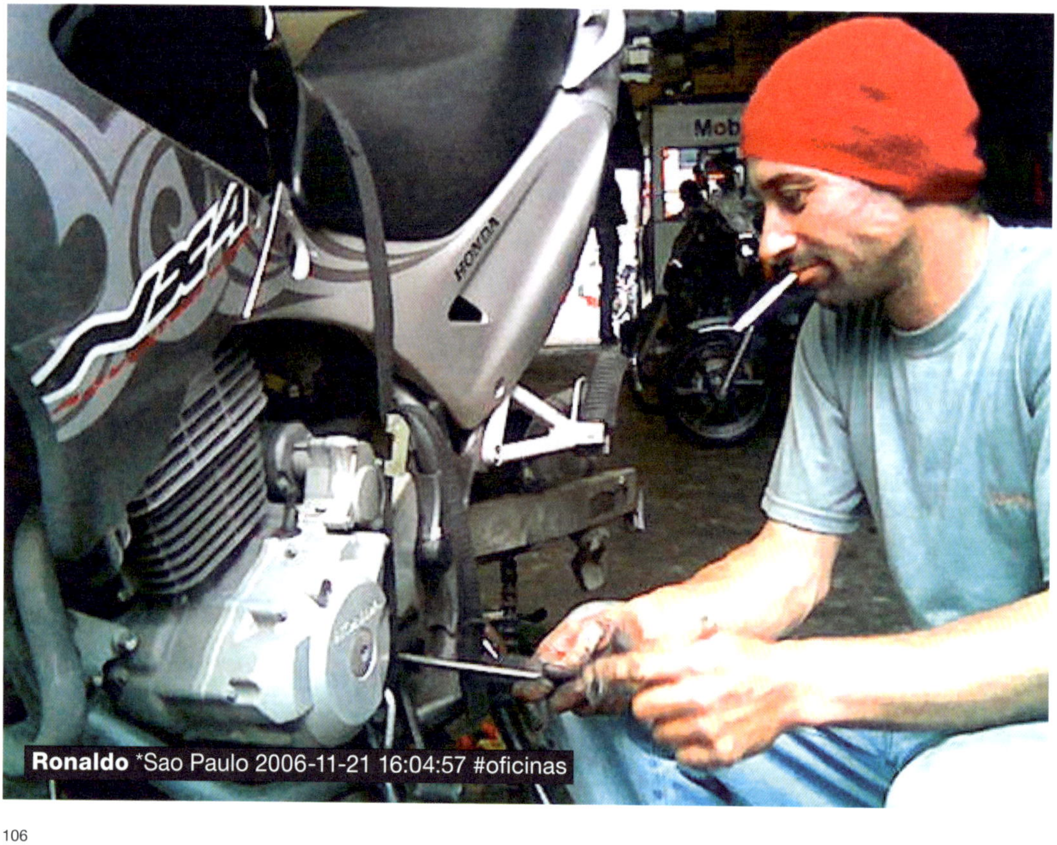

Ronaldo *Sao Paulo 2006-11-21 16:04:57 #oficinas

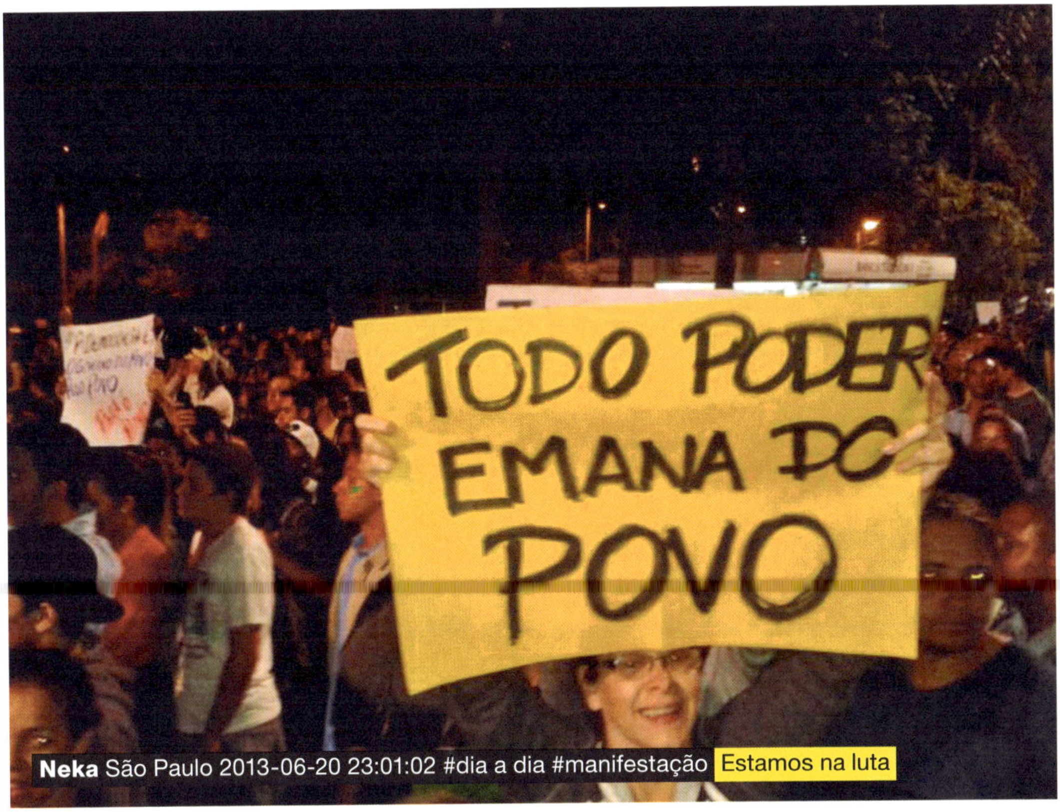

Neka São Paulo 2013-06-20 23:01:02 #dia a dia #manifestação Estamos na luta

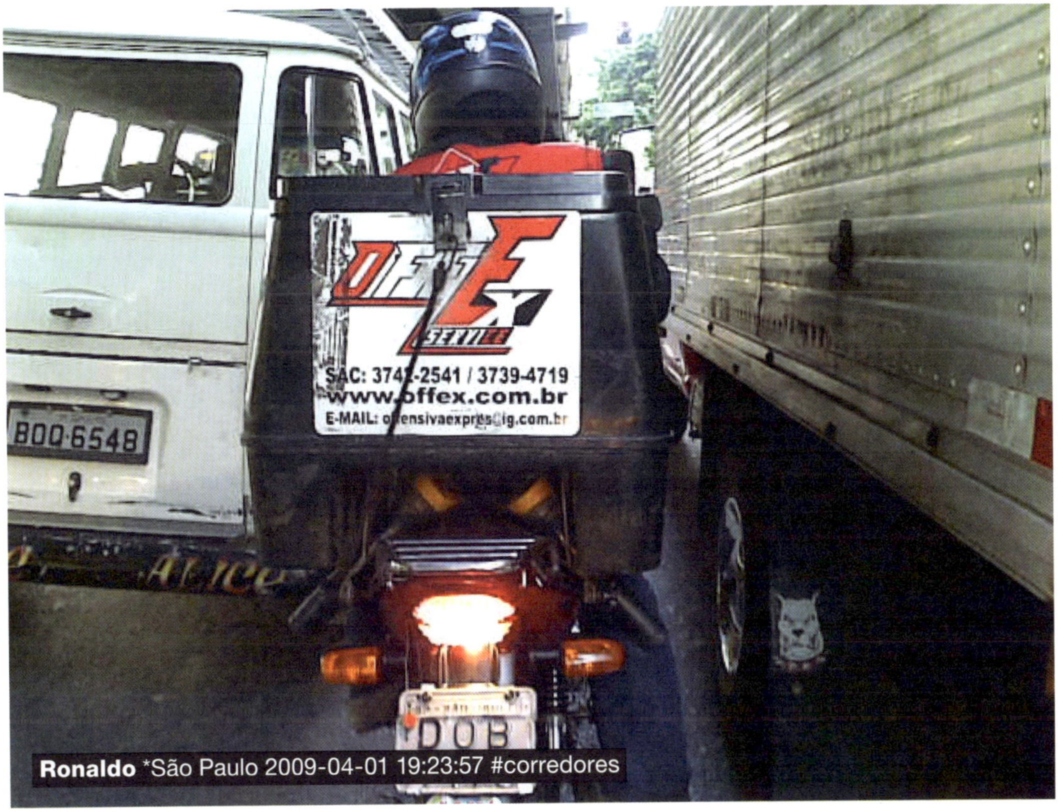

Ronaldo *São Paulo 2009-04-01 19:23:57 #corredores

acces administrations anti-vélos appartements arts ascenseurs

banques bar barrières bibliothèques blanchisseries boulangeries bravo!

cabines téléphonique cafés chien cinemas cirques coiffeurs college coordinateur corinne cuisine

dangers déviations ecran églises émetteurs entrées entreprises

escaliers eugenio fermée gravier graviers handicap

hôtels immeubles impossibilités incivilités interdit isa

jean-bernard jeux joëlle katya laboratoires logements magasins

maisons marches médecins nicola numa offices orthopedie paolo parcs pharmacies

portable radio radio lac rampes régies

immobilières rencontre restaurants sncf supermarché table terrasses tetraplégique

toilettes tourniquets transports trottoirs

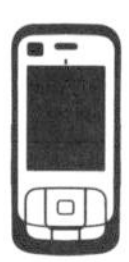

GENÈVE*accessible
People with limited mobility
Geneva, Switzerland
2008

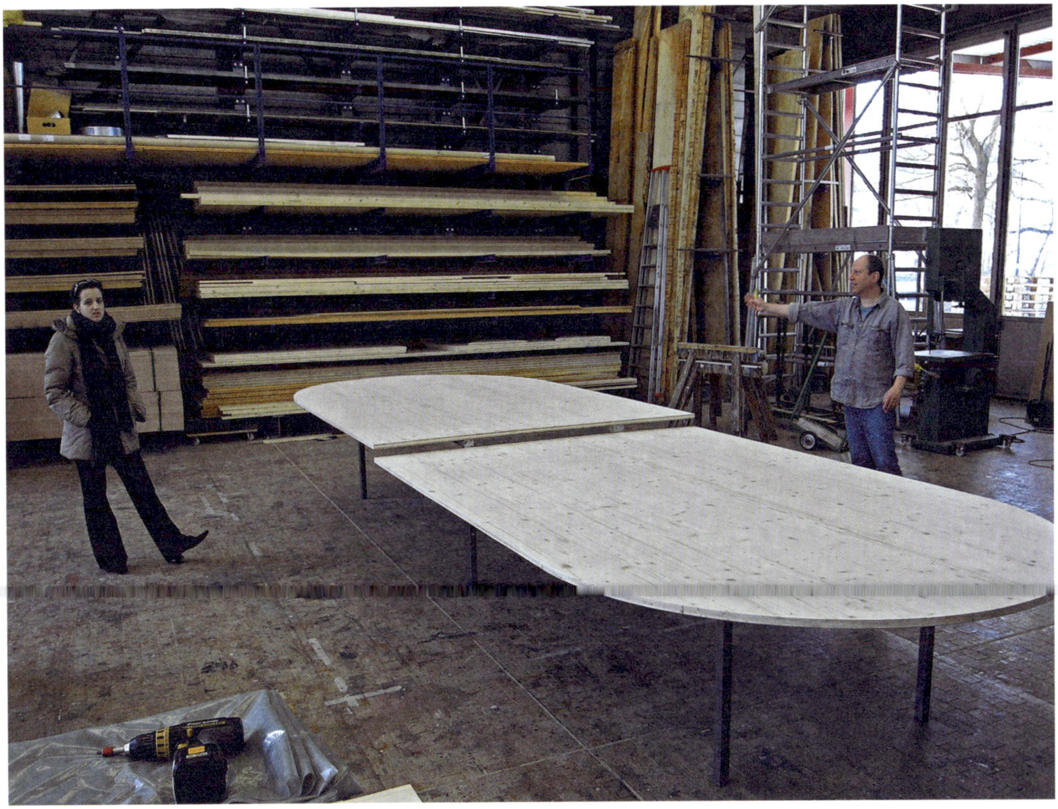

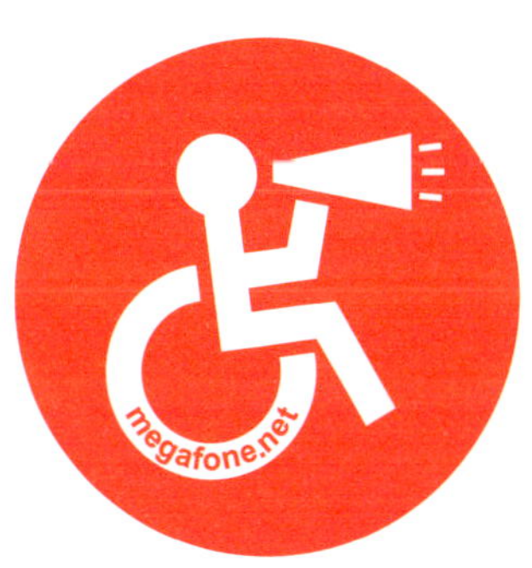

Building the adapted meeting table and logo for the project *GENÈVE*accessible*

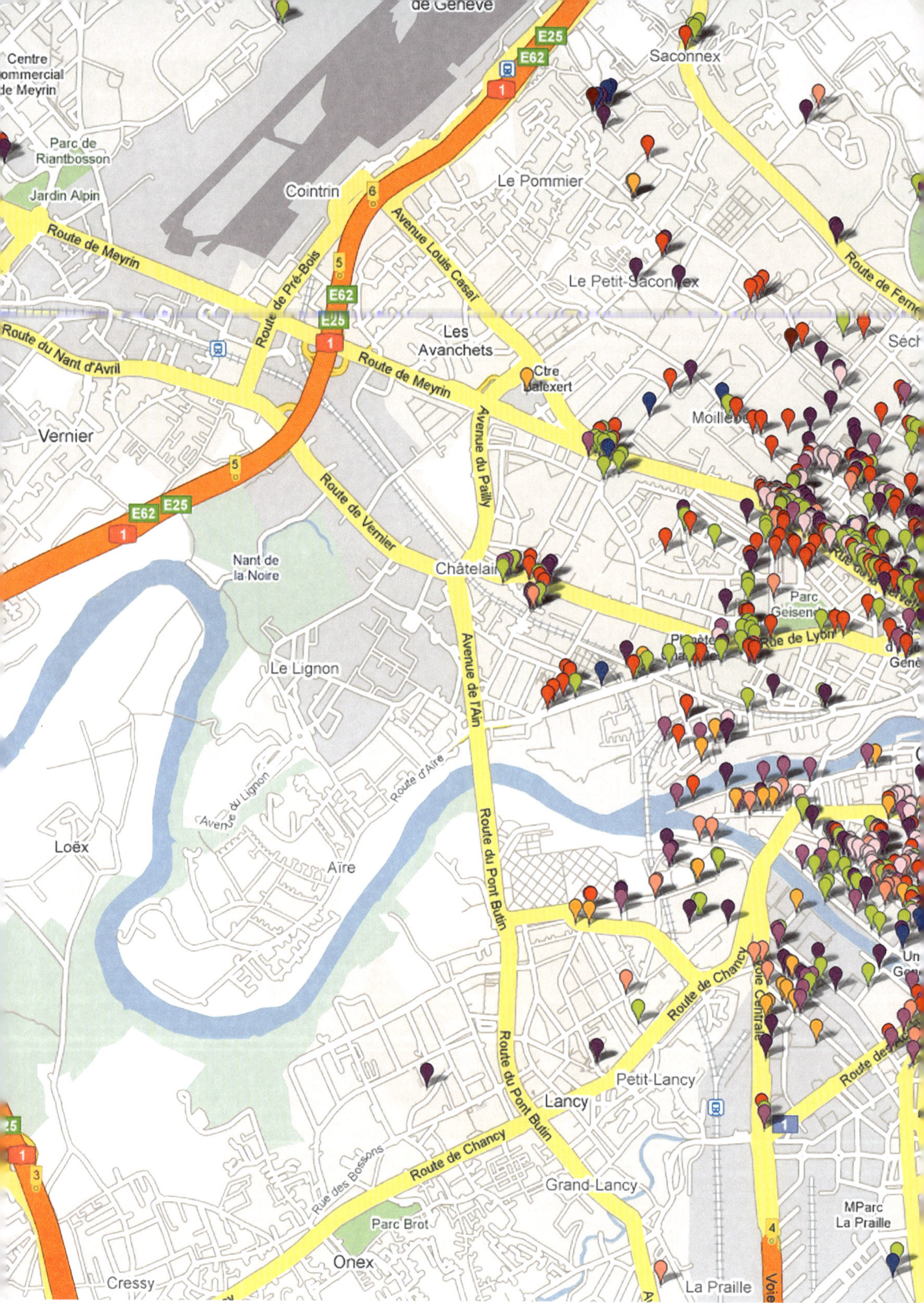

Overall view of the collective mapping of Geneva

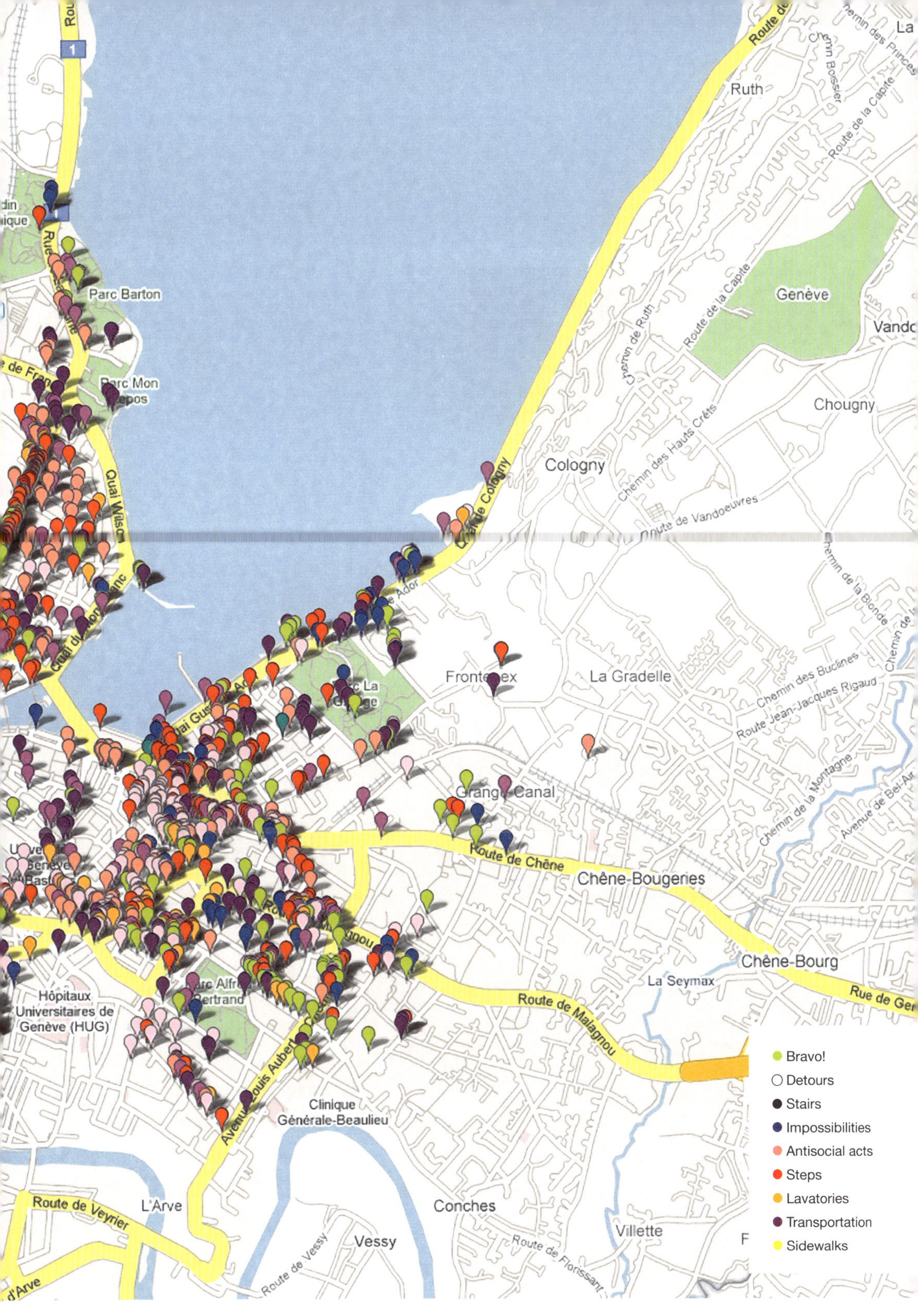

Parc Barton
Parc Mon Repos
Quai Wilson
Quai du Mont-Blanc
Quai Gustave-Ador
Parc La Grange
Frontenex
Cologny
Genève
Chougny
Vando
La Gradelle
Grange-Canal
Route de Chêne
Chêne-Bougeries
Chêne-Bourg
La Seymax
Route de Malagnou
Université de Genève
Uni Bastions
Hôpitaux Universitaires de Genève (HUG)
Parc Alfred Bertrand
Clinique Générale-Beaulieu
Avenue Louis Aubert
Route de Veyrier
L'Arve
Conches
Villette
Vessy
Route de Vessy
Route de Florissant
d'Arve
Ruth
Chemin de Ruth
Route de la Capite
Chemin des Hauts Crêts
Route de Vandoeuvres
Chemin des Bucines
Route Jean-Jacques Rigaud
Chemin de la Montagne
Chemin de la Blonde
Avenue de Bel-Air
Rue de Ger
Chemin des Princes
Chemin Boissier
Chemin de
La

Bravo!
Detours
Stairs
Impossibilities
Antisocial acts
Steps
Lavatories
Transportation
Sidewalks

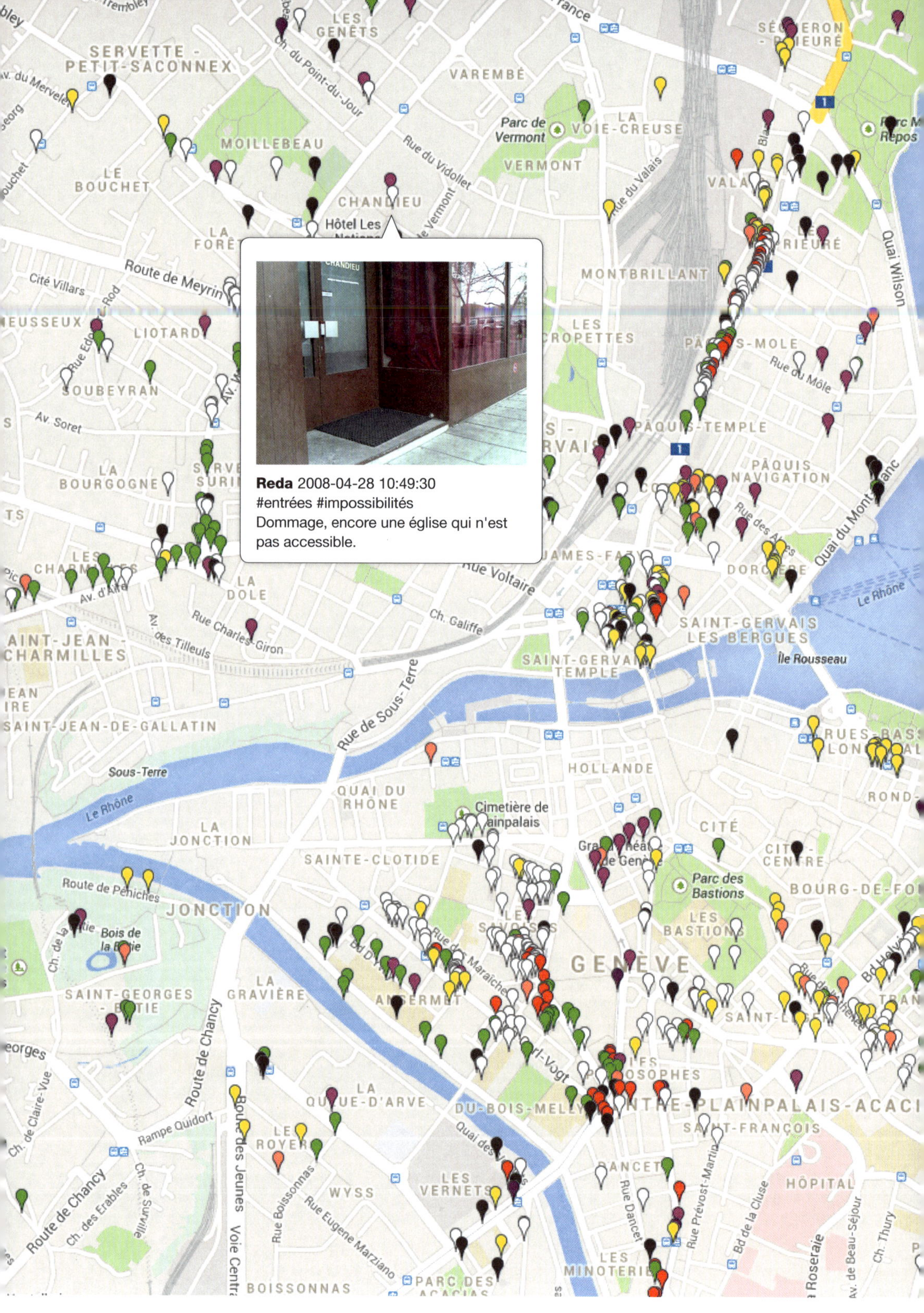

Details of the collective mapping of Geneva

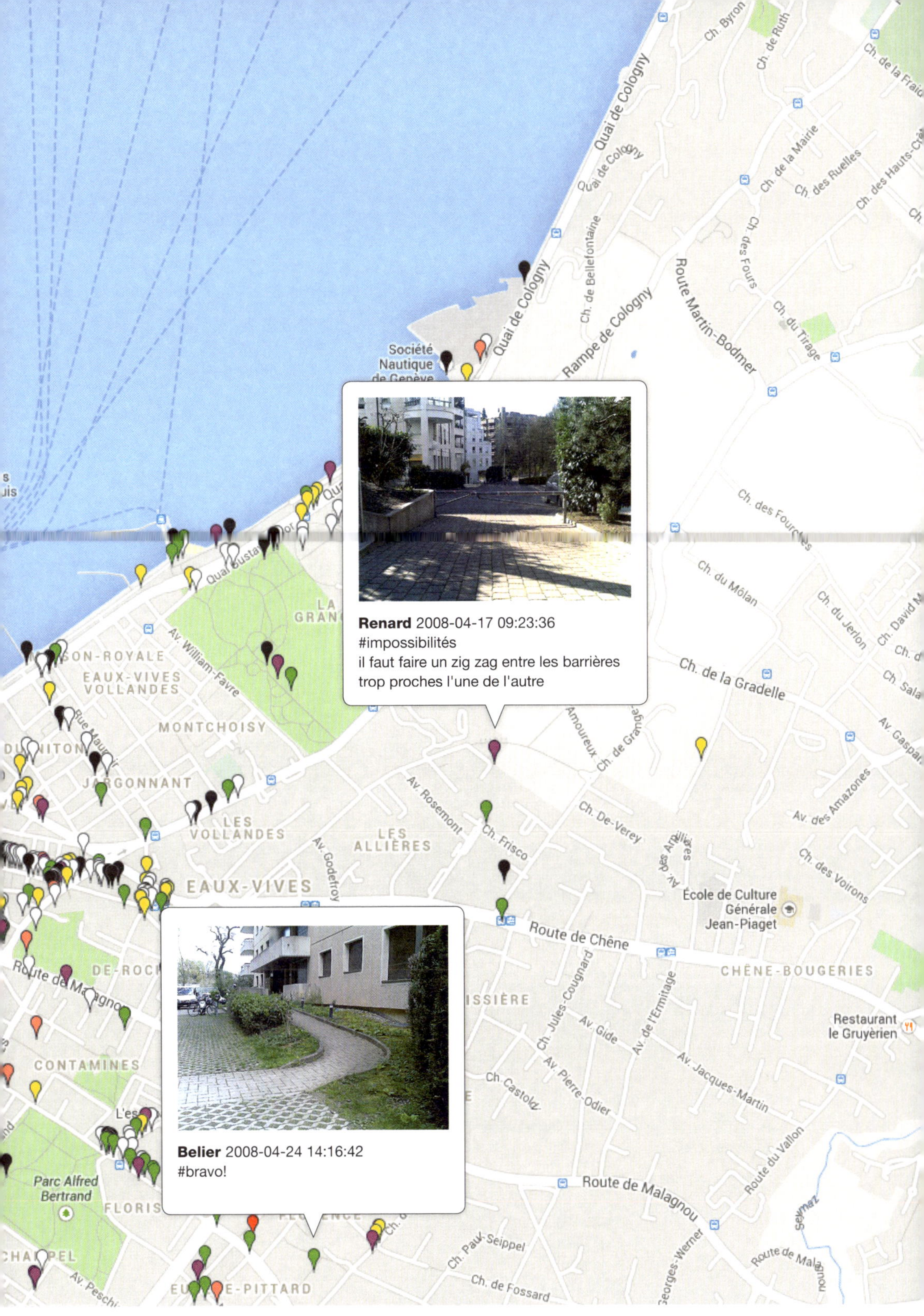

Renard 2008-04-17 09:23:36
#impossibilités
il faut faire un zig zag entre les barrières
trop proches l'une de l'autre
Belier 2008-04-24 14:16:42
#bravo!

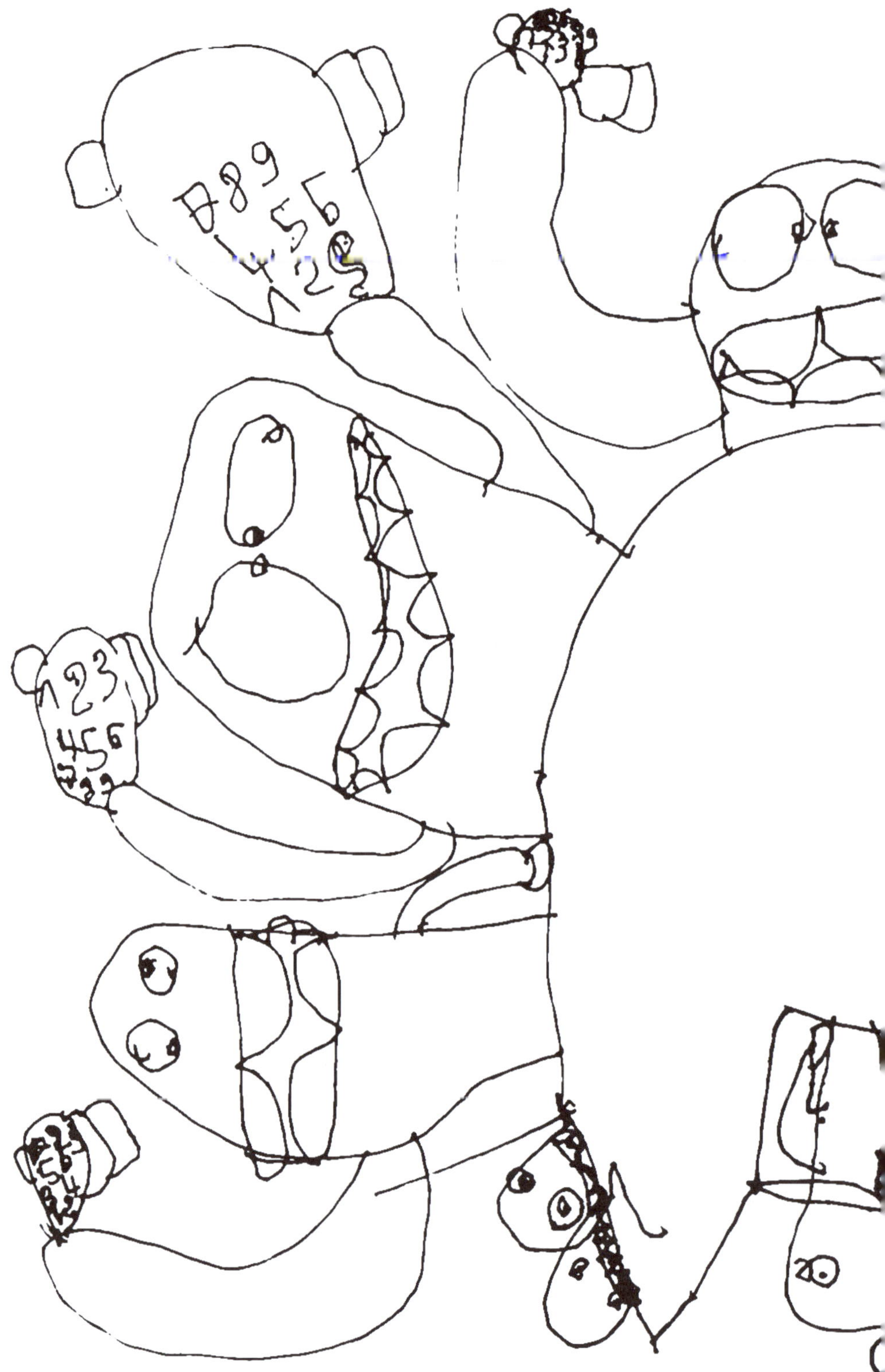

Meeting table drawn by Alex Baumgartner, participant in the project *GENÈVE*accessible*

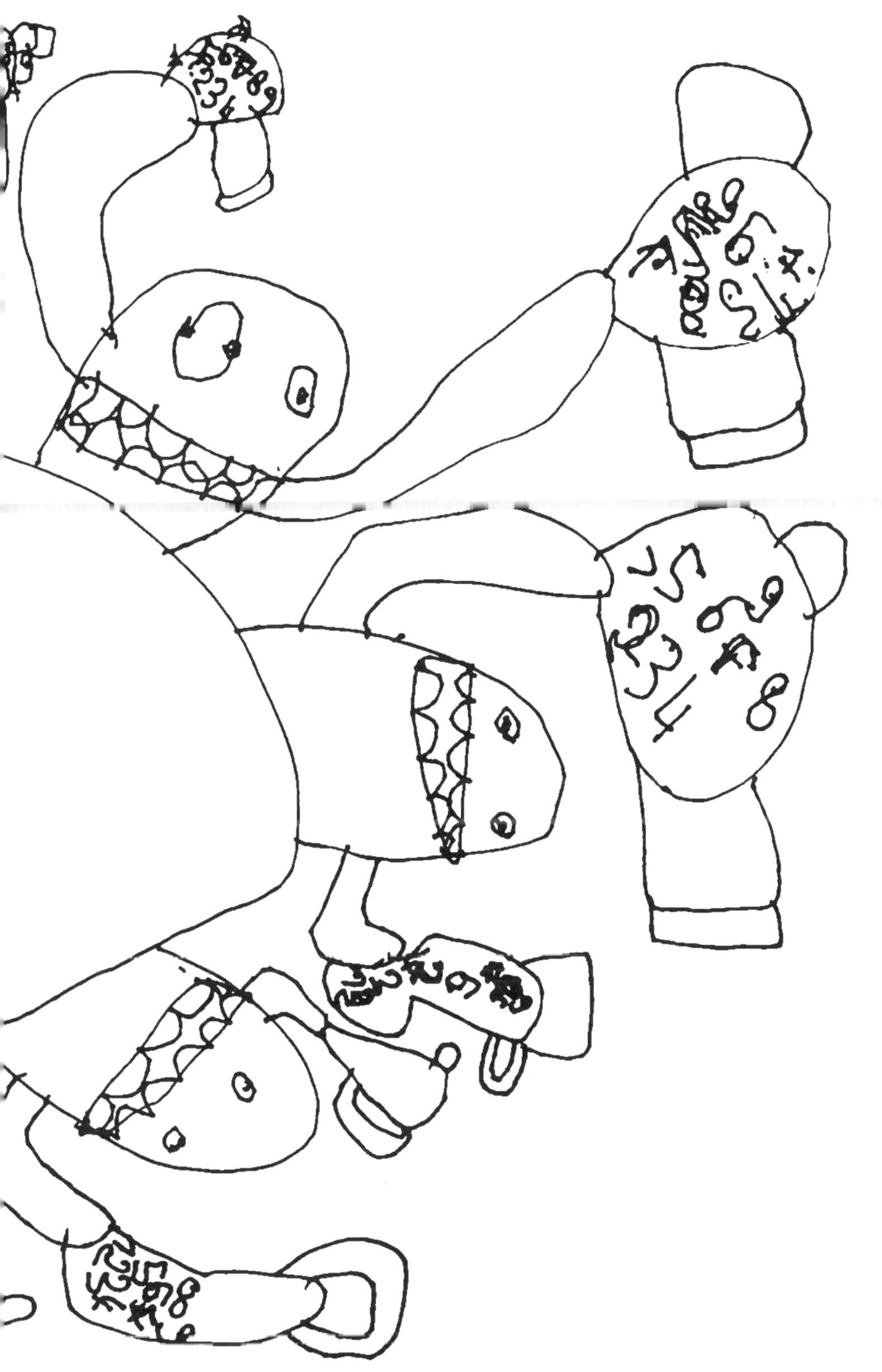

20 años a abandono actual alcanzar alianzas amor anafabetismo años armado aseo asociación atras autoridad bacano bacano tolerancia batuta benefactor camello camino canaltemporal Capacitación casas chiva ciudad de las mujeres clausuras teatrales coca coflicto colombia tambien comida comienzo y final concepto confianza conflicto conflicto armado congreso consejo convivencia cosás cumplidos debate derecho desarrollo deseos despilfarro desplazado dia dialogo diaria diversion ediccion educación el amor elecciones embajador emergencia social? emprendimiento encuentrofamiliar enlaespera entrevista espacio público esperanza estado estar estatuismo exprecion expresión exquisito familia fotografia fugitivo hacinamiento hambre historia inclusión incoder caldas incumple horario infancia inicio instituciones jungla junta ley lanzamiento libertad lista magdalena metas miedos minutos mototáxi mujeres neblinas pasajeras negligencia negócio nevado niños conflicto no vemos nos abandonaron ocio opinión oportunidad orígenes pailas pare pasado paseo paz pedimos peligro persianaamericana pobreza policía política prensa prensa progreso proyecto prueva publicidad reconpensa trabajo recreacion relato religión remando respeto rueda salud saludo servicio sobrevivir sociedad solución sombra sueños teatro temor temores testimonio trabajo transportes trovas vivencias VIVIENDA vuelo

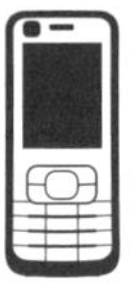

canal*TEMPORAL
Displaced communities and
those demobilised from
armed conflict
Manizales, Colombia
2009–10

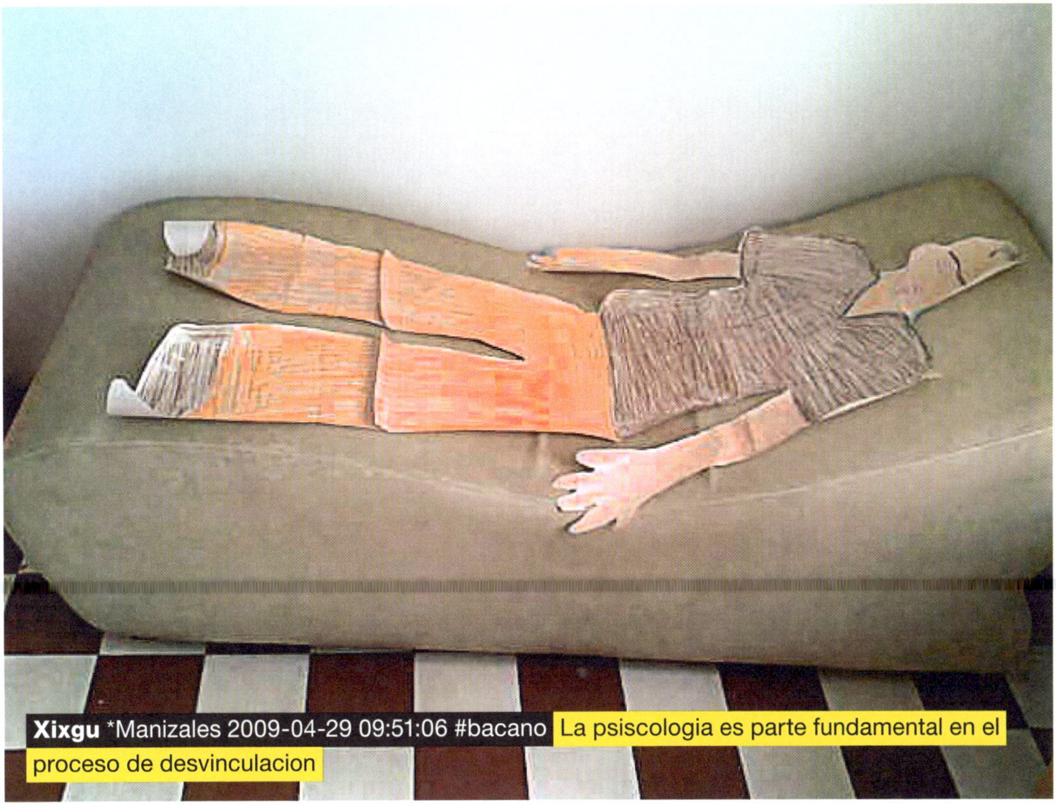

Xixgu *Manizales 2009-04-29 09:51:06 #bacano La psiscologia es parte fundamental en el proceso de desvinculacion

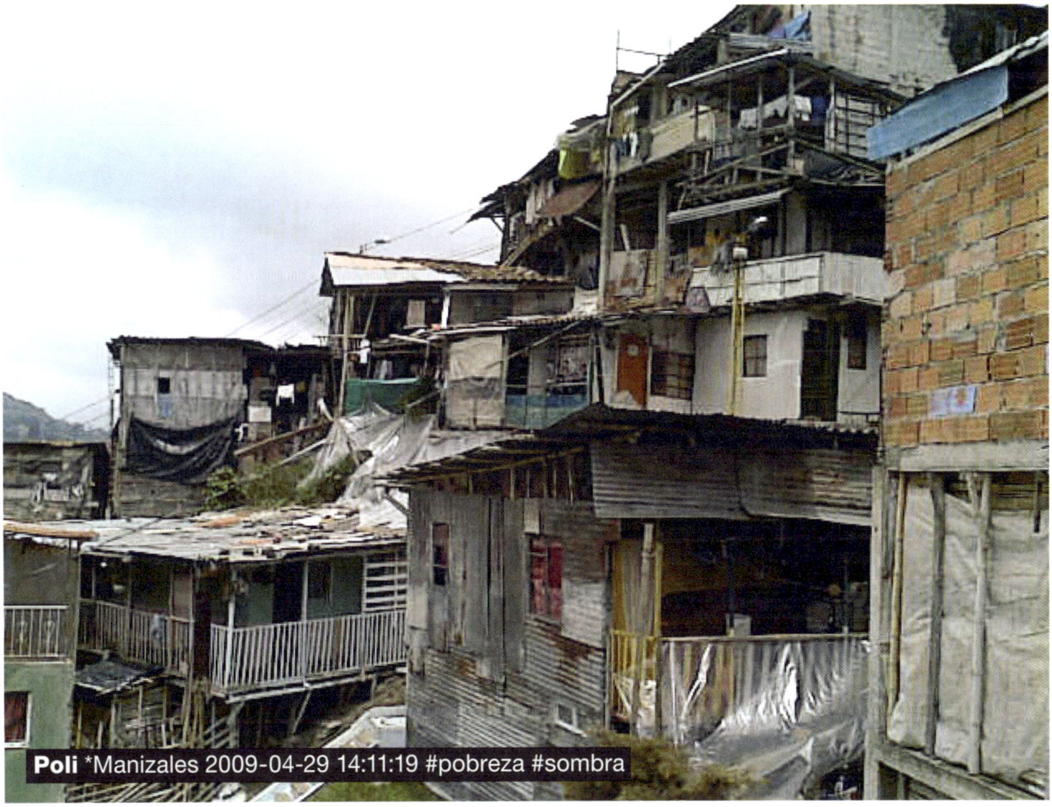

Poli *Manizales 2009-04-29 14:11:19 #pobreza #sombra

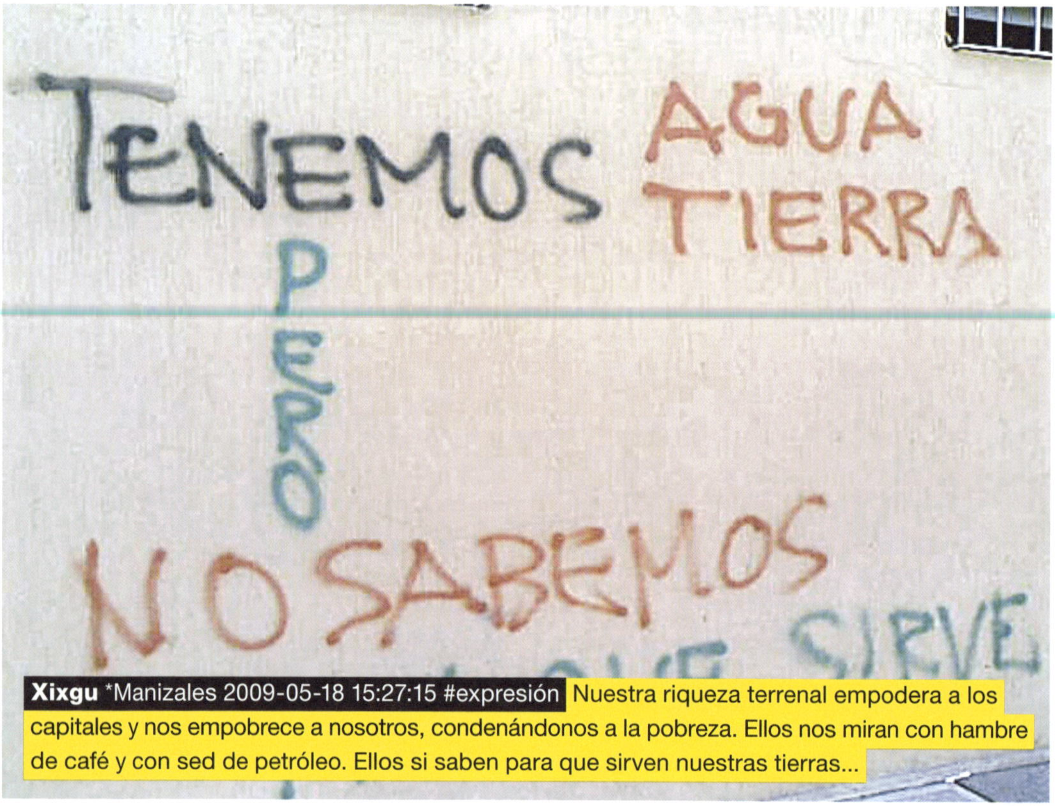

Xixgu *Manizales 2009-05-18 15:27:15 #expresión Nuestra riqueza terrenal empodera a los capitales y nos empobrece a nosotros, condenándonos a la pobreza. Ellos nos miran con hambre de café y con sed de petróleo. Ellos si saben para que sirven nuestras tierras...

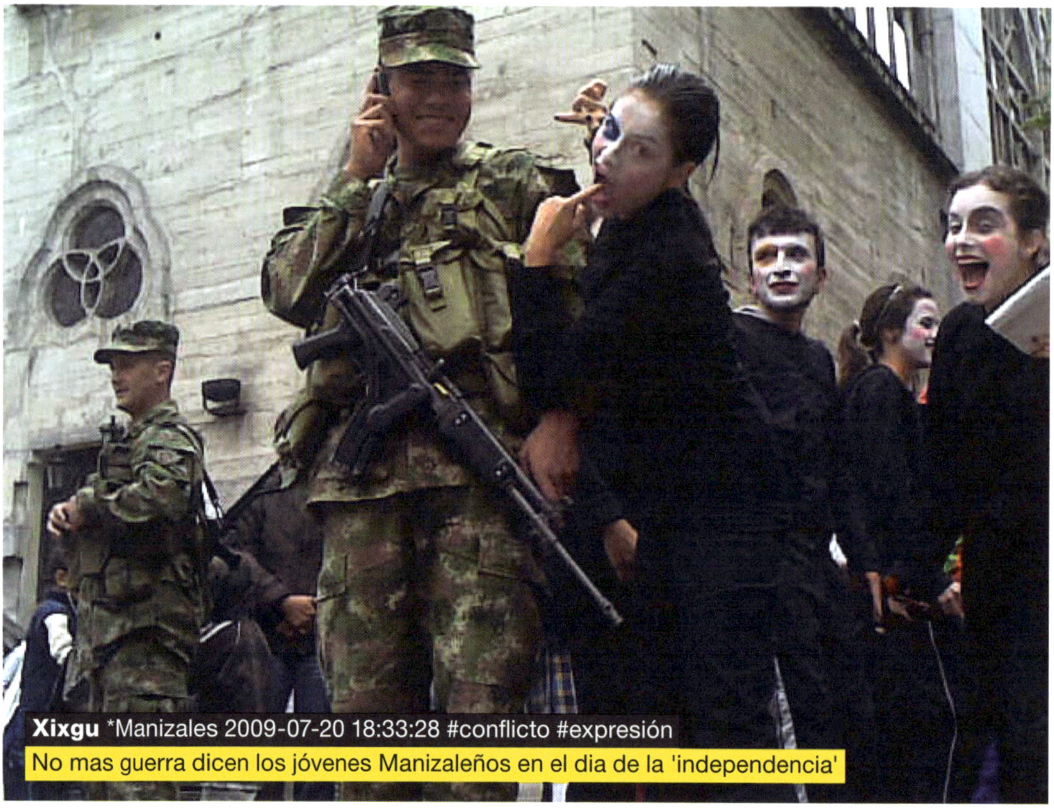

Xixgu *Manizales 2009-07-20 18:33:28 #conflicto #expresión
No mas guerra dicen los jóvenes Manizaleños en el dia de la 'independencia'

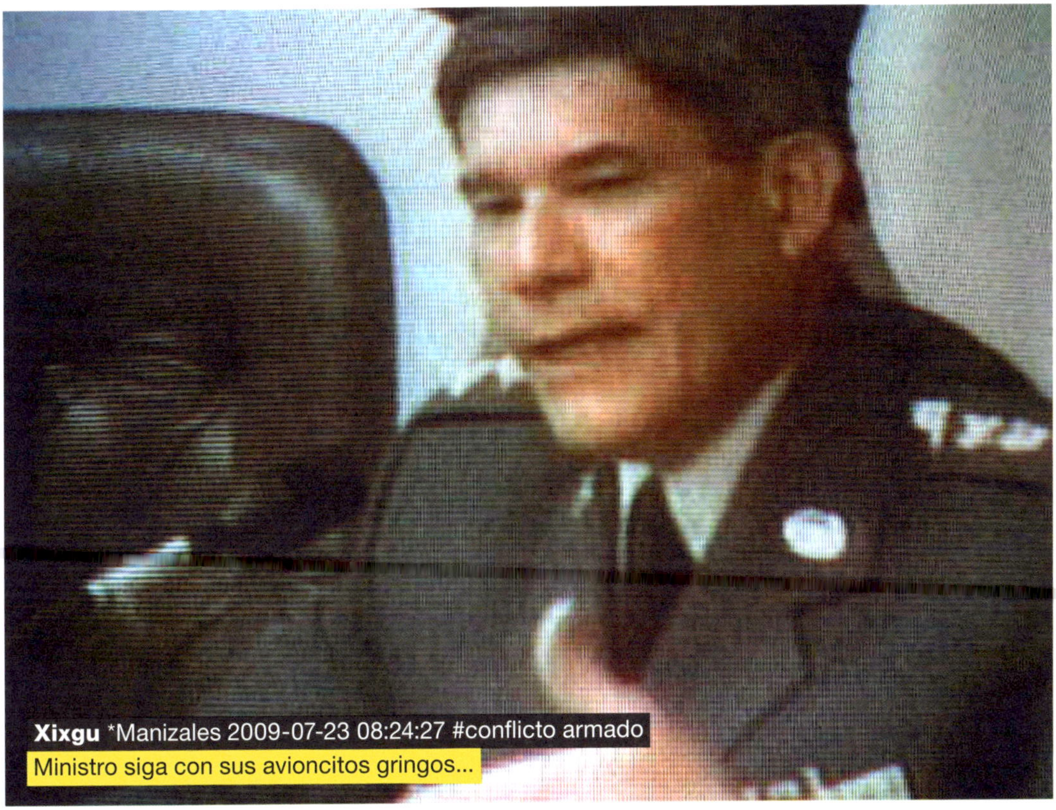

Xixgu *Manizales 2009-07-23 08:24:27 #conflicto armado
Ministro siga con sus avioncitos gringos...

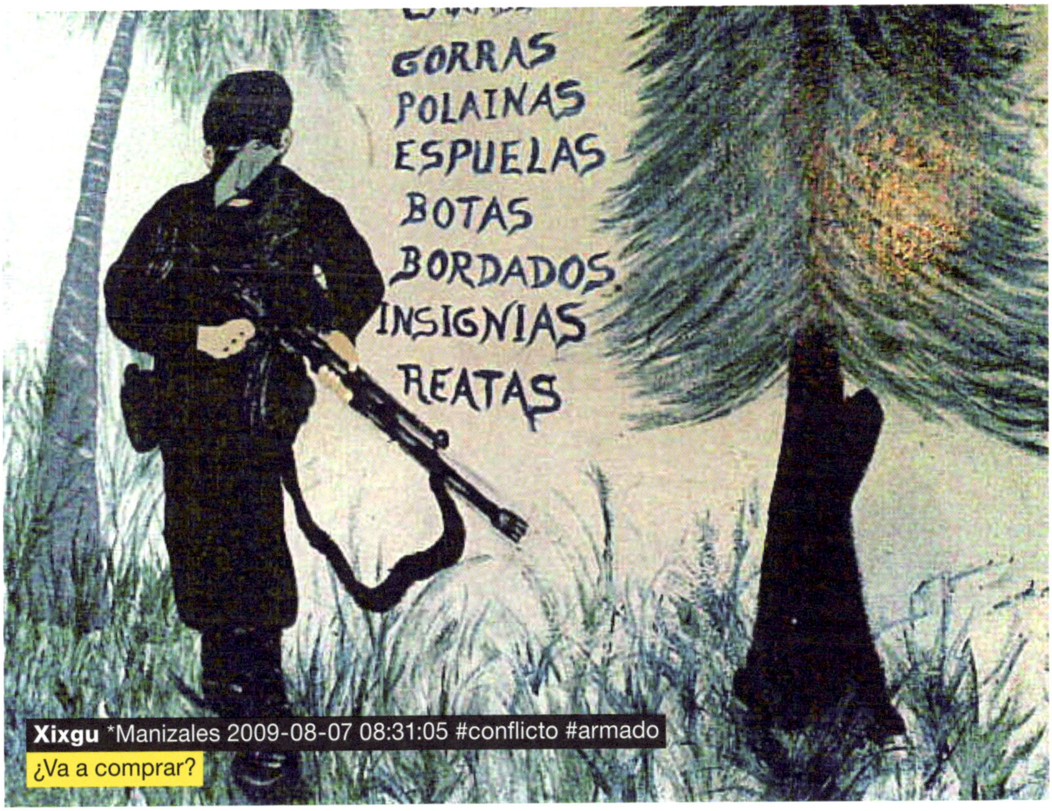

GORRAS
POLAINAS
ESPUELAS
BOTAS
BORDADOS
INSIGNIAS
REATAS

Xixgu *Manizales 2009-08-07 08:31:05 #conflicto #armado
¿Va a comprar?

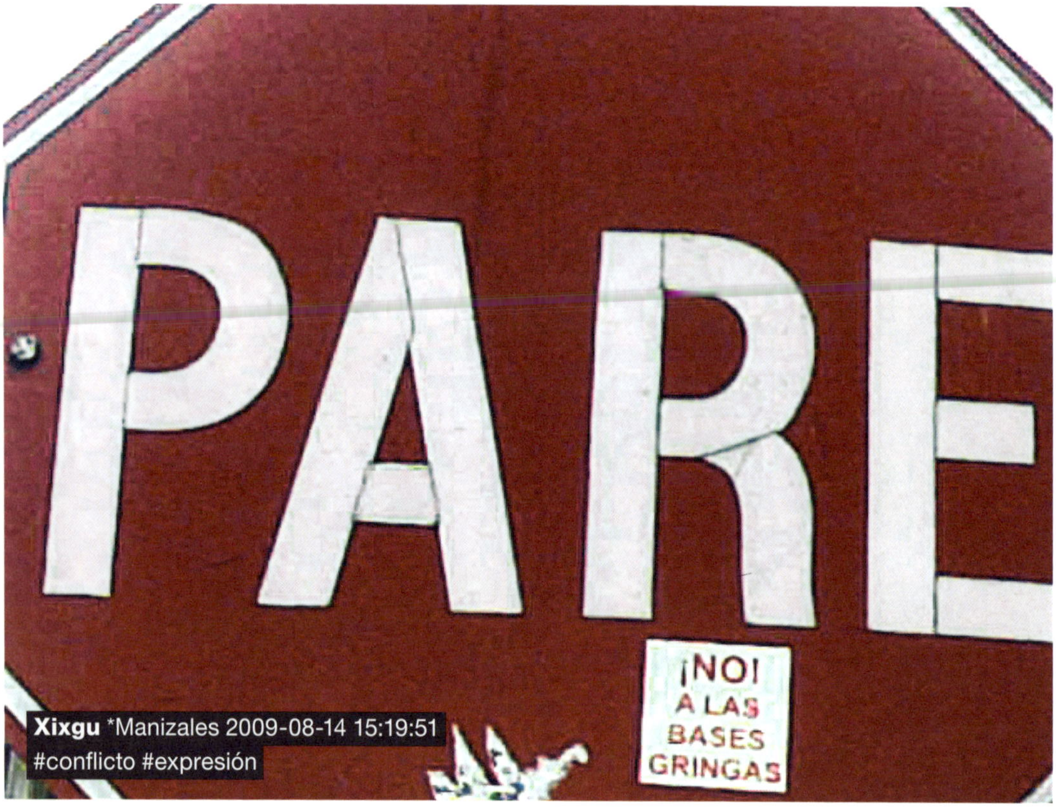

Xixgu *Manizales 2009-08-14 15:19:51
#conflicto #expresión

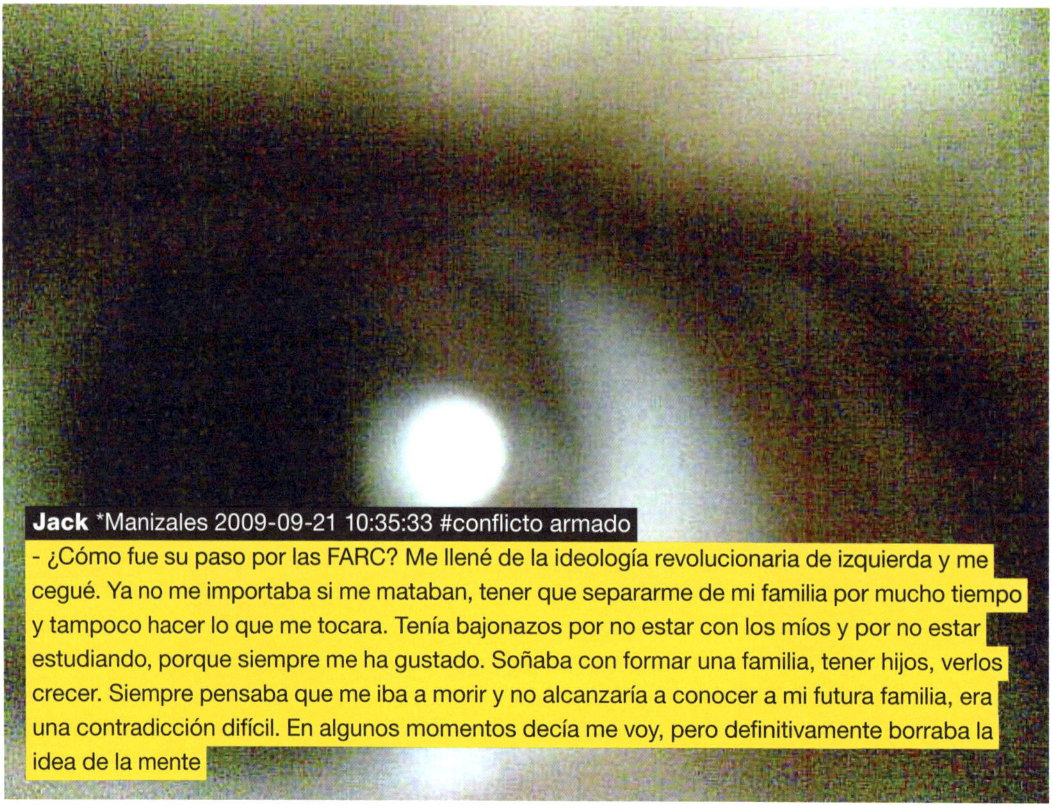

Jack *Manizales 2009-09-21 10:35:33 #conflicto armado
- ¿Cómo fue su paso por las FARC? Me llené de la ideología revolucionaria de izquierda y me cegué. Ya no me importaba si me mataban, tener que separarme de mi familia por mucho tiempo y tampoco hacer lo que me tocara. Tenía bajonazos por no estar con los míos y por no estar estudiando, porque siempre me ha gustado. Soñaba con formar una familia, tener hijos, verlos crecer. Siempre pensaba que me iba a morir y no alcanzaría a conocer a mi futura familia, era una contradicción difícil. En algunos momentos decía me voy, pero definitivamente borraba la idea de la mente

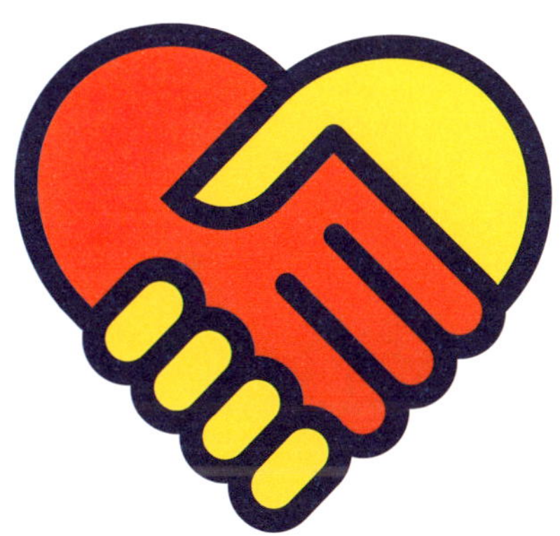

Logo by Ravi Poovaiah (Indian Institute of Technology Bombay) adapted for the project *canal*TEMPORAL*

:ninos actividad cultural activistas activitas afapradesca afrapradesa animales arte-

sania saharaui cabras carreteras casa de la mujer casas coferencia competencia conferencia construccion control

COSTUMBRE saharaui cuidado el tabaco es malo cultura saharaui

discapacitados encuentro familair escuela fapradesca festival de

cultura y arte populares saharauis auserd fotos fotos de memoria gas gracias a megafone y a la ayuda espaÑola!!! guarderia

hombres hosbital hosbital nacional saharaui huerto jaima joven juegos tradicionales saharauis mañana manifestacion

manifestacion en la escuela 27 febrero maratón memoria mensaje mujer trabajo

mujeres museo música natural naturaleza
niños niño político reunión reuniones rezo ruta sombra talleres teatro nacional tierra trabaja
trabajo trbajo viajes víctimas vida visita visita al museo visitas

الارض الاطفال الترجمة الخايمة الذاكرة الطريق

الظل العجز العمل النساء المستشفى الوطني بينارحال رسالة زافت شاب ضحايا

طبيعية لؤلف مدرسا معز منزل

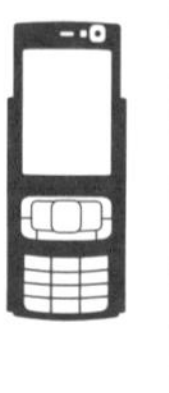

canal*SAHARAUI
Sahrawi refugees
Tindouf, Algeria
2009–11

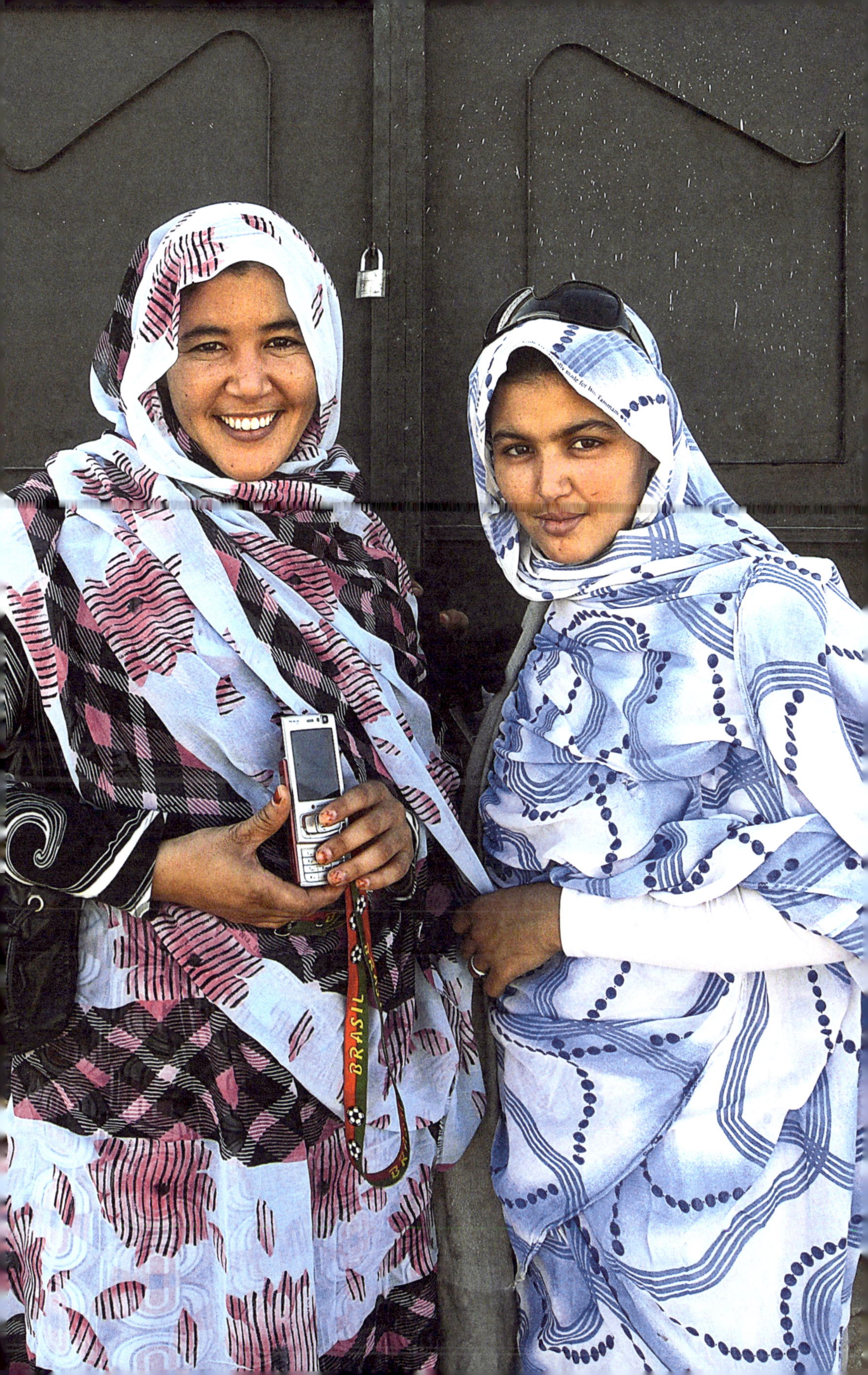

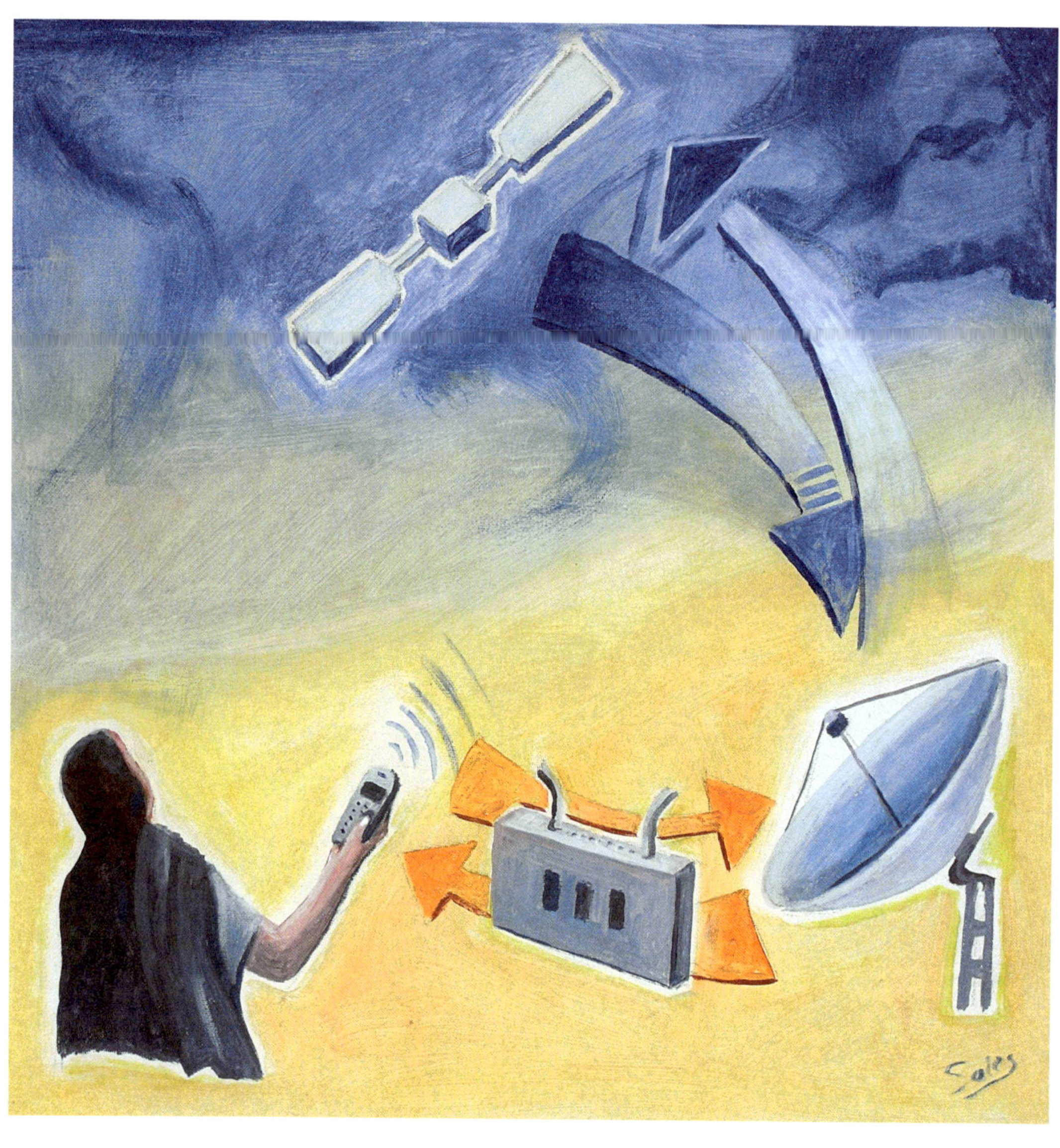

Pictorial interpretation by Saleh Brahim of transmissions in the project *canal*SAHARAUI*
Installing a Wi-Fi antenna at the Sahrawi refugee camp "27 de Febrero"

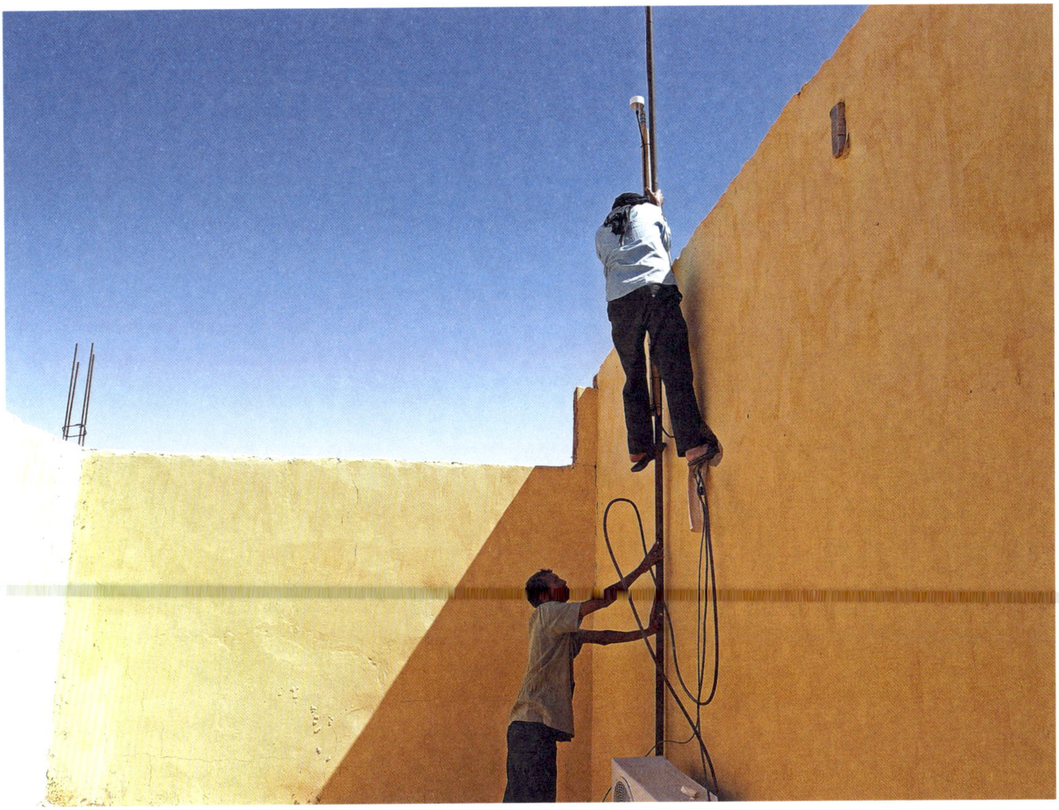

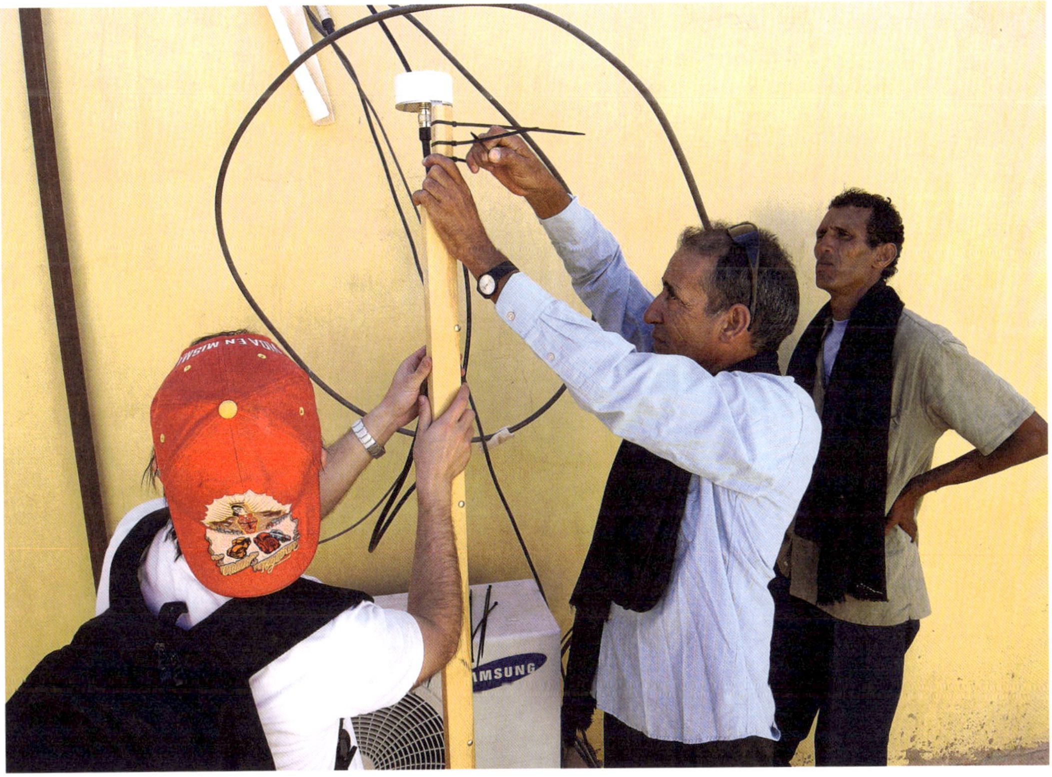

SAMSUNG

LIBERA SU
UNLOCK YO

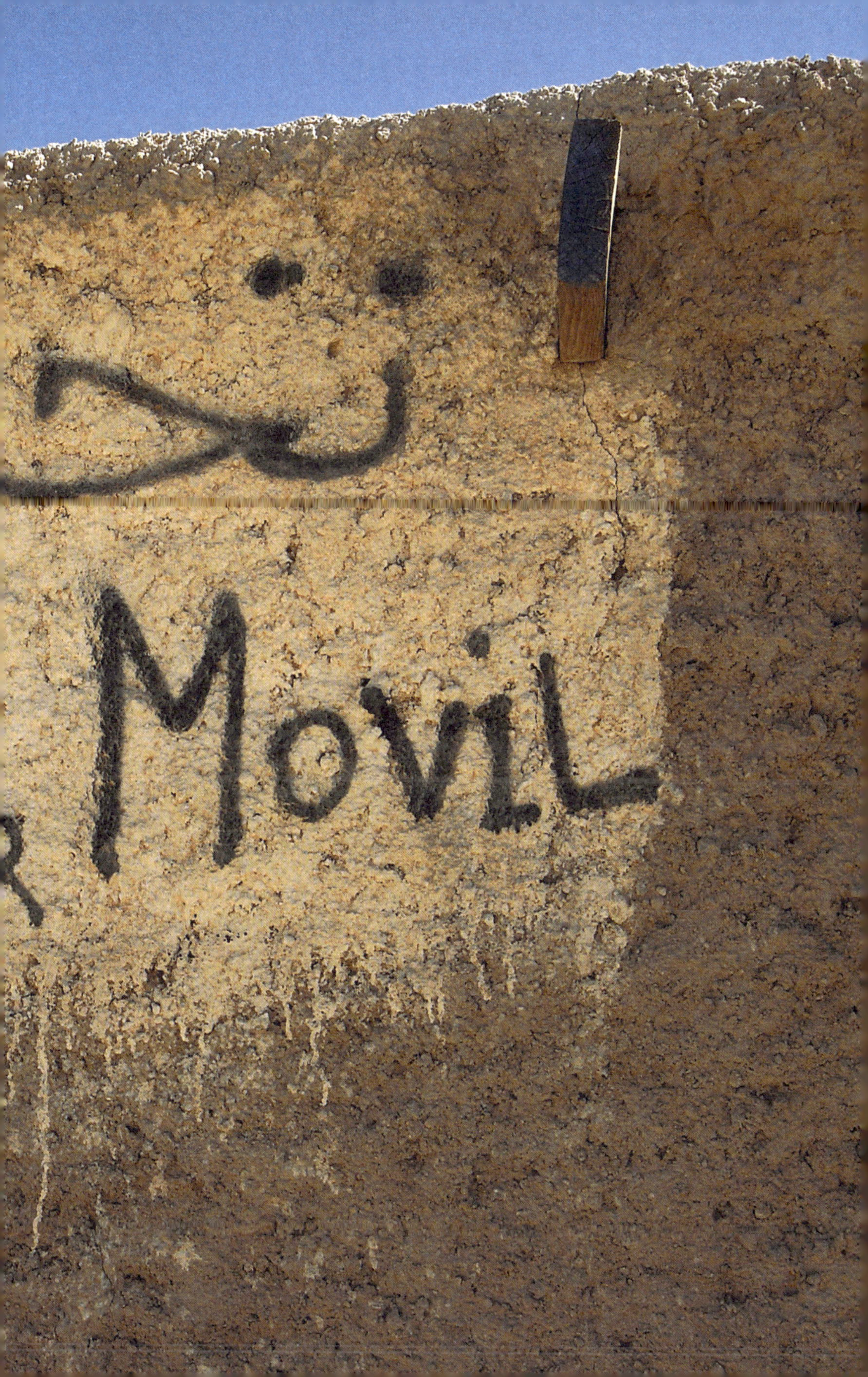
Movil

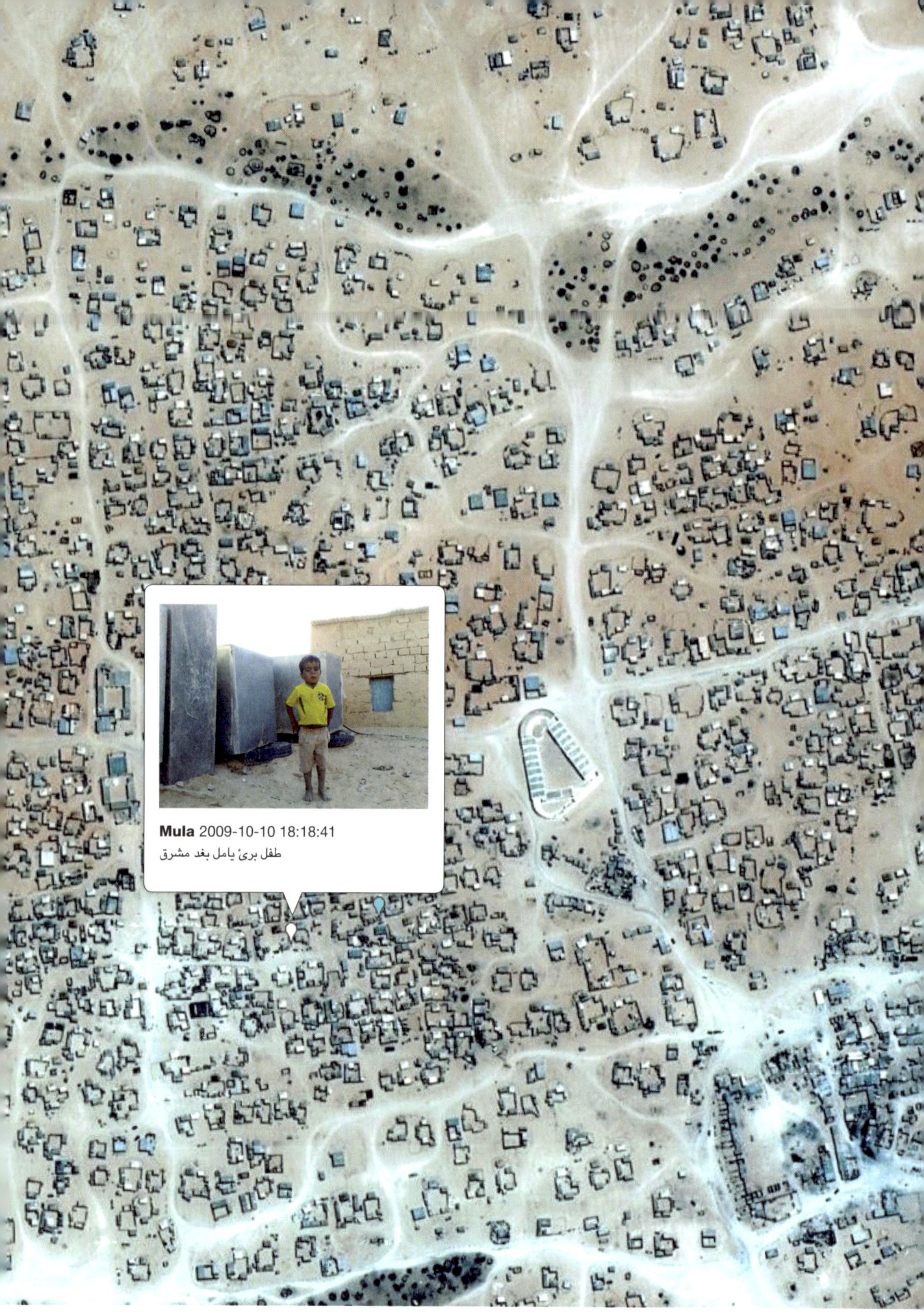

Details of a collective mapping of the Tindouf refugee camps

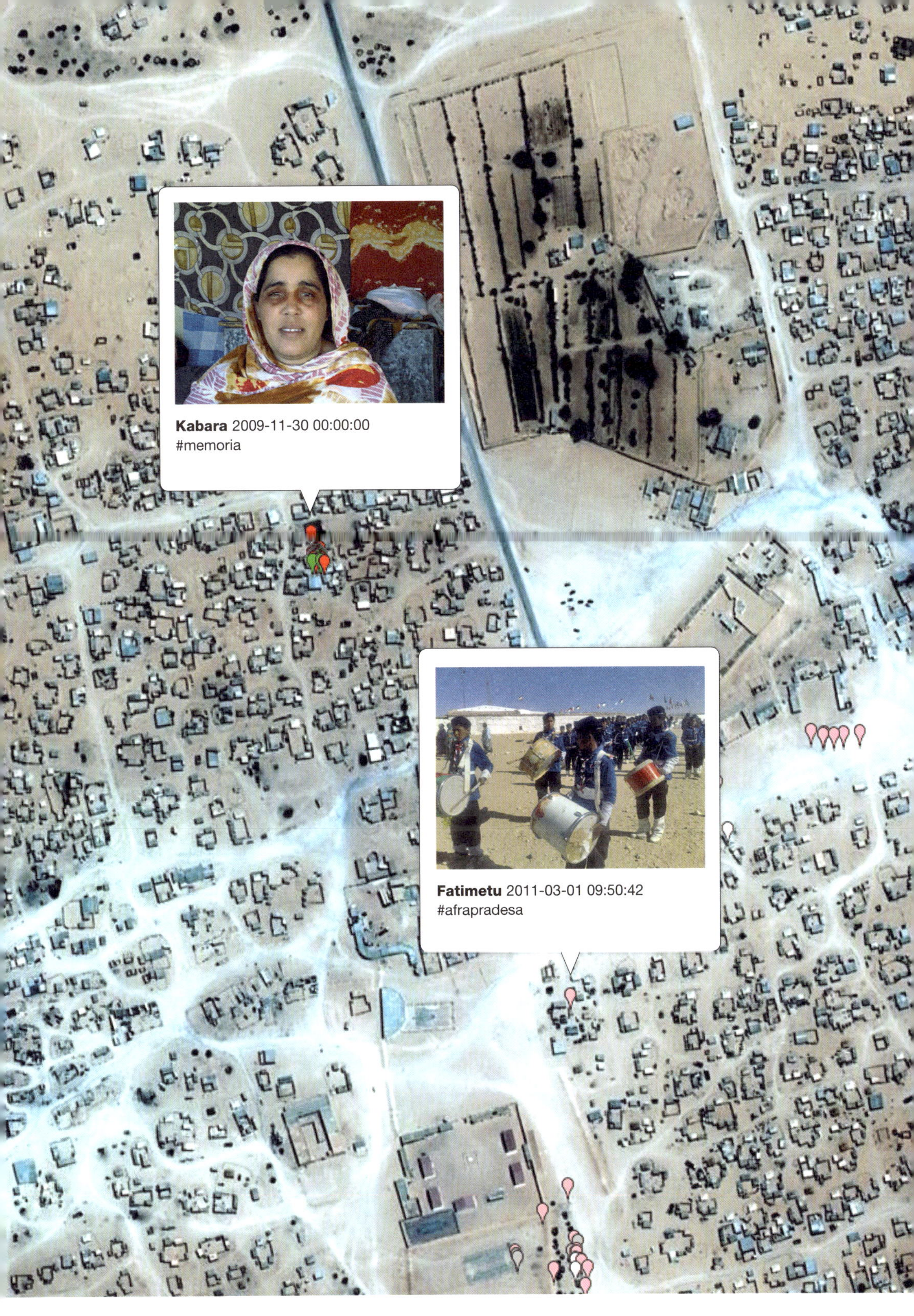

Kabara 2009-11-30 00:00:00
#memoria
Fatimetu 2011-03-01 09:50:42
#afrapradesa

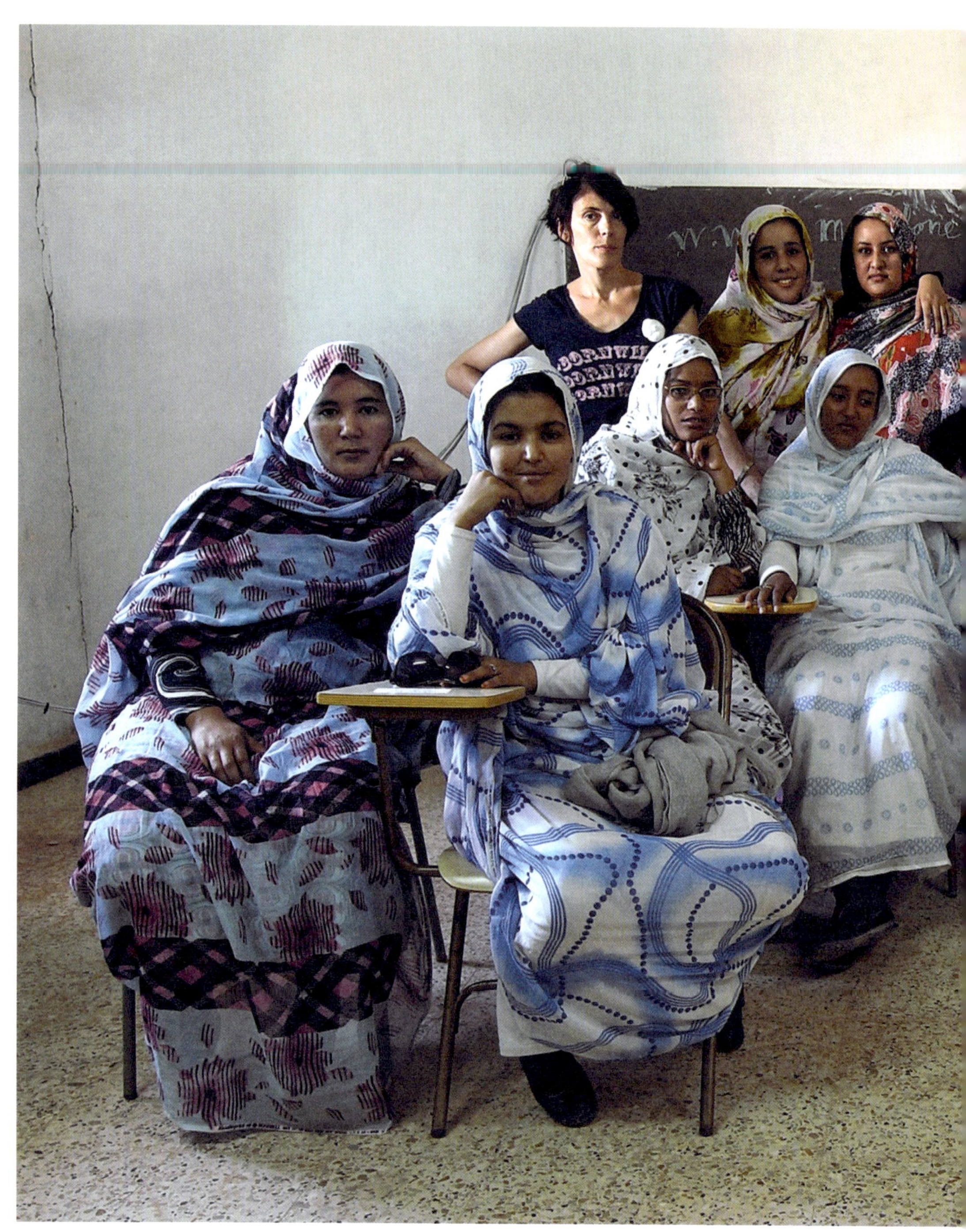

The participants and team of *megafone.net* at the headquarters of the National Union of Sahrawi Women at Tindouf

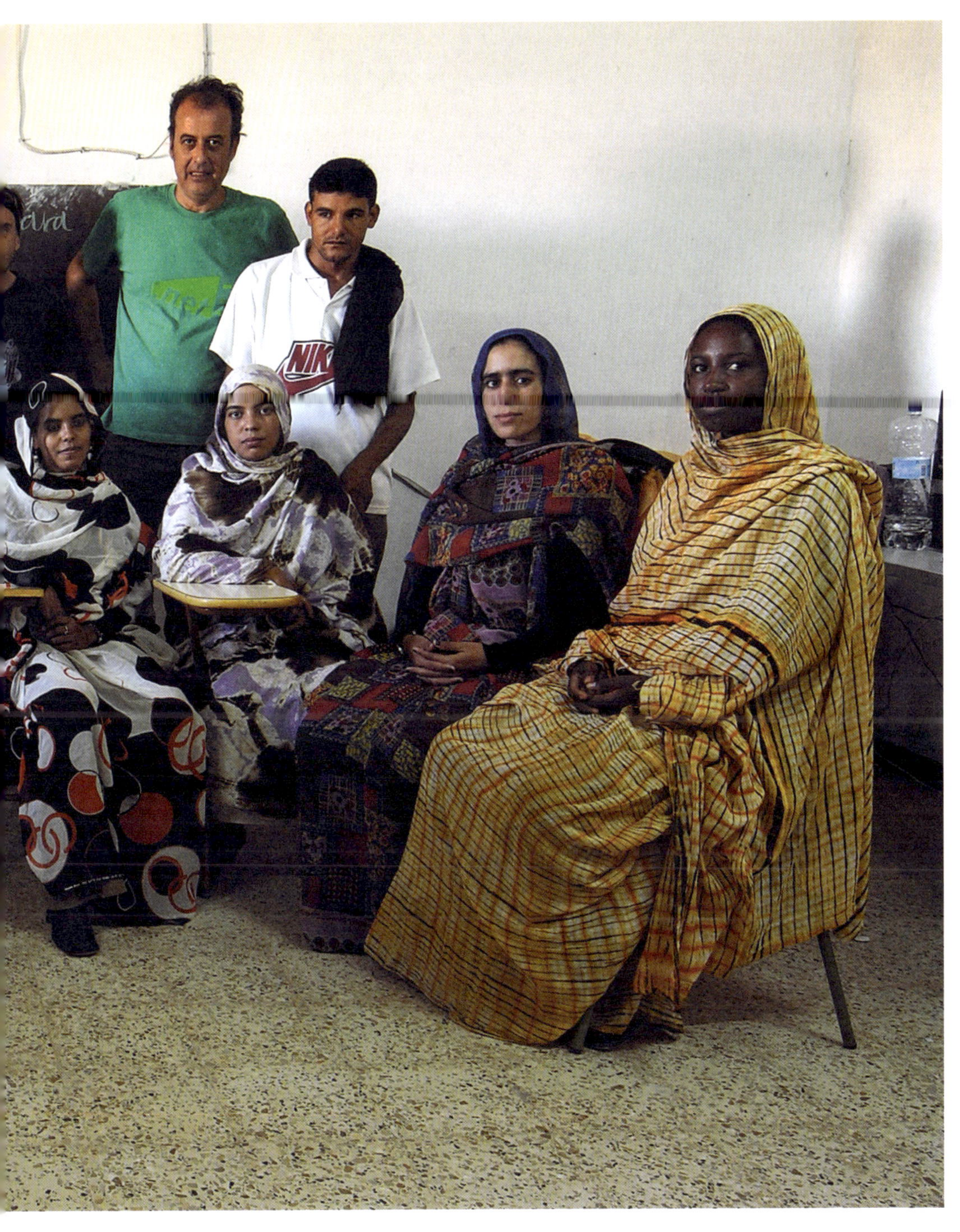

accessibelitat obres accessibilitat obres alumne per recordar amic andamio apaños aprenentatge artes Autobus

b b1b2b3 Braille bravo! cafeteria campus carrer collblanc cuato de piso

cultura accessible cupones emisor entrevista espacio abierto

espacio público fatal golferichs grupo illes per vianants incívics indefinit

informació informàtica maceta maquinas mobiliari privat

mobiliari públic no serveix obra social obres

pal electric papelera paquita parc parkimetro pintada plaça cataluña plaza cívica preuva1 preuva2 primer día

prueva sonido quotidià reunió risc rojo senyalització

temporal trafico trafico coches transports vista

voto accesible

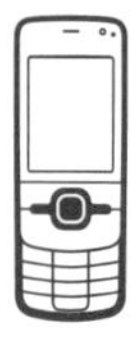

The Blind Point of View
Blind and visually
impaired people
Barcelona, Spain
2010–11

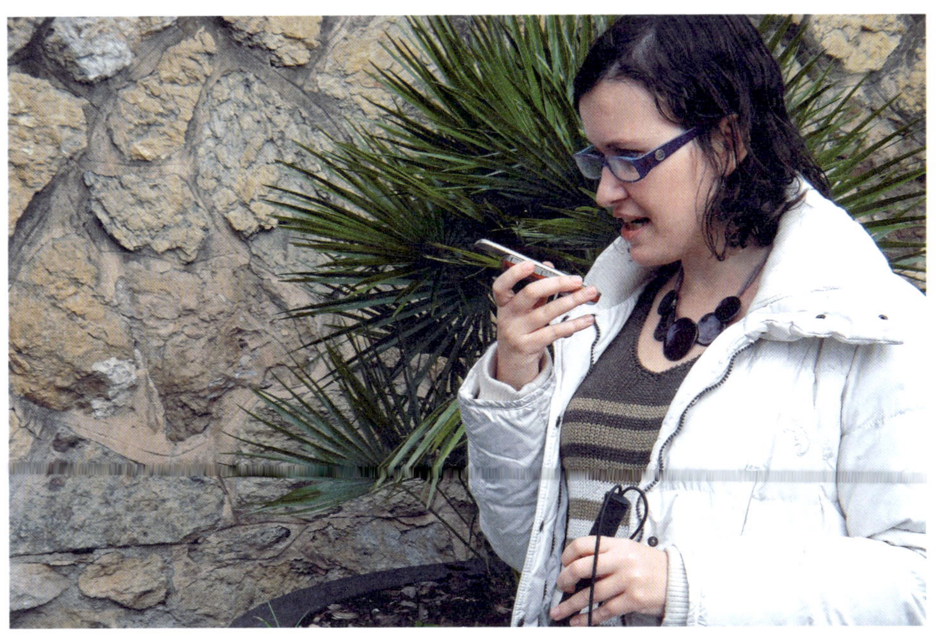

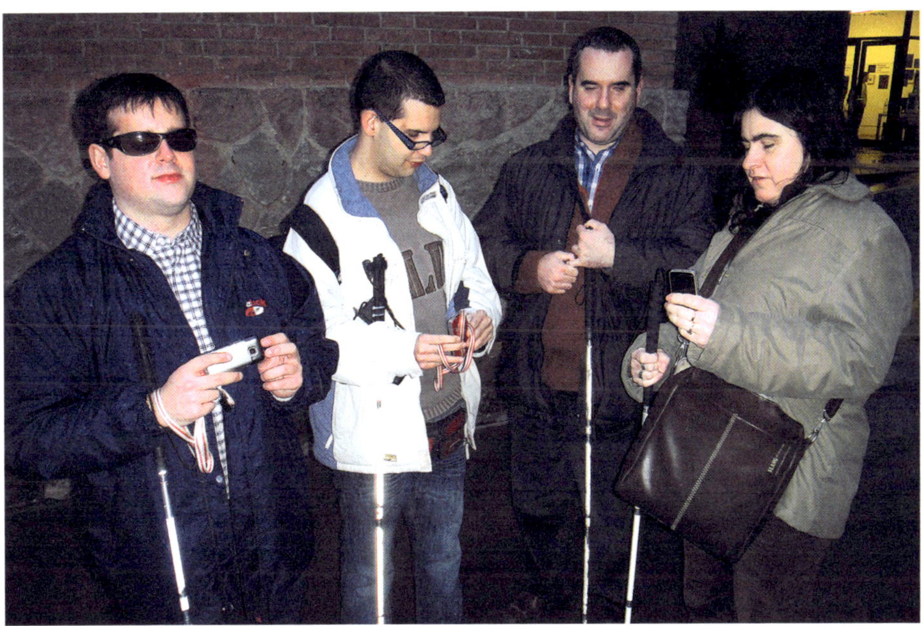

Participants in the project *The Blind Point of View*

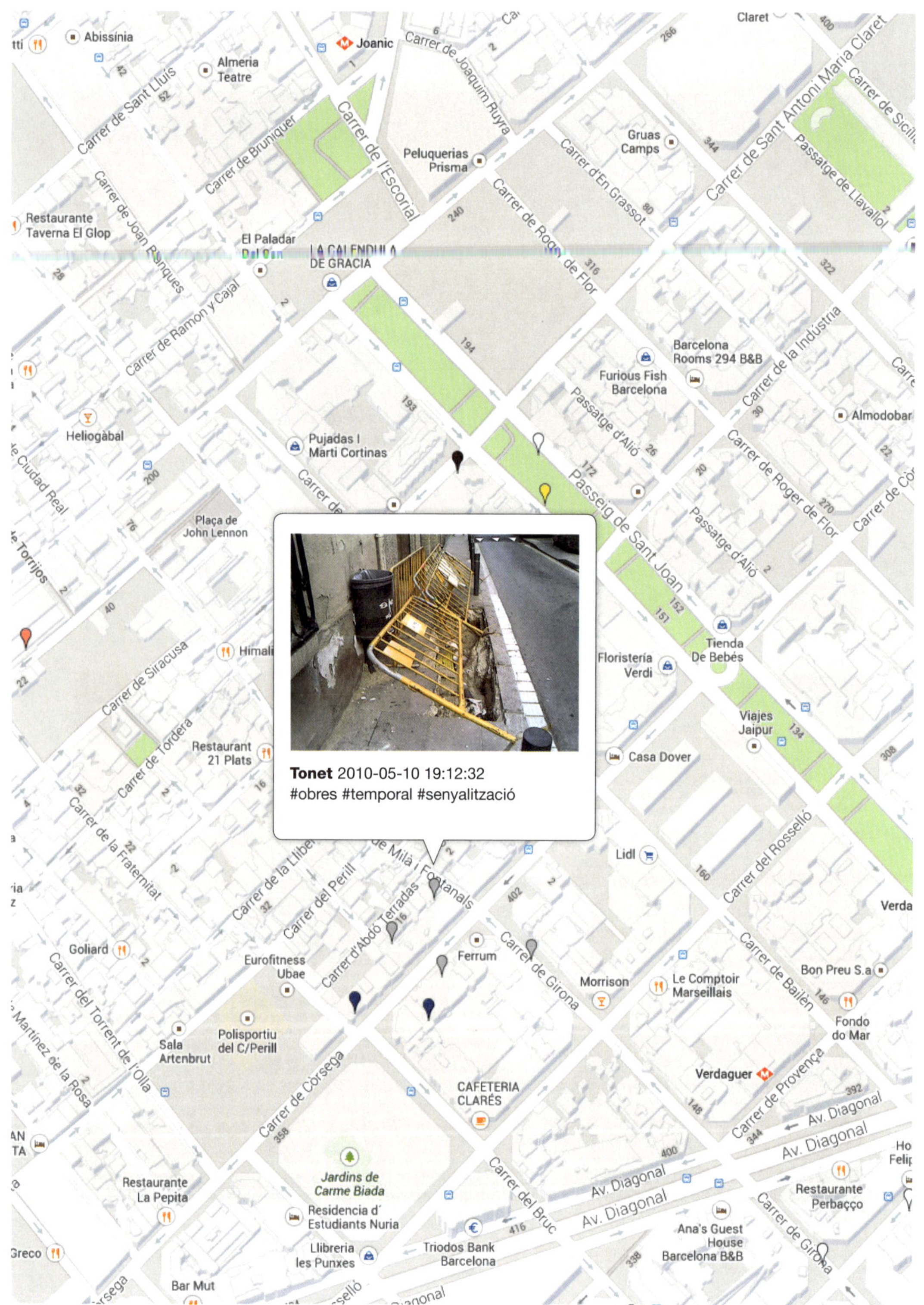

Details of a collective mapping of Barcelona

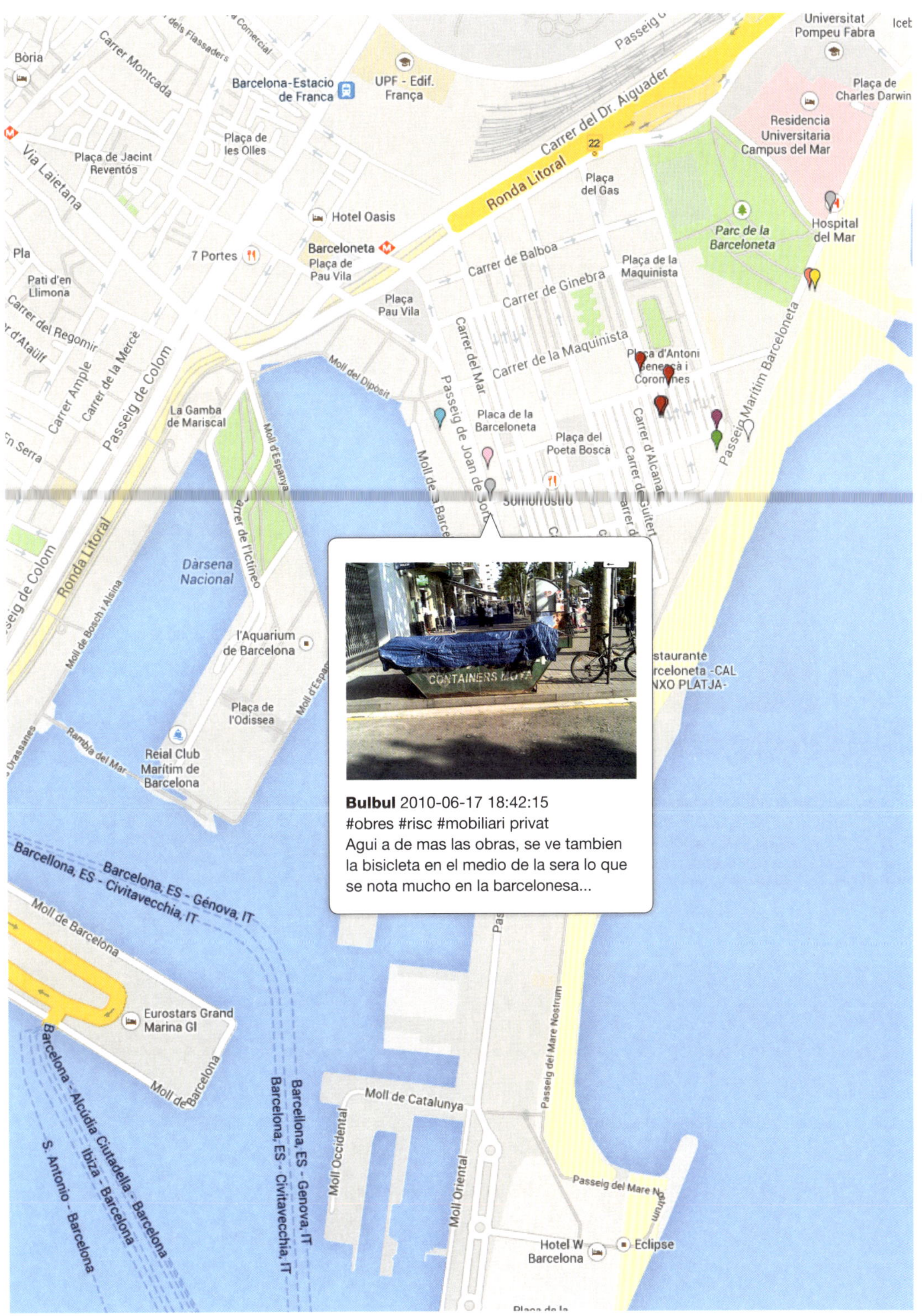

Bulbul 2010-06-17 18:42:15
#obres #risc #mobiliari privat
Agui a de mas las obras, se ve tambien
la bisicleta en el medio de la sera lo que
se nota mucho en la barcelonesa...

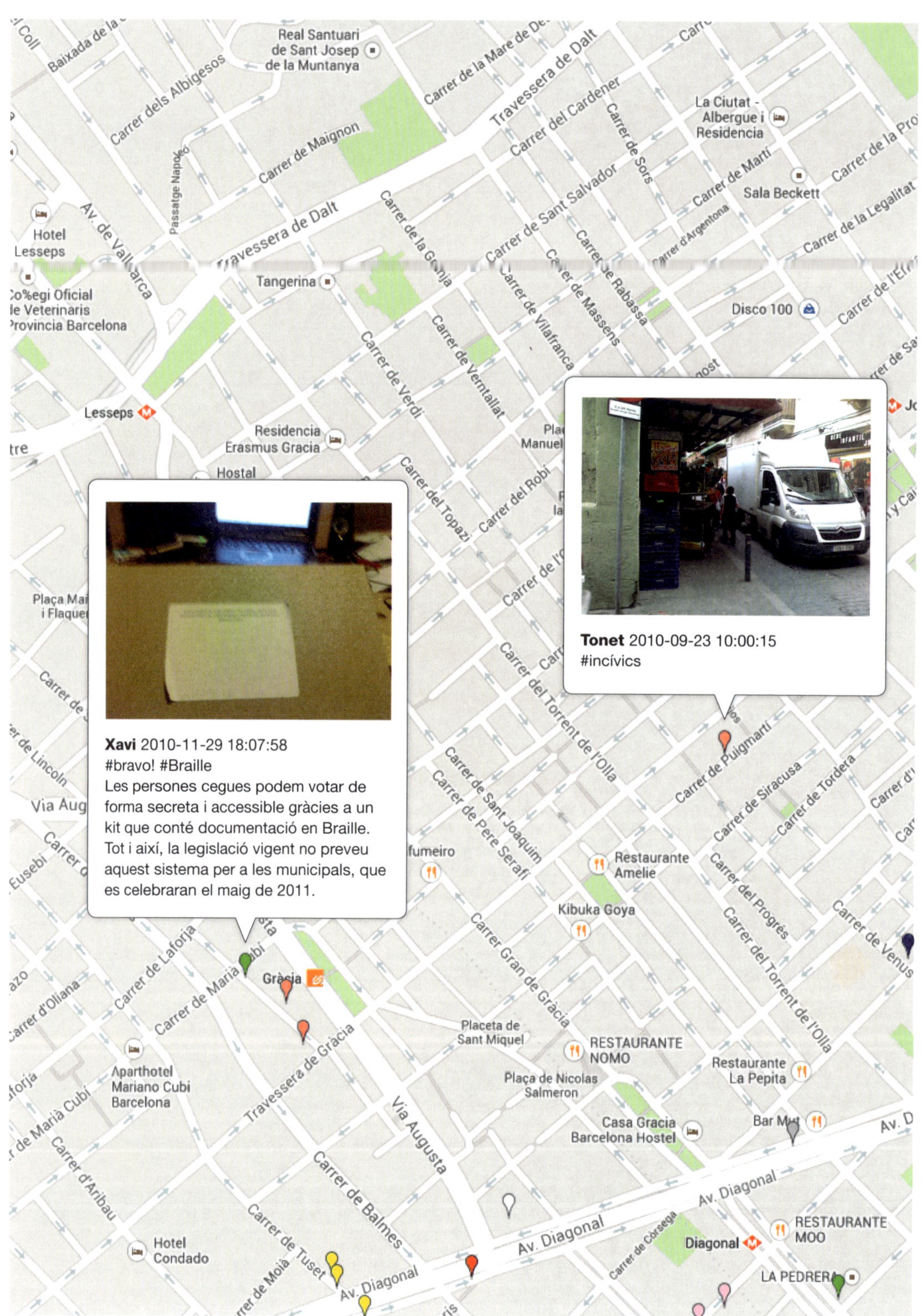

Details of a collective mapping of Barcelona

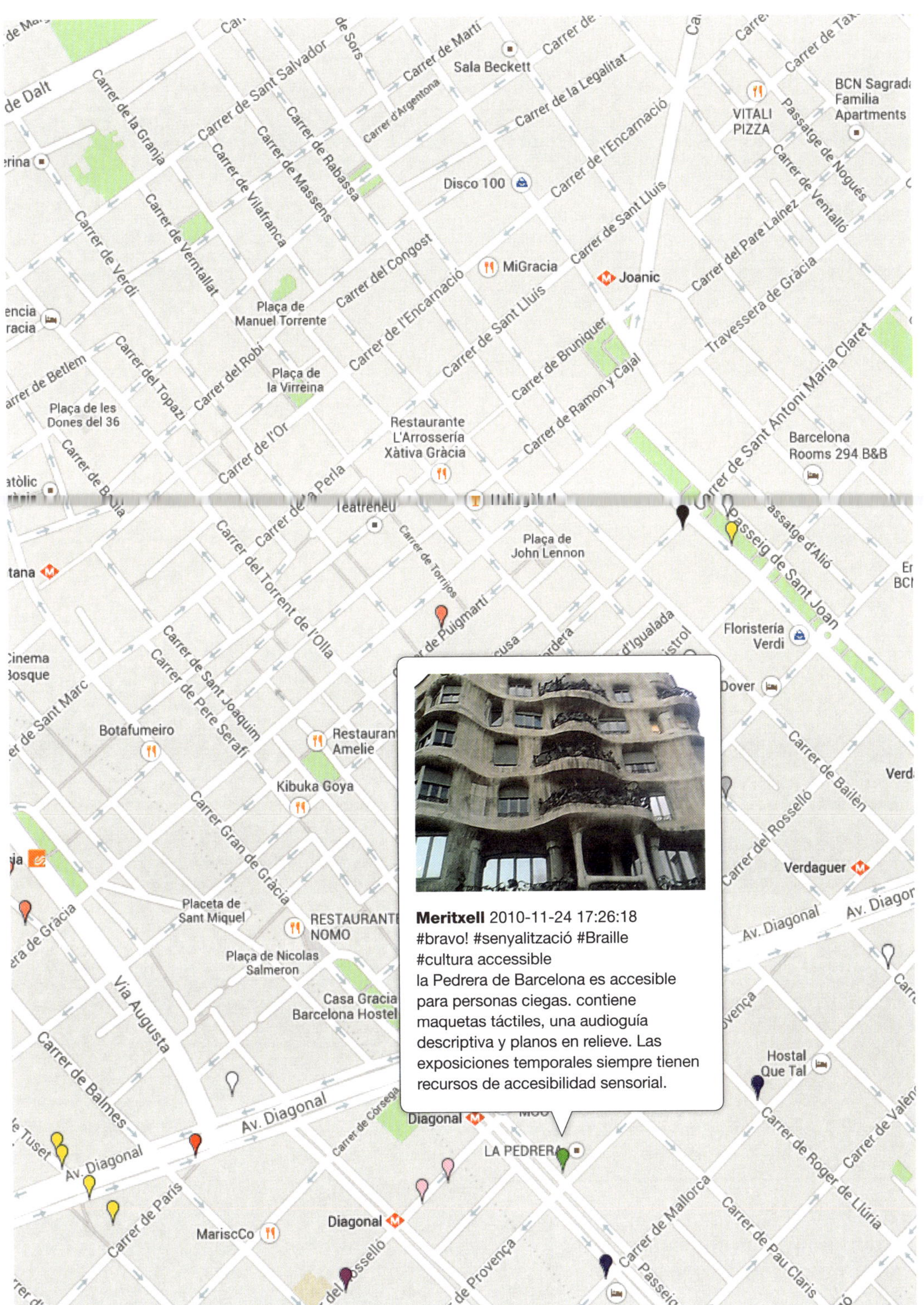

Carrer de Martí
Sala Beckett
Carrer de la Legalitat
Carrer de Dalt
Carrer de la Granja
Carrer de Sant Salvador
de Sots
Carrer d'Argentona
Carrer de l'Encarnació
BCN Sagrada Família Apartments
VITALI PIZZA
Passatge de Nogués
Carrer de la Granja
Carrer de Rabassa
Carrer de Massens
Carrer de Vilafranca
Carrer de Verntallat
Disco 100
Carrer de Sant Lluís
Carrer del Pare Laínez
Carrer de Ventalló
erina
Carrer de Verdi
MiGracia
Joanic
Carrer del Congost
Carrer de l'Encarnació
Carrer de Sant Lluís
Travessera de Gràcia
encia racia
Plaça de Manuel Torrente
Carrer de Bruniquer
Carrer de Sant Antoni Maria Claret
Carrer de Betlem
Carrer del Topazi
Carrer del Robi
Plaça de la Virreina
Carrer de Ramon y Cajal
Barcelona Rooms 294 B&B
Plaça de les Dones del 36
Restaurante L'Arrosseria Xàtiva Gràcia
atòlic
Carrer de Buïa
Carrer de l'Or
de la Perla
Teatreneu
Plaça de John Lennon
Passatge d'Alió
En BCI
tana
Carrer del Torrent de l'Olla
Carrer de Torrijos
Passeig de Sant Joan
Cinema Bosque
Carrer de Sant Marc
Carrer de Pere Serafí
Carrer de Sant Joaquim
de Puigmartí
d'Igualada
Floristería Verdi
Dover
Carrer de Bailèn
Botafumeiro
Restauran Amelie
Carrer del Rosselló
Verd
Kibuka Goya
Carrer Gran de Gràcia
Verdaguer
ia
Placeta de Sant Miquel
RESTAURANTE NOMO
Av. Diagonal
Av. Diagonal
de Gràcia
Plaça de Nicolas Salmeron
Via Augusta
Casa Gracia Barcelona Hostel
Hostal Que Tal
Carrer de Balmes
Av. Diagonal
Carrer de Còrsega
Diagonal
LA PEDRERA
Carrer de Roger de Llúria
Tuset
Av. Diagonal
Carrer de Paris
Diagonal
Carrer de Mallorca
MariscCo
er del Rosselló
de Provença
Carrer de Pau Claris
Passeig d
rer d'Ar

Meritxell 2010-11-24 17:26:18
#bravo! #senyalització #Braille
#cultura accessible
la Pedrera de Barcelona es accesible
para personas ciegas. contiene
maquetas táctiles, una audioguía
descriptiva y planos en relieve. Las
exposiciones temporales siempre tienen
recursos de accesibilidad sensorial.

accident across borderl activity all about new york alterations architecture **arts** authentic food car celebration

chinese new year parade **class** cleanup commerce communication community confetti

consumerism education faith family fatigue feeling friends fruit fun!society future garbage gary hi gary sound

gas **geography** go to hell! goals goodby Petronio green grille harlem harmony heartwarming! hiking housing

ideas immigration kids landscape love magazines market morning music **nature** new occupy! opinion people

queens religion remittances roads shop skeleton upcycle plants 书籍 事故 交流 人们 人物和事件 休闲 传统 信仰

充满爱 的家庭 光 光明 公园 关于皇后区 再见Petronio 出租 创意 勤奋 医疗 午餐 占领！ 危险 参加者 参观访问

喜庆的 图书馆 圣诞节 坚持 墙 夜晚 天堂 奉献 姿态 婚纱照 媒体 孩子 宗教 尊严 少儿卡拉ok比赛 工作 平和 庭院拍卖 引导 感恩节

感觉 手机 摔跤 改变 文化 文学讲座 无标题的 日出 早上 朋友 未来 梦想 汇款 活动 活动, 旅游

派对

活动, 游行 活动, 环保 活动, 艺术 活动, 野餐 活动, 钓鱼 活动, 钓鱼乐 活动, 钓鱼乐, 活动 消费 消费者保护主义 游行 激情

火车 灵魂 照顾残障 爱 猪皮 玩偶 环保 环境 现象 甜美的 电视节目 电话 画展 疲劳 皇后区的艺术

目标 礼物 社会 社区 禁止的 秋天 移民 等待 紧张 职员 聚会 自由 舞蹈 艺术 绘画 花 落差 蒸发 街道

见鬼！ 警察 访谈 购物 足球 边界 运动 运动 足球小子续篇 运输 铁栅栏 长眠的 雀斑 集市 雨 音乐

风景 食物 饮食 骷髅 黄昏

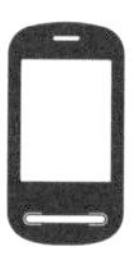

you*PLURAL
Latino and Asian immigrants
New York, United States
2011–13

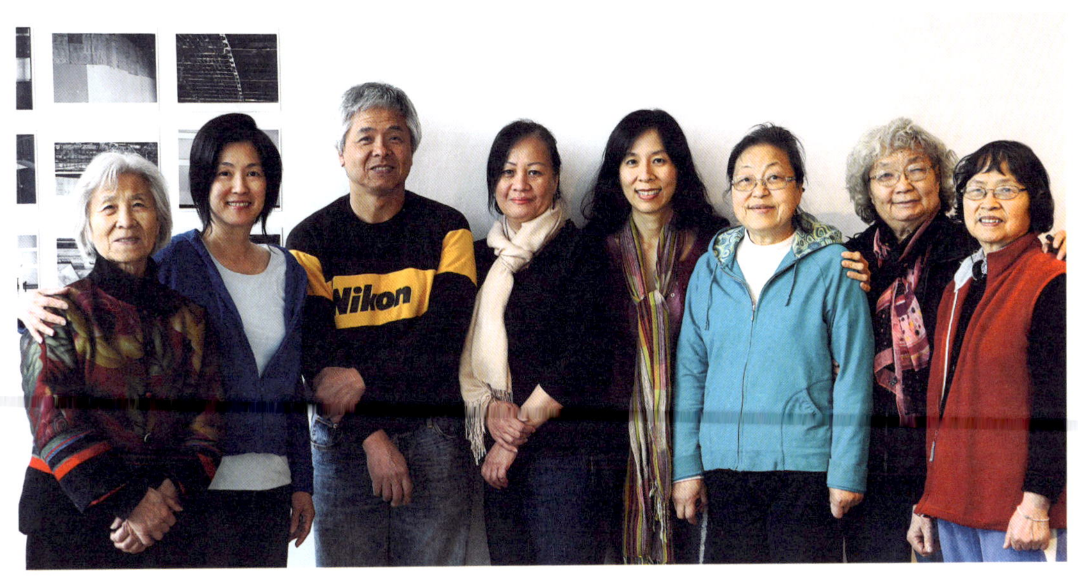

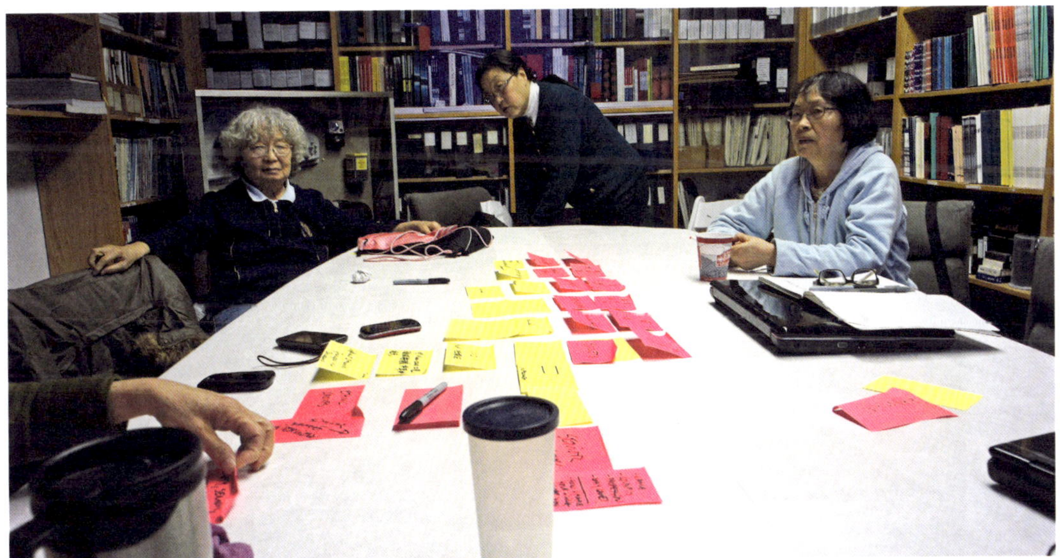

Participants and meeting table for *you*PLURAL*

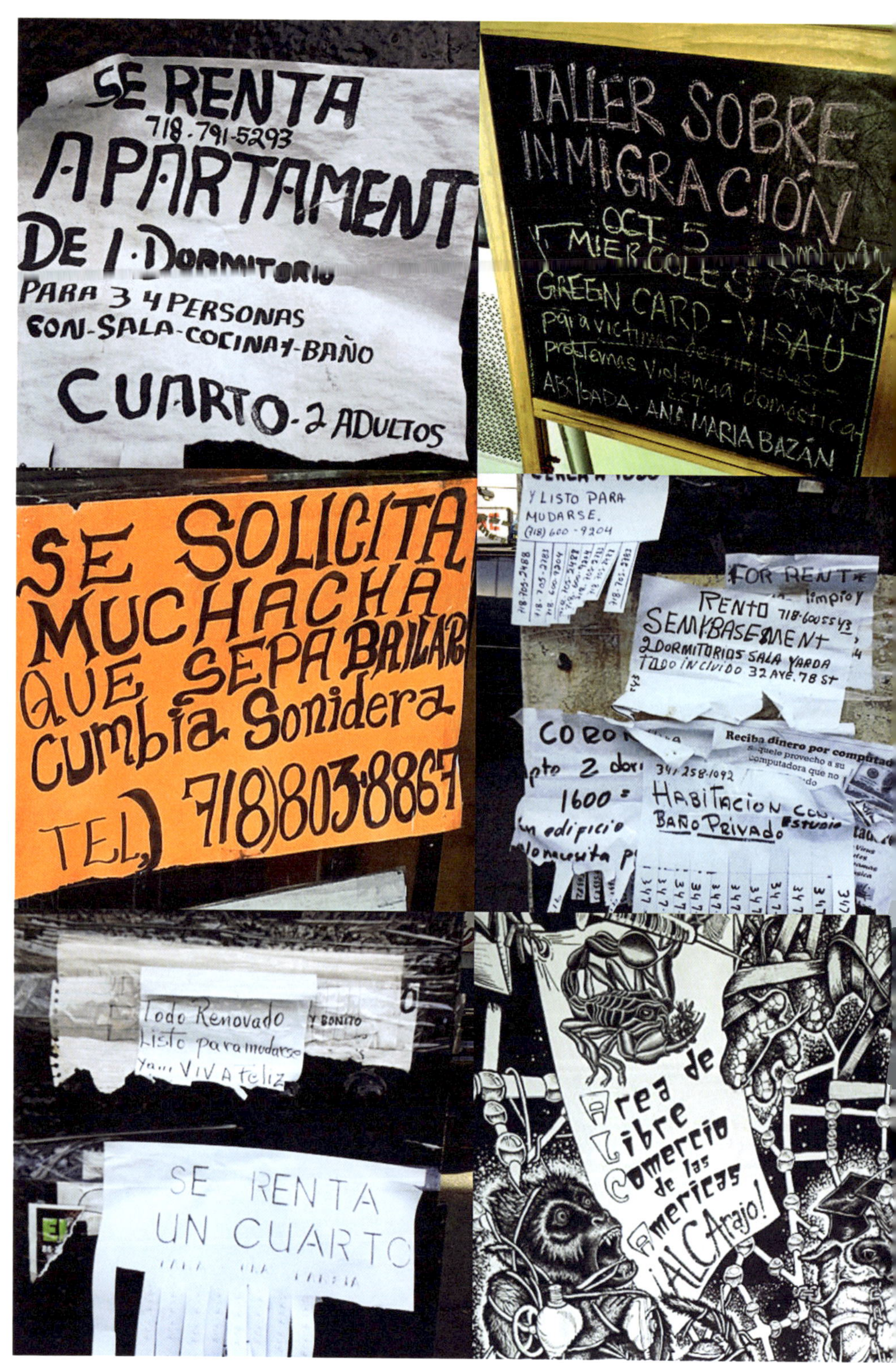

Selection of images of street advertising published by participants in the project *you*PLURAL*

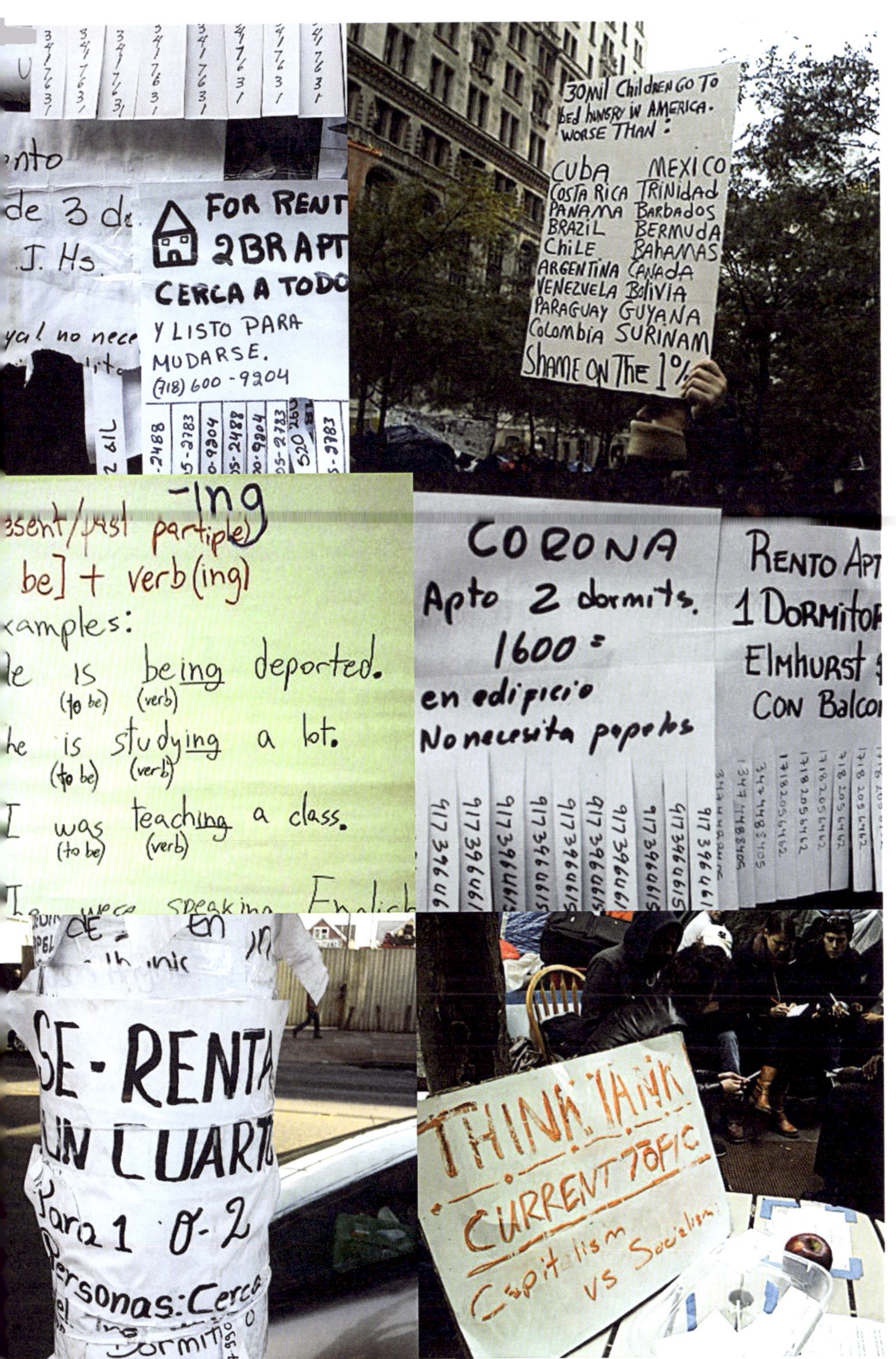
34/763/
FOR RENT
2 BR APT
CERCA A TODO
Y LISTO PARA
MUDARSE.
(718) 600-9204
de 3 d
J. Hs
y al no nece
30 mil children go to
bed hungry in America.
worse than:
CUBA   MEXICO
COSTA RICA   TRINIDAD
PANAMA   BARBADOS
BRAZIL   BERMUDA
CHILE   BAHAMAS
ARGENTINA   CANADA
VENEZUELA   BOLIVIA
PARAGUAY   GUYANA
COLOMBIA   SURINAM
Shame on the 1%
-ing
ssent/past partiple)
be] + verb(ing)
xamples:
e   is   being deported.
   (to be) (verb)
he is studying a lot.
   (to be) (verb)
I was teaching a class.
   (to be)   (verb)
CORONA
Apto 2 dormits.
1600 =
en edificio
No necesita papeles
RENTO APT
1 DORMITOR
Elmhurst $
CON Balco
917 396 46
SE-RENTA
UN CUARTO
para 1 0-2
Personas: Cerca
THINK TANK
CURRENT TOPIC
Capitalism
vs Socialism

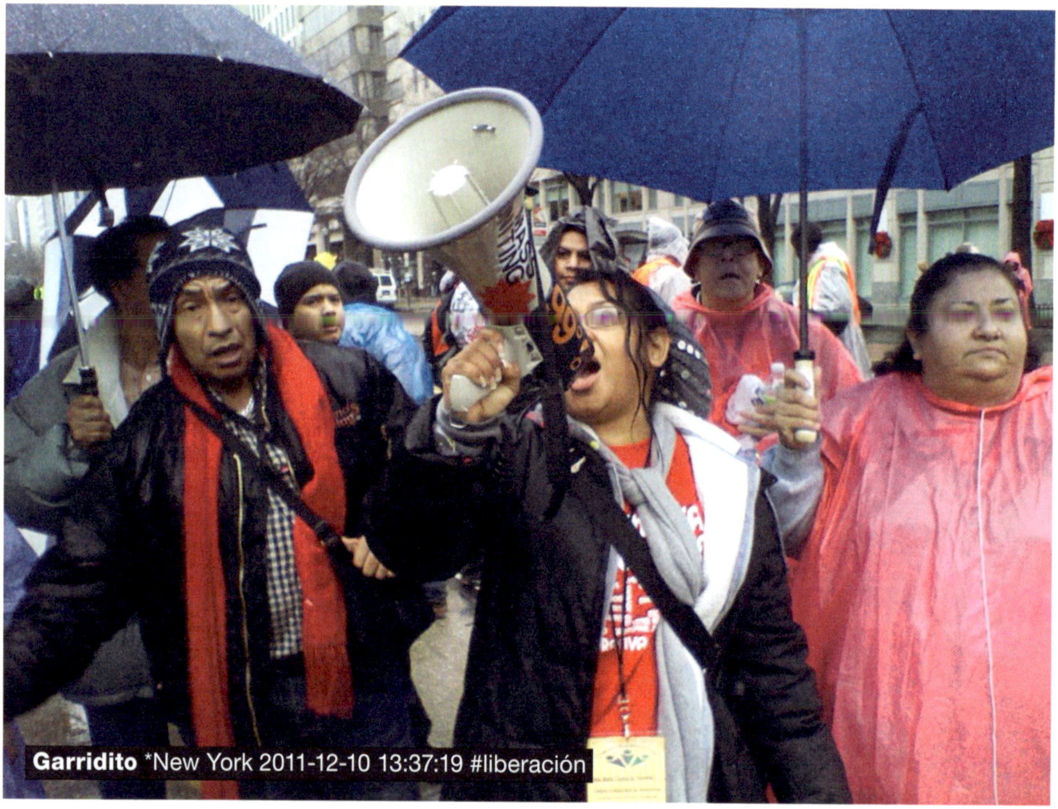

Garridito *New York 2011-12-10 13:37:19 #liberación

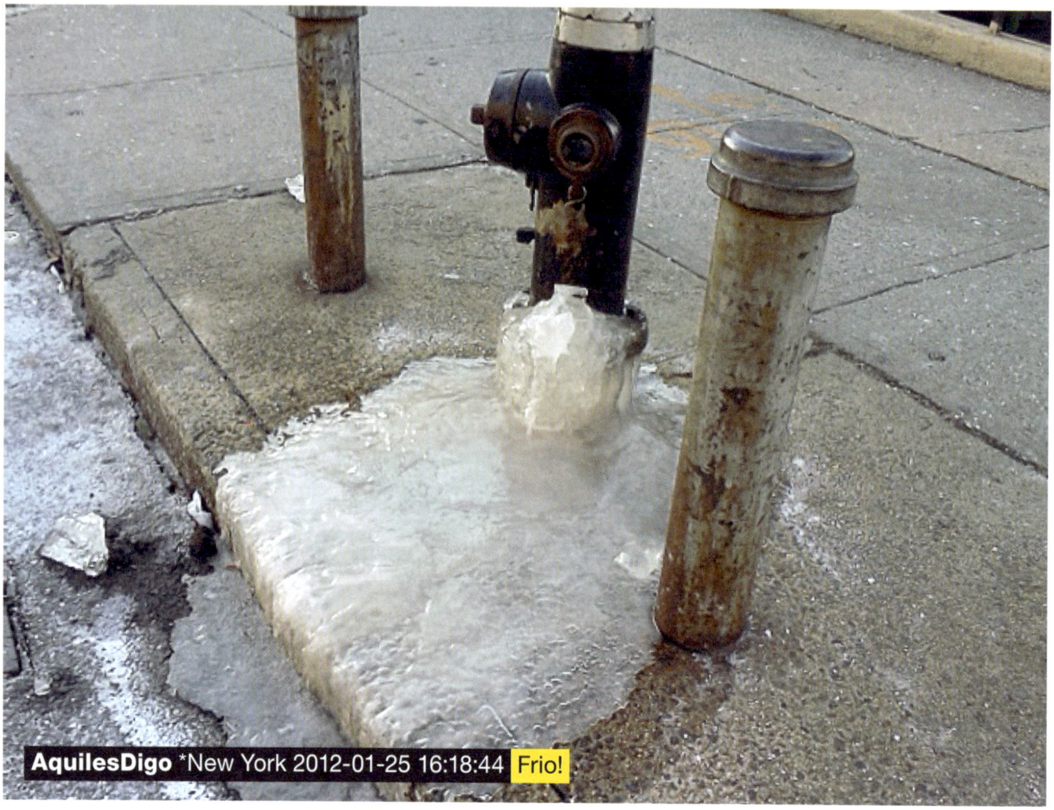

AquilesDigo *New York 2012-01-25 16:18:44 Frio!

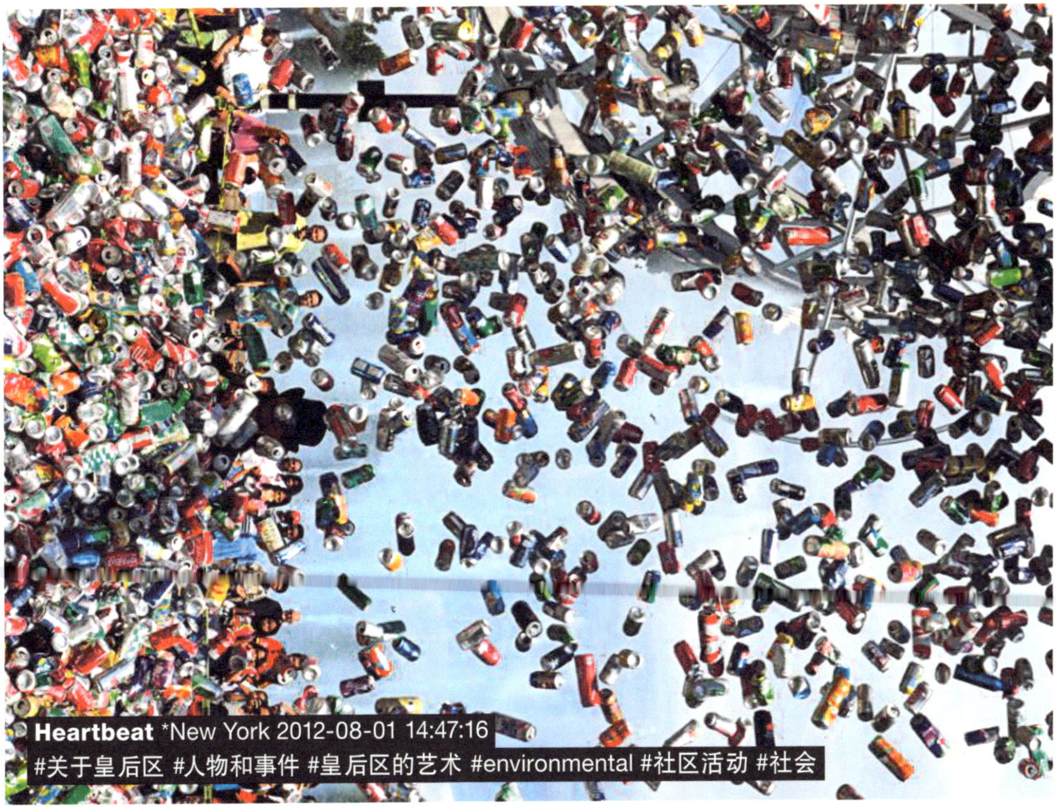

Heartbeat *New York 2012-08-01 14:47:16
#关于皇后区 #人物和事件 #皇后区的艺术 #environmental #社区活动 #社会

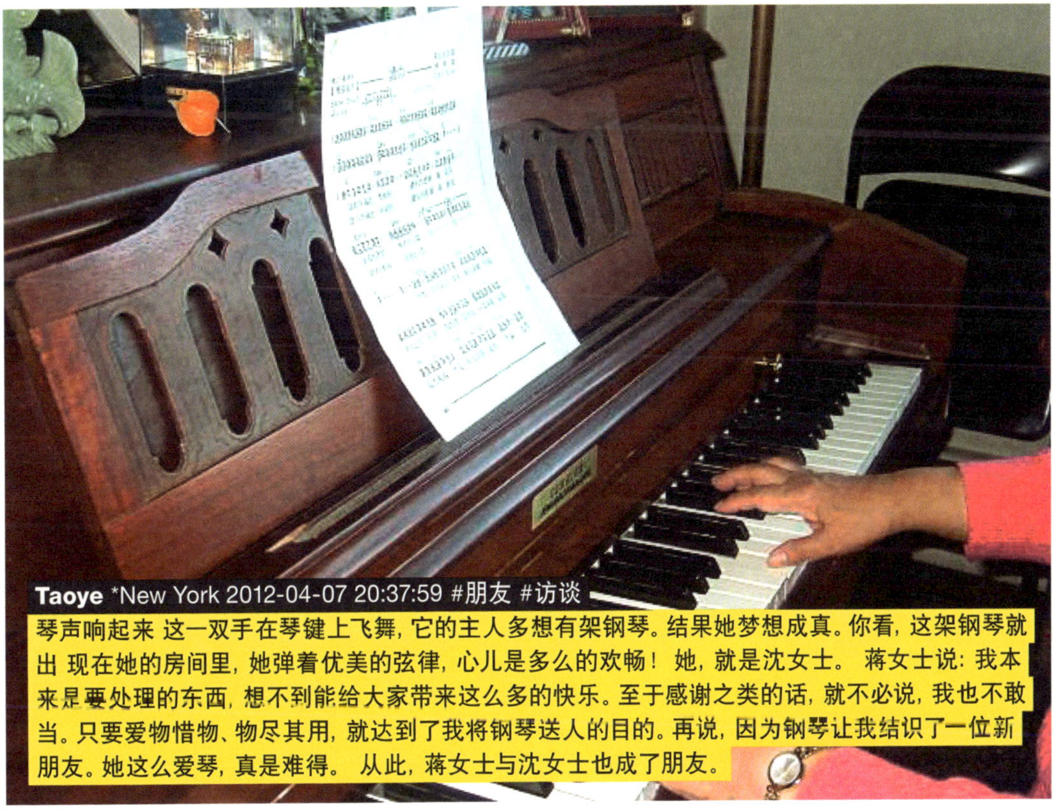

Taoye *New York 2012-04-07 20:37:59 #朋友 #访谈

琴声响起来 这一双手在琴键上飞舞，它的主人多想有架钢琴。结果她梦想成真。你看，这架钢琴就出 现在她的房间里，她弹着优美的弦律，心儿是多么的欢畅！ 她，就是沈女士。 蒋女士说：我本来是要处理的东西，想不到能给大家带来这么多的快乐。至于感谢之类的话，就不必说，我也不敢当。只要爱物惜物、物尽其用，就达到了我将钢琴送人的目的。再说，因为钢琴让我结识了一位新朋友。她这么爱琴，真是难得。 从此，蒋女士与沈女士也成了朋友。

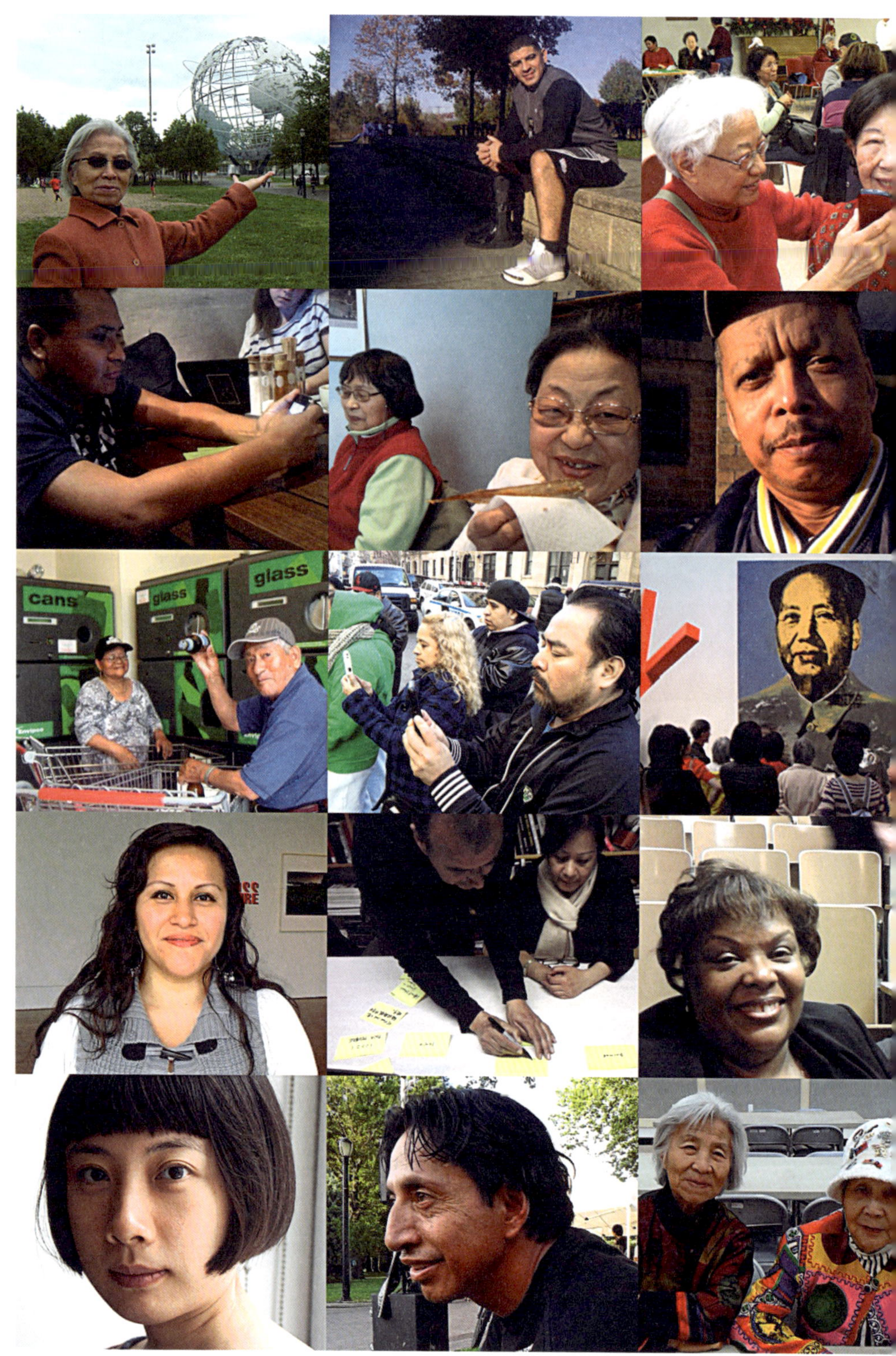

Selection of images taken by participants in the project *you*PLURAL*

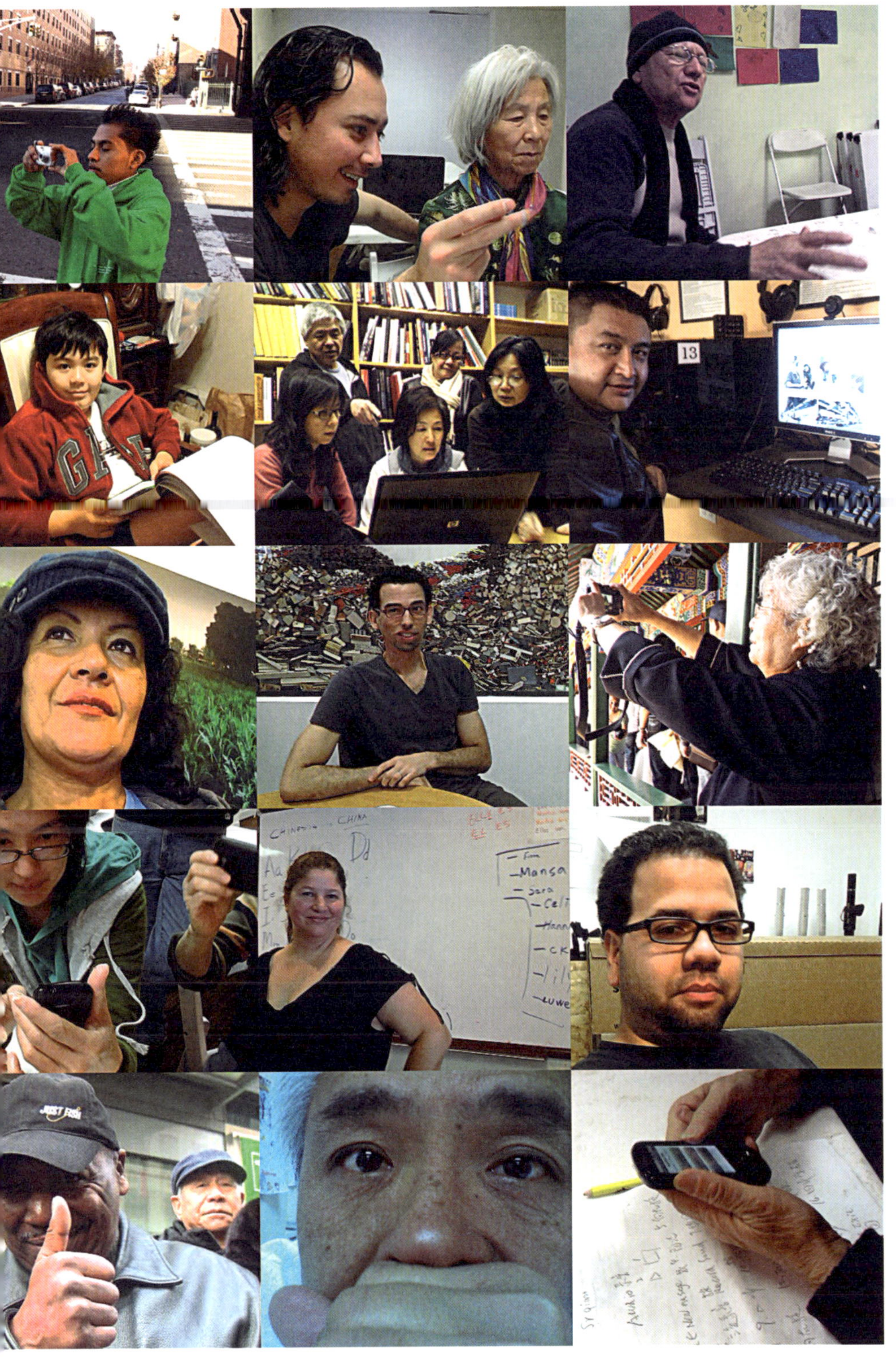

à louer **aberrations** ascenseurs aucune porte automatique **barré!** bars

bravo! cellulaires concordia **constructions** cossins sur le chemin

cul-de-sac danger dépanneurs détour forcé **discrimination** drôle

Échec! education élections QC 2012 entrées equipement adapte

escaliers félicitations fermé à tous **flamblants neufs** habitation hiver

incivilités interviews jazz festival L'ecole du barreau! Maison du barreau du quebec!

marches metrô **mobilier urbain**

neige neuf No push door **Nuitblanche 2013** obstacle

passage piétons portes **presque...** **regard des gens**

rencontre restaurants rue Seuil **sous-terrain** surprise **temporaires**

terrasses toilettes **transports** tres haut

trottoirs Vente trottoir

MONTRÉAL*in/accessible
People with limited mobility
Montreal, Canada
2012–13

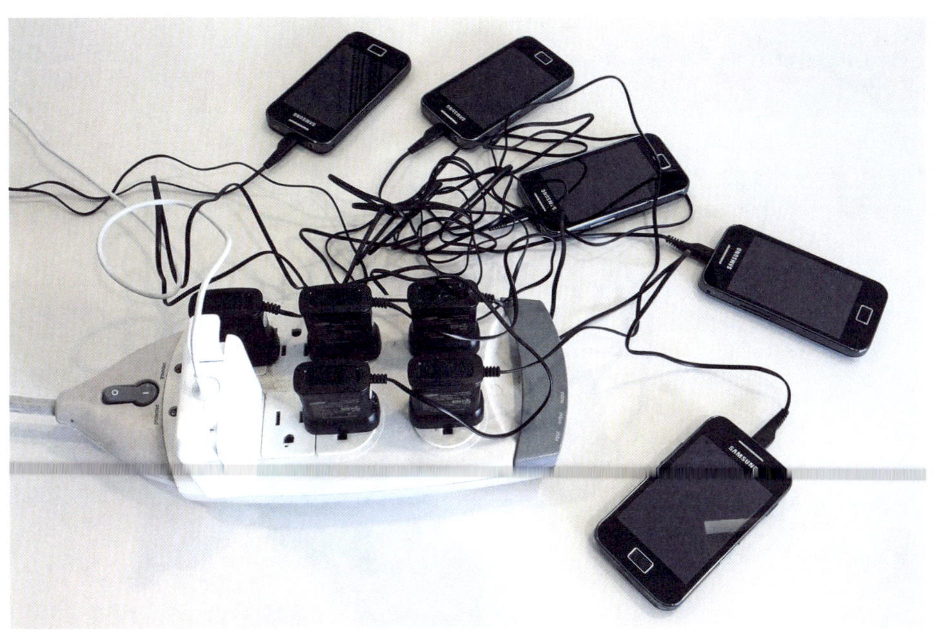

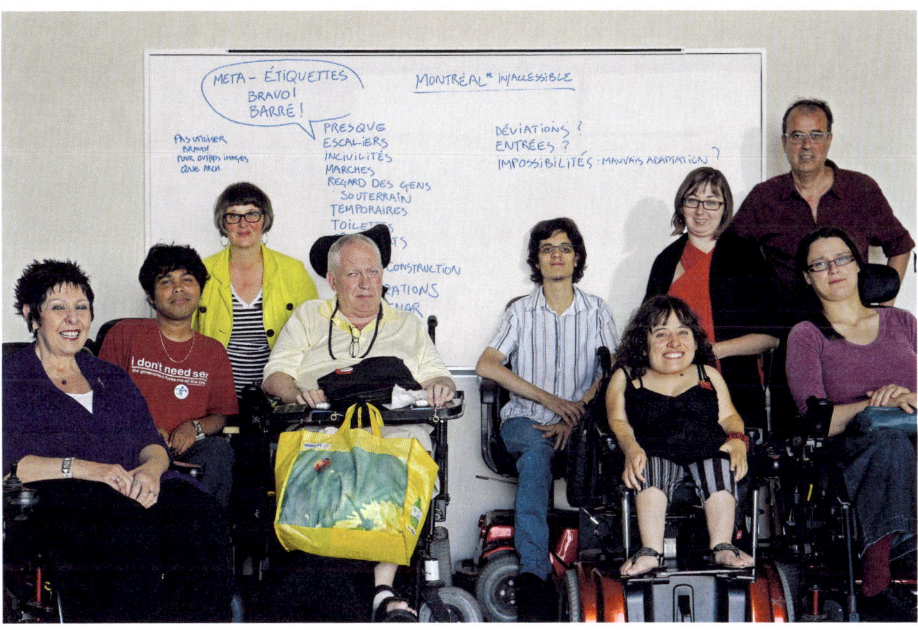

Telephones and participants in the project *MONTRÉAL*in/accessible*

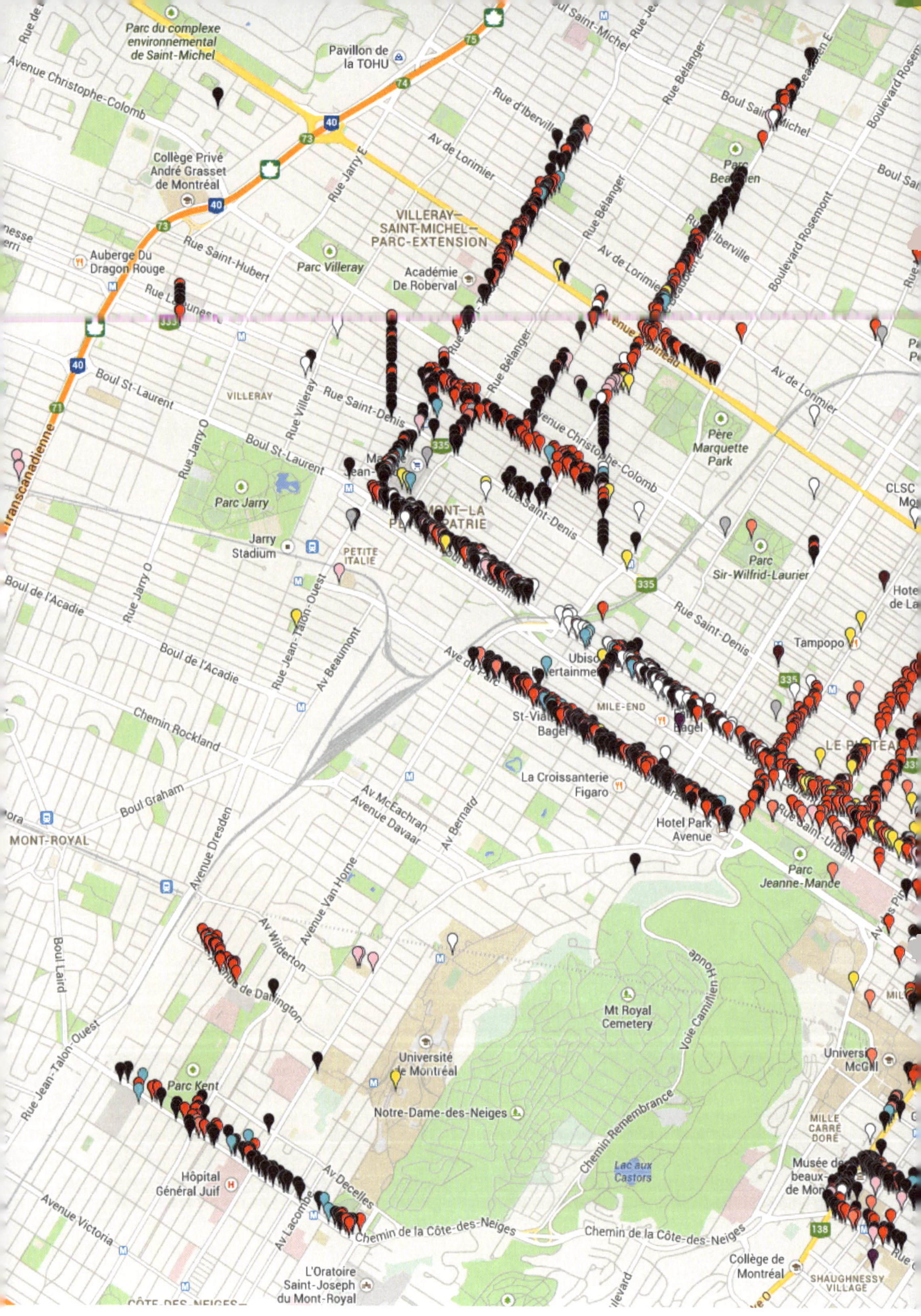

Overall view of the collective mapping of Montreal

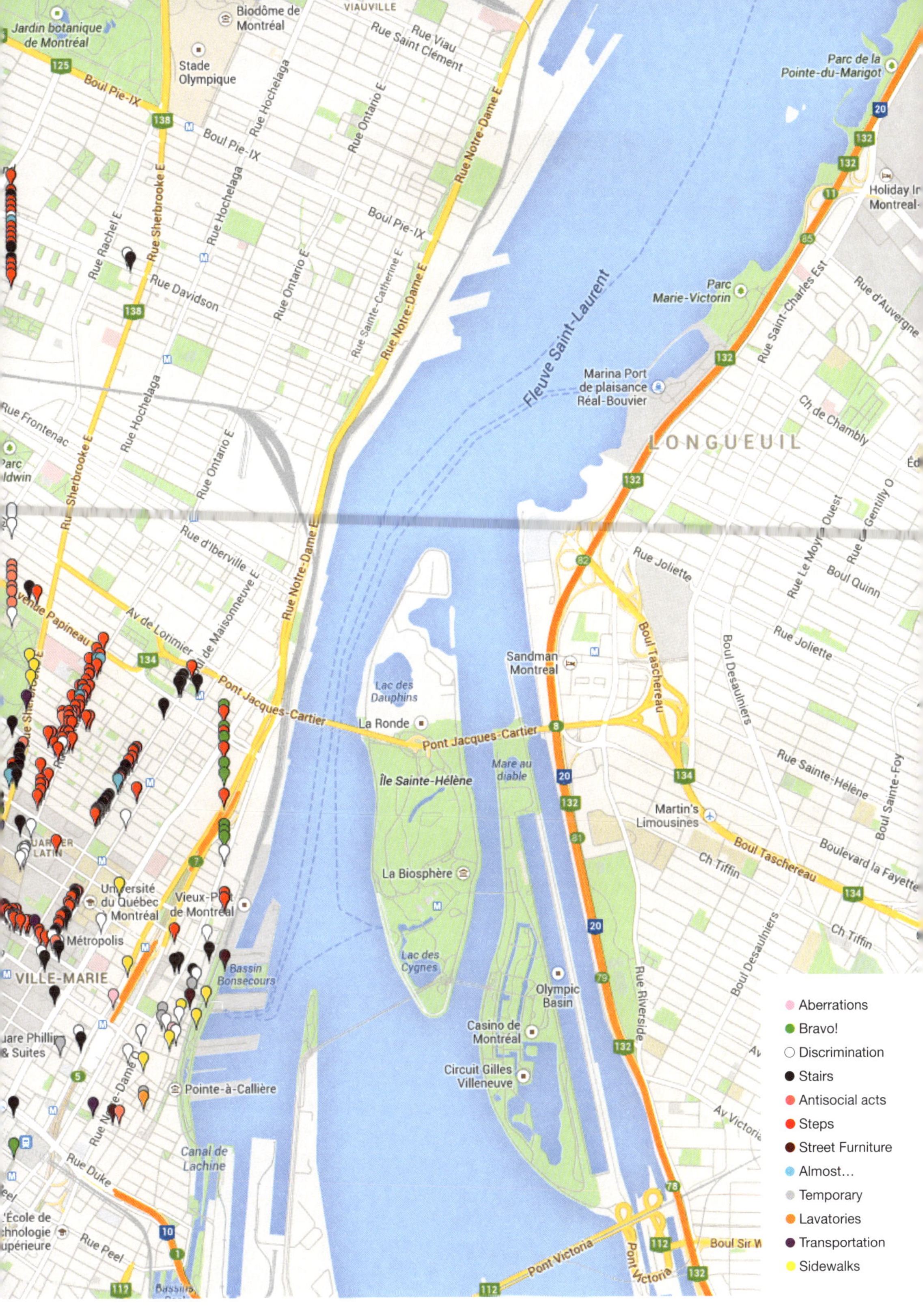
Jardin botanique de Montréal
Biodôme de Montréal
VIAUVILLE
Rue Viau
Rue Saint Clément
Parc de la Pointe-du-Marigot
Boul Pie-IX
Stade Olympique
Boul Pie-IX
Rue Hochelaga
Rue Notre-Dame E
Holiday In Montreal-
Rue Rachel E
Rue Sherbrooke E
Rue Hochelaga
Rue Ontario E
Boul Pie-IX
Rue Saint-Charles Est
Rue d'Auvergne
Rue Davidson
Rue Sainte-Catherine E
Rue Notre-Dame E
Parc Marie-Victorin
Fleuve Saint-Laurent
Rue Frontenac
Rue Hochelaga
Rue Ontario E
Marina Port de plaisance Réal-Bouvier
Ch de Chambly
Parc Idwin
Rue Sherbrooke E
LONGUEUIL
Ed
Rue d'Iberville E
Rue Notre-Dame E
Rue Joliette
Rue Le Moyne Ouest
Rue Gentilly O
Boul Quinn
venue Papineau
Av de Lorimier
Boul de Maisonneuve E
Sandman Montreal
Rue Joliette
Boul Taschereau
Boul Desaulniers
Pont Jacques-Cartier
Lac des Dauphins
La Ronde
Rue Sainte-Hélène
Boul Sainte-Foy
e Sherbrooke
Mare au diable
Martin's Limousines
Boulevard la Fayette
QUARTER LATIN
Île Sainte-Hélène
Ch Tiffin
Boul Taschereau
Université du Québec Montréal
Vieux-Port de Montréal
La Biosphère
Ch Tiffin
Métropolis
Lac des Cygnes
Bassin Bonsecours
Olympic Basin
Rue Riverside
VILLE-MARIE
Casino de Montréal
uare Phillip & Suites
Pointe-à-Callière
Circuit Gilles Villeneuve
Av Victoria
Rue Notre-Dame
Canal de Lachine
Rue Duke
eel
'École echnologie upérieure
Rue Peel
Pont Victoria
Boul Sir W
Pont Victoria
Bassins
Aberrations
Bravo!
Discrimination
Stairs
Antisocial acts
Steps
Street Furniture
Almost...
Temporary
Lavatories
Transportation
Sidewalks

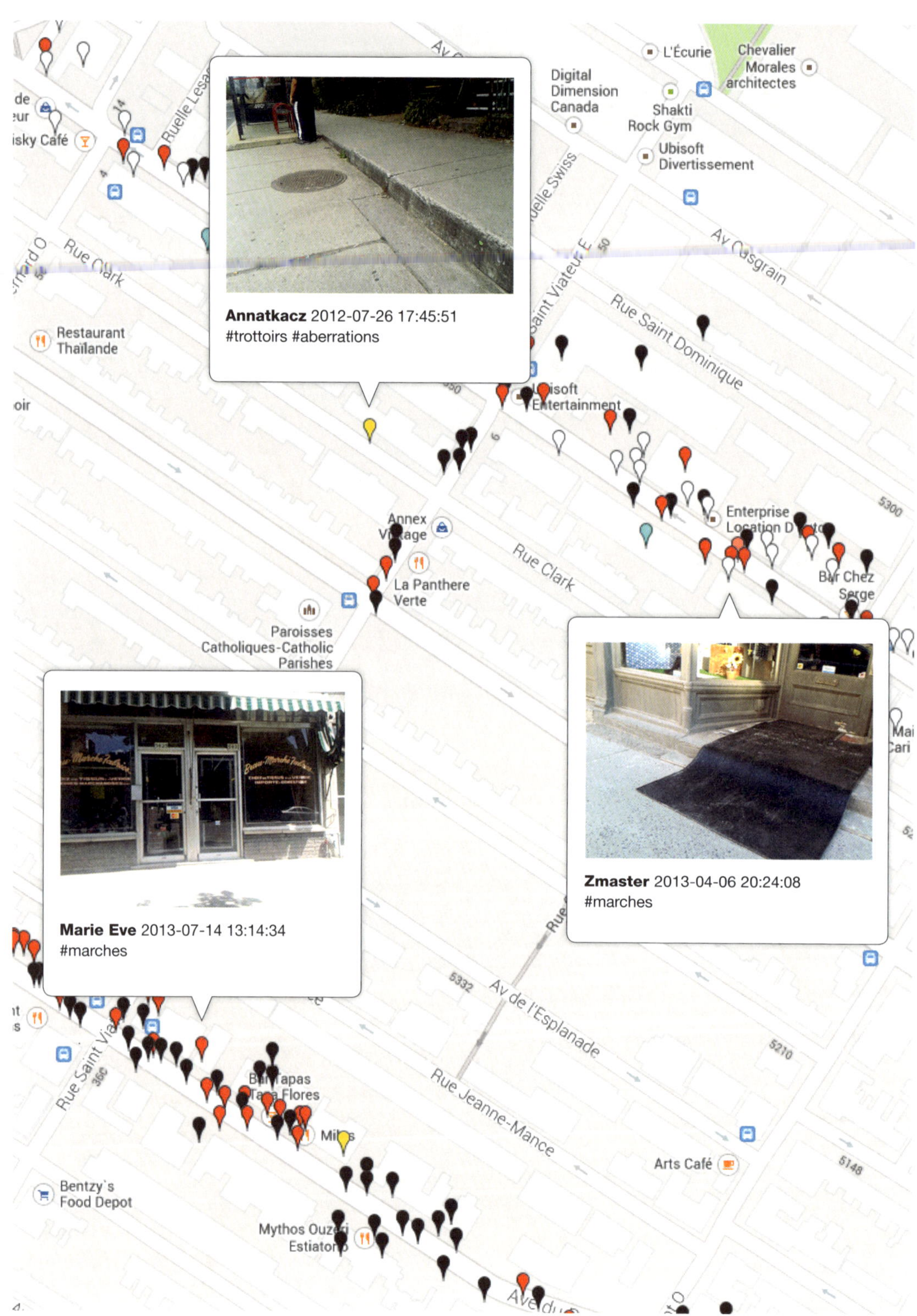

Details of a collective mapping of Montreal

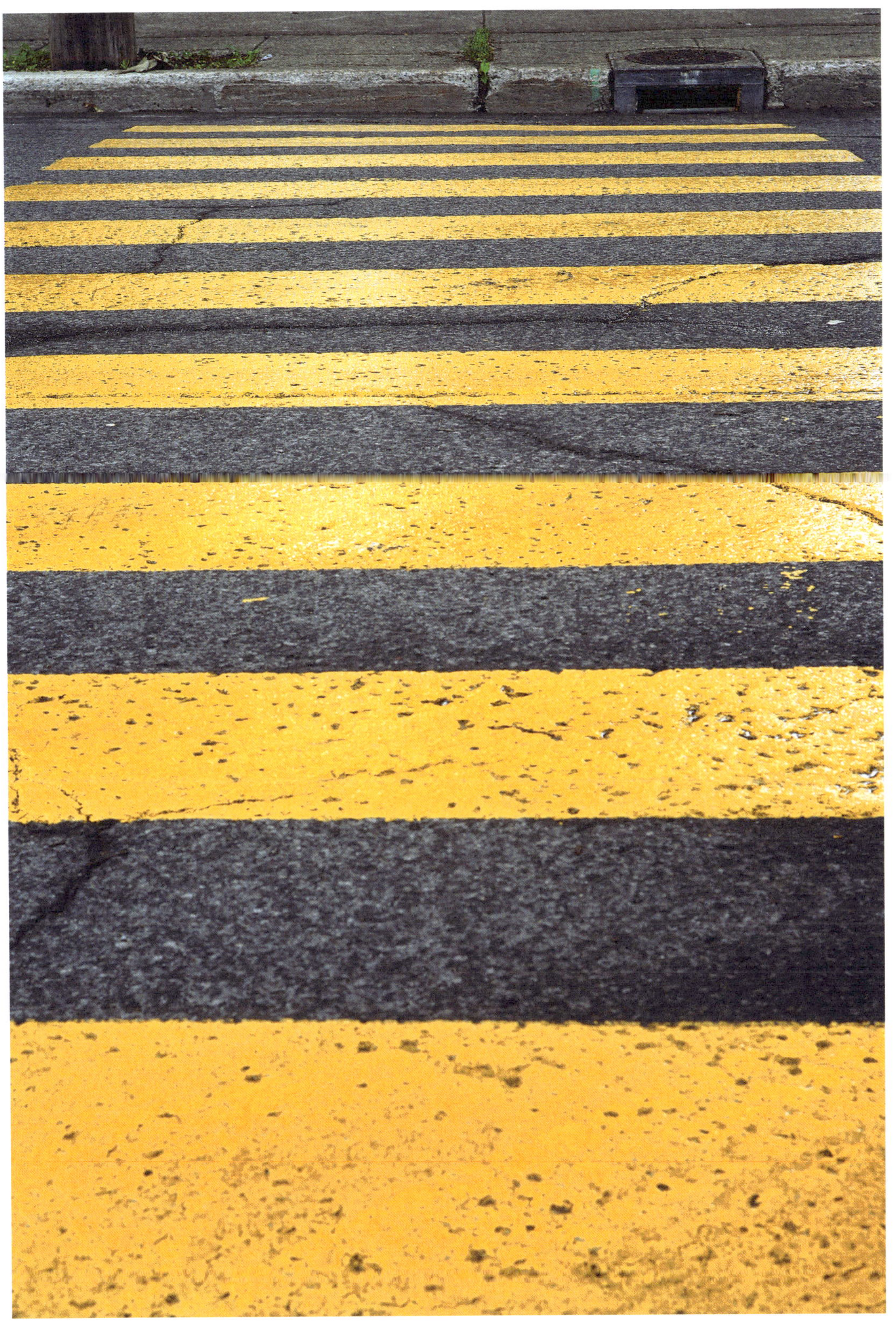

Antoni Abad
Lleida, 1956. Based in Barcelona

EDUCATION

1995–97 MFA, European Media Master, Institut Universitari de l'Audiovisual, Universitat Pompeu Fabra, Barcelona, Spain

1974–79 History of Art University Degree, Facultat de Geografia i Història, Universitat de Barcelona, Barcelona, Spain

GUEST ARTIST IN RESIDENCE

1994–95 *The Nomad Residency*, The Banff Centre for the Arts, Banff, Alberta, Canada

VISITING POSITIONS

2011 **Mobile Art Lab**, Workshop director and tutor, Hangar.org, Barcelona, Spain

2010–14 **University Master in Digital Arts**, Guest lecturer, IDEC, Universitat Pompeu Fabra, Barcelona, Spain

2009 **¿Interactivos? El proceso como paradigma**, Tutor, LABoral Centro de Arte y Creación Industrial, Gijón, Spain

2008 **Almost Perfect Residency**, Peer advisor, The Banff Centre for the Arts, Banff, Alberta, Canada

2007 **canal*BAIRES**, Workshop at Centro Cultural de España, Buenos Aires, Ar-gentina

2003 **ensayo*GENERAL**, Workshop at La Casa Encendida, Madrid, Spain

2000–01 **Artiste-professeur invité** at Le Fresnoy, Studio national des arts contemporains, Tourcoing, France

CONFERENCES

2013 **Differential Mobilities**, Concordia University, Montreal/Quebec, Canada
Catch Forum 2013, Prague, Czech Republic

2012 **The 9th Republic: Dignity of the People** (Key speaker), Nabi Center, Seoul, Korea
Seminário estéticas das periferias, Centro Cultural São Paulo, Brazil

2010 **Imagen, cultura y tecnología: medios**, Universidad Carlos III, Madrid, Spain
Mobilefest 2010, Museum da Imagem e do Som, São Paulo, Brazil

2009 **Arte contemporáneo y público, ¿una relación imposible?**, Valencia, Spain

2008 **Créateurs singuliers**, Centre d'Art Contemporain, Geneva, Switzerland

2007 **Vivo Arte.mov Festival**, Belo Horizonte, Brazil
canal*MOTOBOY, Centro Cultural São Paulo, Brazil

2006 **Ars Electronica Festival**, Linz, Austria

2005 **Padrões aos Pedaços**, Fórum Permanente, Paço das Artes, São Paulo, Brazil
Banquete 05, Centro Cultural Conde Duque, Madrid, Spain

AWARDS

2009 **Innovae**, Fundación Española para la Ciencia y la Tecnología, Madrid, Spain

2008 **Orilaxé/Unesco** award, Rio de Janeiro, Brazil

2006 **Golden Nica Digital Communities**, Prix Ars Electronica, Linz, Austria
Premi Nacional d'arts visuals, awarded by the Catalan Government, Spain

2003 **Multimedia City Award**, Barcelona, Spain
Honorary Mention Net Vision, Prix Ars Electronica, Linz, Austria

1998 **Premi Ciutat de Barcelona** (Plastic arts), Barcelona, Spain

MEGAFONE.NET: COLLABORATIVE PROJECTS USING CELL PHONES

2012–13 **MONTRÉAL*in/accessible** – Limited mobility participants. Concordia University and RAPLIQ Association. Montreal/Quebec, Canada

2011–13 **you*PLURAL** – Latino and Asian Immigrants. Fundación Botín, Queens Museum's New Yorkers program and Immigrant Movement International, New York, USA

2010–11 **The Blind Point of View** – Blind and visually impaired participants. Fundación "la Caixa," Barcelona, Spain

2009–11 **canal*SAHARAUI** – Sahrawi refugees. ARTifariti, Refugee camps near Tindouf, Algeria

2009–10 **canal*TEMPORAL** – Displaced and demobilized participants. Universidad de Caldas, Manizales, Colombia

2008 **GENÈVE*accessible** – Limited mobility participants. Centre d'Art Contemporain and Ville de Genève, Geneva, Switzerland

2007–14 **canal*MOTOBOY** – Motorcycle messengers. Centro Cultural São Paulo, Centro Cultural de España and Seacex, São Paolo, Brazil

2006–07 **canal*CENTRAL** – Nicaraguan migrant workers. Fundación TEOR/éTica and Seacex, San José de Costa Rica

2006/13 **BARCELONA*accessible** – Limited mobility participants. Centre d'Art Santa Mònica, Nokia Spain and Amena, Barcelona, Spain

2005 **canal*INVISIBLE** – Sex workers. La Casa Encendida, Madrid, Spain
canal*GITANO – Young Gypsies. MUSAC, León, Spain
canal*GITANO – Young Gypsies. Centre d'Art la Panera and Nokia Spain, Lleida, Spain

2004–05 **sitio*TAXI** – Taxi drivers. Centro Cultural de España,
/14 Centro Multimedia and Fundación Telefónica, Mexico City, Mexico

NET.ART PROJECTS

2003 **Z**, The Real Royal Trip, MoMA PS1, New York, USA

2002 **Z**, Le Fresnoy, Tourcoing, France
Z, MACBA, Barcelona, Spain

2001 **Z**, www.zexe.net/Z

1999   **Z**, beta, www.mecad.org/net_condition/z, ZKM
       Karlsruhe, Germany
       1.000.000, http://aleph-arts.org/1.000.000
1996   **Sisyphus**, *Macba en línia*, Universitat Pompeu
       Fabra and MACBA, Barcelona, Spain

SOLO EXHIBITIONS

2015   **megafone.net/2004–2014**, Pinacoteca do Estado
       de São Paulo, Brazil
2014   **megafone.net/2004–2014**, Matadero, Madrid,
       Spain
       megafone.net/2004–2014, MACBA, Barcelona,
       Spain
       megafone.net/2004–2014, Laboratorio de Arte
       Alameda y Centro Cultural de España,
       Mexico City, Mexico
2010   **Medidas de emergencia**, site specific installation
       at 3 metro stations, Carmel, Barcelona, Spain
2008   **GENÈVE*accessible**, Centre d'Art Contemporain,
       Geneva, Switzerland
2006   **Taxistas, gitanos y prostitutas**, Galleria Giorgio
       Persano, Turin, Italy
       BARCELONA*accessible, Centre d'Art Santa
       Mònica,   Barcelona, Spain
2005   **canal*GITANO**, Centre d'Art la Panera, Lleida, Spain
2004   **Ciencias naturales**, Centro Cultural de España,
       Mexico City, Mexico
2002   **La última cena**, Galería Oliva Arauna, Madrid, Spain
2001   **Ego**, Media Z Lounge, New Museum of
       Contemporary Art, New York, USA
       Ego, Brito Cimino Arte Contemporánea, São Paolo, Brazil
       Poslednje zelje, Umetnostna Galerija Maribor,
       Slovenia
1999   **Sísifo**, Museo de Arte Moderno, Buenos Aires,
       Argentina
       Vocabulario, Galería Oliva Arauna, Madrid, Spain
1998   **Últimos deseos**, Sala de Verónicas, Murcia, Spain
1997   **Errata**, Metrònom, Barcelona, Spain
       Medidas de emergencia, Espacio Uno, Museo
       Nacional Centro de Arte Reina Sofía, Madrid, Spain
1996   **Últimos deseos**, Museo de San Telmo, San
       Sebastian, Spain
       Sísifo, Galería Oliva Arauna, Madrid, Spain
       Últimos deseos, Círculo de Bellas Artes, Madrid, Spain
1995   **Últimes coincidències**, El Roser, Lleida, Spain
       De fuerza mayor, Museo de Teruel, Teruel, Spain
1994   **En la mesura del possible**, Galeria Antoni Estrany,
       Barcelona, Spain
       Mesures menors, Galeria Antoni Estrany,
       Barcelona, Spain
1991   **Museu Morera**, Lleida, Spain
       Galeria Benet Costa, Barcelona, Spain
       Galería Oliva Arauna, Madrid, Spain
1989   Galeria Benet Costa, Barcelona, Spain
       Esculturas 1985–1987, Universitat de València,
       Valencia, Spain
1987   Chisenhale Gallery, London, United Kingdom
       Galeria Thomas Carstens, Barcelona, Spain
1986   Espai 10, Fundació Joan Miró, Barcelona, Spain

BIENNIALS

2013   **Web Arte**, Bienal de Curitiba, Curitiba, Brazil
       FotobienalMASP, Museo de Arte de São Paulo,
       Brazil
2009   **Projetavéis**, Bienal Mercosul, Porto Alegre, Brazil
2008   **Youniverse**, III Bienal de Arte Contemporáneo de
       Sevilla, Spain
2004   I Bienal de Arte Contemporáneo de Sevilla, Spain
1999   **dAPERTutto**, Biennale di Venezia, Venice, Italy
       II Bienal Iberoamericana, Palacio de Osambela,
       Lima, Peru

GROUP EXHIBITIONS

2014   **Haver fet un lloc**, Fundació Joan Miró, Barcelona,
       Spain
       Sobre (el) paper, Fundació Suñol, Barcelona, Spain
       Double Sense, FRAC Corse, France
2013   **Web Arte**, Bienal de Curitiba, Brazil
       FotobienalMASP, Museo de Arte de São Paulo,
       Brazil
       Continuum, Fundació Suñol, Barcelona, Spain
       Itinerarios, Fundación Botín, Santander, Spain
2012   **299 artistes, 24 comissaris, 23 agents…**, Galeria
       Estrany - De la Mota, Barcelona, Spain
2011   **Barcelona col.lecciona**, Fundació Francisco
       Godia, Barcelona, Spain
       10to10, European Culture Congress, Centennial
       Hall, Wroclaw, Poland
       Mobile Art. Experiències mòbils, Fundació
       Francisco Godia, Barcelona
       Relats encadenats, Centre d'Art la Panera, Lleida,
       Spain
2010   Bienal Internacional de Arte Contemporáneo Ula-
       2010, Mérida, Venezuela
       Marhaba!, Centro Andaluz de Arte Contemporáneo,
       Seville, Spain
       Pixelache Festival, Helsinki, Finland
       III Bienal de Arte Contemporáneo Fundación Once,
       Complejo El Águila, Madrid, Spain
       Libertad, igualdad, fraternidad, Centro Atlántico
       de Arte Moderno, Las Palmas de Gran Canaria,
       Spain
       La fuerza de la palabra, Instituto Cultural
       Cabañas, Guadalajara, Mexico
2009   **Projetavéis**, Bienal Mercosul, Porto Alegre, Brazil
       **banquet_nodes and networks. Netzkultur in
       Spanien**, ZKM, Karlsruhe, Germany
       Libertad, igualdad, fraternidad, La Lonja,
       Zaragoza; Sala Exposiciones Alcalá 31, Comunidad
       de Madrid; Centro de Arte Huarte, Pamplona, Spain
       Cartografías disidentes, Centro Cultural de
       España, Mexico City, Mexico; Centro de
       Formación para la Cooperación, Cartagena
       de Indias, Colombia; Centro de Artes Provinciales,
       Holguín, Cuba; Centro Cultural San Martín, Buenos
       Aires, Argentina; Biblioteca Nacional José Martí,
       Havana, Cuba

2008   **Youniverse**, III Bienal de Arte Contemporáneo de
       Sevilla, Spain
       Cartografías disidentes, Museo de Arte
       Contemporáneo de Santiago de Chile; Centro
       Cultural São Paulo and Oi Futuro de Rio de Janeiro,
       Brazil; Museo de Arte Contemporáneo de Caracas,
       Venezuela
       Máquinas & almas, Museo Nacional Centro de
       Arte Reina Sofía, Madrid, Spain
       Consulta, Centre d'Art Santa Mònica, Barcelona,
       Spain
       banquete_nodos y redes, LABoral Centro de Arte,
       Gijón, Spain
       1970–2001, Fundació Suñol, Barcelona, Spain
       Der diskrete charme der technologie, ZKM,
       Karlsruhe, Germany
       El discreto encanto de la tecnología, MEIAC,
       Badajoz, Spain
2007   **1915–1995**, Fundació Suñol, Barcelona, Spain
       Anamnesis, IV Bienal de Valencia, Spain; Col.lecció
       d'Art Contemporani de l'Ajuntament de
       Lleida, Centre d'Art la Pane-ra, Lleida, Spain
2006   **Contos dixitais**, Centro Galego de Arte
       Contemporànea, Santiago de Compostela, Spain
       Estrecho dudoso: tráficos, Fundación TEOR/
       éTica, San José de Costa Rica
       SonarMàtica, CCCB, Barcelona, Spain
2005   **Síntesis: 15 años de becas Endesa**, Edificio
       Endesa, Madrid, Spain
       Itinerarios y souvenirs, Centro Cultural de España
       en Buenos Aires, Argentina
       Seducidos polo accidente, Fundación Luis
       Seoane, A Coruña, Spain
       Banquete 05, Centro Cultural Conde Duque,
       Madrid, Spain
2004   I Bienal Internacional de Arte Contemporáneo de
       Sevilla, Seville, Spain
       Versâo brasileira, Galeria Brito Cimino, São Paulo,
       Brazil
       Depicting love, Museo Nacional Centro de Arte
       Reina Sofía, Madrid, Spain; Centro Párraga, Murcia,
       Spain; Künstlerhaus Bethanien, Berlin, Germany
       A Arañeira. A Colección, Centro Galego de Arte
       Contemporánea, Santiago de Compostela, Spain
2003   **El real viaje real / The Real Royal Trip**, MoMA
       PS1, New York, USA
       Prix Ars Electronica 2003, Linz, Austria
       La conquista de la ubicuidad, CAAM, Las Palmas
       de Gran Canaria and Centro Párraga, Murcia, Spain
       25 hrs, Mostra Internacional de Videoart, Barcelona,
       Spain
       C2, Centre d'Art la Panera, Lleida, Spain
       **Himmel Schwer: Transformationen der
       Schwerkraft**, Kunshalle Brandts Odense, Denmark
       and Landesmuseum, Graz, Austria
       25 años de arte en España, Atarazanas,
       Valencia, Spain
       Pintar palabras, Instituto Cervantes, Berlin,
       Germany; New York, USA
2002   **Big Sur**, Hamburger Banhof, Berlin, Germany
       //Paralela, São Paulo, Brazil

       Necessità di relazione, Galleria Civica di Arte
       Contemporanea, Trento, Italy
       Gótico..., pero exótico, Artium, Vitoria, Spain
       brg 2000, Braga, Portugal
2001   **Revolving Doors**, Apexart, New York, USA
       It doesn't work, Künstlerhaus Palais Thurn und
       Taxis, Bregenz, Austria
       Sem Fronteiras, Santander Cultural, Porto Alegre,
       Brazil
       Vostestaquí, Palau de la Virreina, Barcelona Art
       Report 2001, Barcelona, Spain
       A Kiss is Just a Kiss, Galeria Estrany - De la Mota,
       Barcelona, Spain
       Escenarios domésticos, Koldo Mitxelena, San
       Sebastian, Spain
       Panorama 2, Le Fresnoy, Tourcoing, France
       El segle de Cristòfol, Centre Cultural de la
       Fundació "la Caixa," Lleida, Spain
2000   **Art Forum**, Berlin, Germany
       Mostra d'Arts Electròniques, Centre d'Art Santa
       Mònica, Barcelona, Spain
       **2 milenios en la historia de España: año 1000 -
       año 2000**, Centro Cultural de la Villa, Madrid, Spain
       Indoméstico, Imatra, Bilbao, Spain
       Festival Penedès, Capella de l'Antic Hospital,
       Sant Sadurní, Spain
1999   **dAPERTutto**, Arsenale, Biennale di Venezia,
       Venice, Italy
       II Bienal Iberoamericana, Palacio de Osambela,
       Lima, Peru
       net_condition, ZKM, Karlsruhe, Germany
       Ragtime, Galería Estrany - De la Mota, Barcelona,
       Spain
       Tuscia Electa, Greve in Chianti, Italy
       Cuerpos contaminados, Museo Alejandro Otero,
       Caracas, Venezuela
       II Biennal Leandre Cristofol, Lleida, Spain
       Dobles vides, Museu de Zoologia, Barcelona,
       Spain
       SonarMàtica, CCCB, Barcelona, Spain
       Cuerpo y habitat, Centro Cultural Montehermoso,
       Vitoria-Gasteiz, Spain
       PHE99, Galería Oliva Arauna, Madrid, Spain
       Fardel de Dissidências I, Fundación Luis Seoane,
       A Coruña, Spain
       Existencias agotadas, Mercado de Fuencarral,
       Madrid, Spain
1998   **Het subjective daarzijn**, Museum van
       Hedendaagse Kunst Antwerpen, Antwerp,
       Belgium
       Novas incorporacións, Centro Galego de
       Arte Contemporánea, Santiago de Compostela,
       Spain
       Fisuras na percepción, 25 Bienal de Pontevedra,
       Pontevedra, Spain
       Mostra d'Arts Electròniques, Centre d'Art Santa
       Mònica, Barcelona, Spain
       Coincidències, Museum Dhondt-Dhaenens,
       Deurle, Belgium
       Iluminar y oscurecer, St. Michael's Church,
       Honiton, United Kingdom

1997 **Procesos**, Casa Grace, Lima, Peru
Projected Sites, Cummings Art Center, New
London (Conn), USA
Of Mudlarkers and Measurers, Agnes Etherington
Art Centre, Kingston and Ottawa Art Gallery, Canada
Transformación, Fundación Marcelino Botín,
Santander, Spain
Carambolage, Centre d'Art Santa Mònica,
Barcelona, Spain
Adlan i el Circ Frediani, Can Palauet, Mataró,
Barcelona, Spain

1996 **Hide and Seek**, Art Focus, Teddy Stadium,
Jerusalem, Israel
Thinking of you, Göteborg Konsthallen,
Gothenburg, Sweden
Container'96, Copenhagen, Denmark

1995 **Grøne gnister**, Charlottenborg Udstillingsbygning,
Copenhagen, Denmark
Seeing Things, Galeria Antoni Estrany, Barcelona,
Spain
Peninsulares, Galeria Graça Fonseca, Lisbon,
Portugal

1993 **El lloc enlloc**, Galeria Antoni Estrany, Barcelona,
Spain
Sembla Útil, Sala Vinçon, Barcelona, Spain
Los universos lúcidos, Arco'94, Madrid, Spain
Becarios Endesa, Arco'94, Madrid, Spain
Europa'94, Münchner Order Center, Munich,
Germany
Paradoja y metáfora, Galeria Fúcares, Almagro,
Spain

1992 **12 esculturas CE**, Expo'92, Seville, Spain
Izoztea, Arteleku, San Sebastian, Spain
Summer Invitational, Cold City Gallery, Toronto,
Canada
Becarios Endesa, Museo de Teruel, Teruel, Spain

1991 **Confrontaciones**, Palacio de Velázquez, Madrid,
Spain
Mòdul, Galeria Antoni Estrany, Barcelona, Spain
Becarios Endesa, Centre d'Art Santa Mònica,
Barcelona, Spain
L'avantgarde de la sculpture: la Catalogne,
Merignac, France
Emergences, Centre Culturel Espagnol, Paris,
France
P/A, Galeria Benet Costa, Barcelona, Spain
11 escultures, Museu de Granollers, Barcelona,
Spain

1990 **L'avantguarda de l'escultura catalana**,
Sa Llonja, Mallorca, Spain
A 4 mans, Galeria Benet Costa, Barcelona, Spain
Global Art at the Galleria, Brent Gallery, Houston,
Texas, USA
6 Katalanische Kunstler, Kunstverein
Ludwigsburg, Germany
Liquen, Galeria Àngels de la Mota, Barcelona, Spain
Ceci n'est pas une sculpture, Mosel &
Tschechow, Munich, Germany

1989 **L'avantguarda de l'escultura catalana**,
Centre d'Art Santa Mònica, Barcelona, Spain
Biennal de Barcelona, Casa de la Caritat,
Barcelona, Spain

Paper de paret, Galeria Paral.lel 39, Valencia, Spain
Escultura/Objeto, Galería Rafael Ortiz, Seville,
Spain
III Premio de Escultura Pablo Gargallo, Espacio
Pignatelli, Zaragoza, Spain

1988 **Culminació d'un Entorn**, Moll de Costa,
Tarragona, Spain
Del sòl al mur, Galeria Angels de la Mota,
Barcelona, Spain
L'H.Art, Hospitalet, Barcelona, Spain

1987 **Itinerario**, Le Plan K, Brussels, Belgium

1986 **Actitudes**, Palacio de Velázquez, Madrid, Spain

COLLECTIONS

Artium Centro-Museo Vasco de Arte
Contemporáneo, Vitoria, Spain
Auditori de Lleida, Spain
CEGAC – Fundación ARCO, Centro Galego de Arte
Contemporanea, Santiago de Compostela,
Spain
Centre d'Art la Panera – Col.lecció d'Art
Contemporani, Ajuntament de Lleida, Lleida,
Spain
Colección Caja de Ahorros del Mediterráneo,
Alicante, Spain
Colección Sanitas, Madrid, Spain
Endesa, Museo de Teruel, Teruel, Spain
Fundació "la Caixa," Barcelona, Spain
Fundación Unión Fenosa, Spain
Marugame Hirai Museum, Marugame, Japan
Museo de Arte Contemporáneo de Castilla y León
(MUSAC), León, Spain
Museo de Bellas Artes de Murcia, Spain
Museo Nacional Centro de Arte Reina Sofía
(MNCARS), Madrid, Spain
Museo Pablo Gargallo, Zaragoza, Spain
Museu d'Art Contemporani de Barcelona (MACBA),
Barcelona, Spain
Museu de Granollers, Barcelona, Spain
Museu Morera, Lleida, Spain

Projects Assistants
Berta Cervantes
Meritxell Colina
Imma Duñach

COLLECTION

**Head of the Collection,
Curator**
Antònia Maria Perelló

**Deputy Curator
of Collection**
Maria Victoria Fuentes
Ainhoa González

**Assistant Curator
of Collection**
Anna Garcia

Collection Assistant
Núria Montclús

PUBLIC PROGRAMMES
AND EDUCATION

**Head of Public Programmes
and Education**
Tonina Cerdà

**Academic Programmes
Coordinator**
Myriam Rubio

**Public Programmes
Coordinators**
Alicia Escobio
Yolanda Nicolás

Education Coordinators
Yolanda Jolis
Ariadna Miquel

Audience Attention Technician
Marta Velázquez

**Public Programmes and
Education Assistant**
David Malgà

STUDY CENTRE

Head of Archive
Maite Muñoz

Head of Library
Marta Vega

Study Centre Technician
Èric Jiménez

Archive Technician
Núria Gallissà

Librarian
Iraïs Martí

Library Assistants
Andrea Ferraris
Noemí Mases
Sònia Monegal

Archive Assistant
Llorenç Mas

Study Centre Assistants
Mª Carmen Bueno
Ariadna Pons

PUBLICATIONS

Head of Publications
Clara Plasencia

Editorial Coordinators
Ester Capdevila
Clàudia Faus

Graphic Coordinator
Gemma Planell

Publications Assistant
Begoña Azcorreta

PRODUCTION AREA

Director of Production
Anna Borrell

Head of Production
Lourdes Rubio

AUDIOVISUALS

Audiovisual Technicians
Miquel Giner
Jordi Martínez

REGISTRAR

**Head of Logistics
and Registrar**
Ariadna Robert i Casasayas

Registrars
Guim Català
Denis Iriarte
Mar Manen
Patricia Sorroche

Registrar Assistant
Eva López

CONSERVATION -
RESTORATION

**Head of Conservation -
Restoration**
Silvia Noguer

Conservator - Restorer
Xavier Rossell

**Conservation - Restoration
Assistant**
Eva López

ORGANISATION AREA

Director of Management
Imma López Villanueva

FINANCIAL MANAGEMENT

Head of Financial Management
Montse Senra

Accounting Technician
Beatriz Calvo

Accounting Assistant
Meritxell Raventós

CONTROLLING

Controller
Aitor Matías

HUMAN RESOURCES

Head of Human Resources
Carme Espinosa

Human Resources Technician
Marta Bertran

Human Resources Assistant
Angie Acebo

Receptionist - Telephonist
Erminda Rodríguez

INTERNAL SERVICES AND
CONTRACTS

**Head of Internal Services
and Contracts**
Mireia Calmell

Internal Services Assistant
Jordi Rodríguez

Contracts Assistant
Mª Carmen Bueno

ORGANISATION AND SYSTEMS

**Process and Organisation
Technician**
Alba Canal

IT Technician
Toni Lucea

Technical Support
Albert Martínez

**Process and Organisation
Assistant**
Begoña Azcorreta

MARKETING AND
AUDIENCE AREA

Marketing and Audience Director
Bel Natividad

MARKETING

Head of Marketing
Teresa Lleal

Marketing Coordinators
Guillem Edo
Beatriz Escudero
Marc López

Marketing Assistants
Judith Menéndez
Cristina Mercadé

PRESS

Head of Press
Mireia Collado
Ainhoa Pernaute

Press Assistant
Victòria Cortés

DIGITAL MEDIA

Head of Digital Media
Sònia López

Digital Media Coordinator
Anna Ramos

Digital Media Assistant
Lorena Martín

GRANT AND
SPACE MANAGEMENT

**Head of Grant and
Space Management**
Gemma Romaguera

Space Management Coordinator
Georgina Filomeno

Space Management Assistant
Ariadna Pons

This catalogue is published on the occasion of the Antoni Abad *megafone.net/2004–2014* project presented in the Museu d'Art Contemporani de Barcelona (MACBA) from 19 February to 24 June 2014.

The exhibition is organized and produced by Museu d'Art Contemporani de Barcelona (MACBA) and Acción Cultural Española (AC/E) in collaboration with Laboratorio de Arte de Alameda and the Centro Cultural de España en México (Mexico City), Matadero Madrid (Spain), and the Pinacoteca do Estado de São Paulo (Brazil).

EXHIBITION

Curatorial Team
Cristina Bonet
Soledad Gutiérrez
Roc Parés

Coordination
Cristina Bonet (MACBA)
Marta Rincón (AC/E)

Coordination Assistants
Susan Anderson
Guim Català

Registrar
Denis Iriarte

Conservation and Restoration
Lluís Roqué

Architecture
Isabel Bachs
Núria Guarro

Audiovisuals
Albert Toda
Miquel Giner

PUBLICATION

Published by
Museu d'Art Contemporani de Barcelona (MACBA)
Acción Cultural Española (AC/E)
TURNER

Scientific Direction
Roc Parés

Publishing Coordination
Clara Plasencia (MACBA)
Raquel Mesa (AC/E)
TURNER

Design and layout
Setanta

Translations
Wade Matthews

Copyediting
Tessa Milne

Production
Artes Gráficas Palermo

© in the printed edition: MACBA, AC/E, TURNER, 2014
© in the texts: their authors, 2014
© in the photographs and images: their authors and owners, 2014
© Alexandre Baumgartner (pp.114–15)
© in the original maps:
2006 Servei de Cartografia de l'Ajuntament de Barcelona / 2014 Google / 2014 Google-BCN IGN España / 2014 CIVES/Astrium Digital Globe

ISBN AC/E:
978-84-15272-56-4
ISBN TURNER:
978-84-16142-38-5
LEGAL DEPOSIT:
M-14644-2014

Distributed in the United States by:
DAP
orders@dapinc.com
www.artbook.com

Distributed in Europe by:
IDEA BOOKS
webform@ideabooks.nl
www.ideabooks.nl

Distributed in the United Kingdom by:
ART DATA
orders@artdata.co.uk
www.artdata.co.uk

SPANISH AND CATALAN EDITIONS AVAILABLE
Distributed in Spain by:
Machado Grupo de Distribución
machadolibros@machadolibros.com
and
Les Punxes Distribuidora
punxes@punxes.es
www.punxes.es

Distributed in Latin America by:
Océano
info@oceano.com
www.oceano.com

MABCA and AC/E acknowledge the support of Mobile World Capital, and the collaboration of Tania Aedo, Carlota Álvarez Basso, Ivo Mesquita, Ana Tomé, and Carme Sais.